Ultimate Machine Learning with Scikit-Learn

Unleash the Power of Scikit-Learn and Python to Build Cutting-Edge Predictive Modeling Applications and Unlock Deeper Insights Into Machine Learning

Parag Saxena

www.orangeava.com

Copyright © 2024, Orange Education Pvt Ltd, AVA™

All rights reserved. No part of this book may be reproduced, stored in a retrieval system, or transmitted in any form or by any means, without the prior written permission of the publisher, except in the case of brief quotations embedded in critical articles or reviews.

Every effort has been made in the preparation of this book to ensure the accuracy of the information presented. However, the information contained in this book is sold without warranty, either express or implied. Neither the author nor **Orange Education Pvt Ltd** or its dealers and distributors, will be held liable for any damages caused or alleged to have been caused directly or indirectly by this book.

Orange Education Pvt Ltd has endeavored to provide trademark information about all of the companies and products mentioned in this book by the appropriate use of capital. However, **Orange Education Pvt Ltd** cannot guarantee the accuracy of this information. The use of general descriptive names, registered names, trademarks, service marks, etc. in this publication does not imply, even in the absence of a specific statement, that such names are exempt from the relevant protective laws and regulations and therefore free for general use.

First published: May 2024
Published by: Orange Education Pvt Ltd, AVA™
Address: 9, Daryaganj, Delhi, 110002, India

275 New North Road Islington Suite 1314 London,
N1 7AA, United Kingdom

ISBN: 978-81-97223-94-5

www.orangeava.com

Dedicated To

My Beloved Mother:

Whose Unwavering Belief in My Dreams has been a Constant Source of Strength and Inspiration

It is also Dedicated to the Spirit of Relentlessness that Drives Every Data Scientist on their Quest for Applied Knowledge

About the Author

Parag Saxena, a seasoned AI ML Data Scientist, embodies a unique blend of academic excellence and industry expertise. With a master's degree in Data Science and Analytics, his career spans vital sectors like banking, retail, and power generation. Parag is a visionary, having deployed sophisticated machine learning models, authored research papers, and shared his expertise on prestigious platforms.

His technical prowess is matched by a heartfelt dedication to mentorship and collaboration, as evidenced by his leading roles in Generative AI and Machine Learning Operations. Parag is not just a Data Scientist; he is a storyteller who uses data to narrate tales of trends, predictions, and insights.

Beyond his professional pursuits, Parag's life is a testament to the power of continuous learning and growth. He stands as an embodiment of the belief that our work is not just about what we build, but also the knowledge we share and the communities we uplift.

About the Technical Reviewer

Dr. Alok Tiwari holds a Ph.D. in Biomedical Engineering from IIT-BHU, following his Master's degree in the same field from NIT Kurukshetra and a Bachelor's degree in Electronics and Communication from IET Sitapur.

He is currently working as an Assistant Professor of Big Data Analytics at the esteemed Goa Institute of Management (GIM), located in Sanquelim, Goa. He brings a comprehensive skillset across Data Science, Data Engineering, Artificial Intelligence, and Machine Learning, making him adept at tackling complex problems with robust solutions.

His expertise extends beyond traditional data analysis. He is proficient in a variety of programming languages and tools, including Python, R, SQL, Git, and CI/CD pipelines. This allows him to work seamlessly with diverse databases (MySQL, MongoDB) and leverage high-performance computing resources like GPU Workstations for large-scale projects.

Dr. Tiwari's background in Biomedical Engineering fuels his passion for applying advanced data science techniques to healthcare challenges. His Ph.D. research focused on medical image analysis, specifically using transfer learning for COVID-19 classification and cardiac MRI segmentation. This experience positions him well to contribute to the growing field of AI-powered healthcare solutions.

In his leisure time, he enjoys indulging in various activities such as listening to music, singing songs, playing cricket, badminton, and chess.

Acknowledgements

Writing "*Ultimate Machine Learning with Scikit-Learn*" has been both a professional accomplishment and a personal journey of growth and self-discovery. This book represents the culmination of a decade's worth of learning, exploration, and passion for data science—a path that many of you have walked alongside me.

I am deeply grateful to the academic and professional communities that have been an integral part of my life, particularly the teams at the University of North Carolina Charlotte, where the seeds for many of these chapters were first planted. I extend my heartfelt thanks to my mentors, whose guidance has been invaluable, and to my peers, whose challenges and inspiration have pushed me to greater heights.

My family deserves a special mention for their unwavering support and encouragement, which have been my guiding light through the challenges. To my parents, whose sacrifices have paved the way for me to pursue my ambitions, this book is a testament to your unconditional love.

To my colleagues in the field, your camaraderie and competition have been a source of inspiration that pushes me out of my comfort zone. And to you, the reader, who is embarking on this journey with me—may you find within these pages the tools to unlock the vast potential that lies dormant within your data.

Preface

"*Ultimate Machine Learning with Scikit-Learn*" is more than just a technical guide; it is a narrative crafted from the fabric of real-world challenges in the realm of data science. Each chapter reflects a part of my journey, translating complex concepts into relatable insights, akin to the models we strive to build.

The chapters are as follows:

Chapter 1. Data Preprocessing with Linear Regression: This chapter recalls the foundational lessons established in earliest projects, setting the stage for the powerful analytics to follow.

Chapter 2. Structured Data and Logistic Regression: This chapter reflects the strategic thinking honed during my first Kaggle competition—a victory that showcased the might of simple yet effective models.

Chapter 3. Time-Series Data and Decision Trees: Drawing on experiences in stock market prediction, this chapter emphasizes the importance of understanding historical data to forecast future trends.

Chapter 4. Unstructured Data Handling and Naive Bayes: The chapter mirrors the endeavors to decode the complexity of natural language, turning unstructured murmurs into structured insights.

Chapter 5. Real-time Data Streams and K-Nearest Neighbors: Inspired by real-time data applications, this chapter highlights the critical role of both speed and accuracy in such scenarios.

Chapter 6. Sparse Distributed Data and Support Vector Machines: This chapter encapsulates experiences in harnessing the power of distributed systems to predict and plan with greater precision.

Chapter 7. Anomaly Detection and Isolation Forests: This chapter acknowledges the development of models to safeguard systems from the unexpected, finding patterns in the outliers.

Chapter 8. Stock Market Data and Ensemble Methods: This chapter captures the essence of crafting scalable solutions for the ever-expanding universe of big data.

Chapter 9. Data Engineering and ML Pipelines for Advanced Analytics: This chapter demonstrates a credit case fraud case study which combines data engineering, model building and deployment.

This book is an invitation to embark on a journey of exploration and enlightenment. It aspires to serve as a beacon for those who seek to navigate the rich and complex world of machine learning.

Downloading the code bundles and colored images

Please follow the links or scan the QR codes to download the
Code Bundles and Images of the book:

https://github.com/ava-orange-education/Ultimate-Machine-Learning-with-Scikit-Learn

The code bundles and images of the book are also hosted on
https://rebrand.ly/ise1rec

In case there's an update to the code, it will be updated on the existing GitHub repository.

Errata

We take immense pride in our work at **Orange Education Pvt Ltd,** and follow best practices to ensure the accuracy of our content to provide an indulging reading experience to our subscribers. Our readers are our mirrors, and we use their inputs to reflect and improve upon human errors, if any, that may have occurred during the publishing processes involved. To let us maintain the quality and help us reach out to any readers who might be having difficulties due to any unforeseen errors, please write to us at :

errata@orangeava.com

Your support, suggestions, and feedback are highly appreciated.

DID YOU KNOW

Did you know that Orange Education Pvt Ltd offers eBook versions of every book published, with PDF and ePub files available? You can upgrade to the eBook version at **www.orangeava.com** and as a print book customer, you are entitled to a discount on the eBook copy. Get in touch with us at: **info@orangeava.com** for more details.

At **www.orangeava.com**, you can also read a collection of free technical articles, sign up for a range of free newsletters, and receive exclusive discounts and offers on AVA™ Books and eBooks.

PIRACY

If you come across any illegal copies of our works in any form on the internet, we would be grateful if you would provide us with the location address or website name. Please contact us at **info@orangeava.com** with a link to the material.

ARE YOU INTERESTED IN AUTHORING WITH US?

If there is a topic that you have expertise in, and you are interested in either writing or contributing to a book, please write to us at **business@orangeava.com**. We are on a journey to help developers and tech professionals to gain insights on the present technological advancements and innovations happening across the globe and build a community that believes Knowledge is best acquired by sharing and learning with others. Please reach out to us to learn what our audience demands and how you can be part of this educational reform. We also welcome ideas from tech experts and help them build learning and development content for their domains.

REVIEWS

Please leave a review. Once you have read and used this book, why not leave a review on the site that you purchased it from? Potential readers can then see and use your unbiased opinion to make purchase decisions. We at Orange Education would love to know what you think about our products, and our authors can learn from your feedback. Thank you!

For more information about Orange Education, please visit **www.orangeava.com**.

Table of Contents

1. Data Preprocessing with Linear Regression 1
    Introduction 1
    Structure 2
    Introduction to Data Preprocessing 2
    Role of Data Preprocessing in Data Science 3
        Common Oversight of Preprocessing in the Rush to Analysis 4
        Example 1: The Impact of Misclassification in Medical Diagnoses 5
        Example 2: Predictive Policing and Biased Data 5
    Understanding Linear Regression 6
    A Closer Look at the Applied Linear Regression Model 9
        Intercept and Coefficients 10
        Error Term 10
        Core Assumptions of Linear Regression 11
    Practical Application: Fitting a Linear Regression Model 14
        Diving Deep into Data Preprocessing 15
        Model Deployment: From Development to Production 19
    Python Code – Comprehensive Exploratory Data Analysis 25
    Comprehensive Data Preprocessing 28
        Feature Importance and Feature Selection 31
    Conclusion 36
    Points to Remember 36

2. Structured Data and Logistic Regression 39
    Introduction 39
    Structure 39
    APIs and Structured Data 40
    Handling Categorical Variables 40
    Introduction to Logistic Regression 41

xii

    Implementation 41

    Evaluation 42

End-of-Chapter Project: Predicting Loan Defaults 43

    Dealing with Missing Values 44

Project: Customer Churn Prediction 47

    Delving Deeper into Logistic Regression 47

    Implementing and Evaluating Retention Strategies 60

Final Project: Overview 62

    Model Training and Evaluation 70

    Challenges and Future Directions 74

Conclusion 75

3. Time-Series Data and Decision Trees 77

Introduction 77

Structure 77

Significance of Time-Series Data in Stocks 78

    The Stock Market 78

    Decision Trees for Stock Market Prediction 78

Delving into Decision Trees 84

    Benefits of Decision Trees 84

    Limitations of Decision Trees 84

    Decision Trees for Binary Classification 85

    Setting up the Problem 85

Techniques to Visualize Time-Series Data 91

    Handling Missing Values and Outliers 92

    Transformations and Stationarity in Time-Series Data 93

    Time-Series Forecasting with ARIMA 94

Preparing Data for Decision Trees 94

    Decision Trees for Predicting Price Direction 94

End-of-Chapter Project 98

    Data Exploration: Starting with INFY 100

    Application to INFY Data 107

Learning Outcomes 110

Conclusion	111
Points to Remember	111

4. Unstructured Data Handling and Naive Bayes 113

Introduction	113
Structure	114
Problem Statement	114
Unstructured Data Preprocessing	115
Naive Bayes Algorithm	116
Sentiment Analysis	116
Unstructured Data	116
Web scraping	117
Naïve Bayes Algorithm	130
Understanding the "Naiveness"	133
Gaussian Naive Bayes: A Quick Overview	135
Multinomial Naive Bayes: A Quick Overview	136
Bernoulli Naive Bayes: A Quick Overview	137
End-of-Chapter Project	145
Conclusion	155

5. Real-time Data Streams and K-Nearest Neighbors 157

Introduction	157
Structure	157
K-Nearest Neighbors (KNN): A Powerful Tool for Real-Time Data Analysis	158
Real-Time Data Streams: Nature and Modern-Day Relevance	159
Modern-Day Relevance	160
Real-Time Data Streams: The Pulse of the Modern World	160
Demand Forecasting with KNN in Python	163
Deeper Insights into Anomalies and Conclusion	169
Additional Considerations	173
Foundations and Mechanisms of KNN	180
KNN in Action: Uber's Real-time Demand Prediction	181
End-of-Chapter Project: Predicting Emojis in Tweets Using KNN	183

    Twitter Data Collection and Preprocessing 183
    Conclusion 193

6. Sparse Distributed Data and Support Vector Machines 195
    Introduction 195
    Structure 196
    Sparse Data 196
        Characteristics of Sparse Data 196
    Dealing with Sparse Data 197
    Introduction to Support Vector Machines (SVM) 197
        Working of SVM 198
        Key Components of SVM 198
    High-dimensional Contexts and SVM 200
    Distributed Systems and SVM 200
        The Promise of SVM in Distributed Sparse Datasets 200
    Sparse Data in Financial Contexts: Challenges and Opportunities 200
    Data Storage and Processing: A New Paradigm for Sparse Datasets 201
        Handling Sparse Data Structures in Distributed Systems 202
        Compression Techniques 202
        Distributed Representations 202
        Parallel Computation 203
        Combining Distributed Systems and SVM 203
        NameNode and DataNodes 203
    Using SVMs to Predict Loan Defaults 204
        Sparse Data in Financial Contexts 204
        The Mokka Dataset 205
        Problem Statement 205
        Solution: Support Vector Machines 205
        The Necessity of Preprocessing 208
        Mathematics of SVM 208
        SVM Modeling for Mokka's Data 210
        Implementation and Evaluation of SVM for Mokka's Dataset 210
    Libraries for Distributed SVM 215

	Performance Considerations and Optimizations for Sparse Datasets 215
	Hands-on with Distributed SVM on Sparse Datasets 216
	Optimizing Distributed SVM for Sparse Data 217
	PySpark: The Powerhouse for Big Data Machine Learning 218
	Setting up PySpark.. 219
	MLLib: PySpark's Machine Learning Library............................. 219
	Fraud Detection in Sparse Financial Datasets using SVM 220
	End-of-the-Chapter Project: Optimizing Marketing Campaign Responses (Company: SparkCognition) 221
	Diving into the Data: A Comprehensive Description................ 222
	Pre-processing the Data: Laying a Robust Foundation 223
	Visualization and Feature Engineering: Creating New Insights 226
	Model Development and Validation: From Theory to Action................. 229
	Dealing with Imbalances and Model Refinement..................... 232
	Taking Actions and Recommendations.................................... 233
	Future Directions and Long-Term Vision................................. 235
	Conclusion.. 236
	Points to Remember 237
7.	**Anomaly Detection and Isolation Forests** **239**
	Introduction..239
	Structure 239
	The Significance of Anomalies 240
	Real-World Applications and Implications of Anomaly Detection 240
	Isolation Forests..241
	Deep Dive into Isolation Forests 241
	Isolation Forest Algorithm 241
	Explaining Conceptual Isolation of Anomalies 242
	Mechanism: Working of Isolation Forests..............................244
	i-Trees: The Building Blocks..244

  Practical Insights for Using Isolation Forests 249
  Traditional Statistical Methods for Anomaly Detection 252
  Clustering-Based Methods for Anomaly Detection 253
  Neural Networks (Autoencoders) for Anomaly Detection 254
  Autoencoders 254
  Robust Covariance (Elliptic Envelope) 255
  Working of Elliptic Envelope method 255
  One-Class Support Vector Machines (SVMs) 257
  Advantages of Isolation Forests for Multi-Modal Datasets 259
  Example of Using Isolation Forests 259
 Implementation of Isolation Forests with Revolut's
 Fraudsters Detection Project 260
  Introduction to the Dataset 260
  Data Preprocessing 260
  Applying Isolation Forests 261
  Visualizations and Interpretation of Results 261
  Methods for Model Validation and Performance Improvement 263
 End of the chapter Project: Outlier Detection in Financial Data 269
  Project Overview 269
  Data Overview 269
  Outlier Interpretation and Documentation 279
 Conclusion 280

8. Stock Market Data and Ensemble Methods **281**
 Introduction 281
 Structure 282
 Stock Market Data: A Catalyst for Financial Decisions 282
  The Power of Ensemble Methods 282
  Distinguishing Between the Projects 282
 Collecting Stock Market Data 283
  The Importance of Quality Data 283
  Sources of Stock Market Data 284

  Understanding Sentiment Analysis in the Financial Context 284
  Preprocessing Composite Stock Data 286
Introduction to Ensemble Methods 287
  Types of Ensemble Methods 287
  Advantages of Ensemble Methods 288
Getting Hands-On: Ensemble with Stock Data 288
  Implementing the Ensemble Model for Sentiment Score Calculation 289
  Step-by-Step Implementation 289
  Decoding the Ensemble Diagram 292
  Ensemble Diagram 292
  Ensemble Philosophy 293
  Ensemble Methods Outperform Single Models 294
  Use Ensemble Methods for Stock Market Forecasting 294
Deep Dive into Bagging 295
  Benefits of Bagging 295
  Random Forest 296
Boosting 296
  Advantages of Boosting 297
Understanding Stacking 298
  Basic Steps of Stacking 298
  Advantages of Stacking 299
Sentiment Analysis using Time Series with Ensemble Techniques 299
  Time Series Analysis 300
  Ensemble Techniques 300
  Project Objective 300
  Data 300
  Methodology 300
Ensemble Methods for Sentiment Analysis 301
  Traditional Approaches and Limitations 301
  Need for Ensemble in Sentiment Analysis 301

Ensemble Architecture 302
Evaluation 302
Logistic Regression for Text Classification with TF-IDF 302
Naive Bayes for Text Classification with Word Embeddings 303
Random Forest for Text Classification with N-grams 305
Evaluating the Sentiment Analysis Ensemble 306
Evaluation Metrics 306
Validation Approach 306
Comparison to Baseline Models 306
Model Analysis 306
Future Work 309
End of the Chapter Project: Literature Review on
Stock Market Prediction 310
Traditional Statistical Models 310
Machine Learning Approaches 310
Ensemble Techniques 311
Features Used in Stock Prediction Models 311
Stock Market Data Collection and Preprocessing 312
Model Selection and Ensemble Strategy for Stock
Market Direction Prediction 314
*Model Evaluation and Validation for Stock Market
Direction Prediction* 317
Evaluation Metrics 317
Validation Techniques 317
*Feature Engineering and Selection for Stock
Market Direction Prediction* 319
*Model Training, Tuning, and Conclusion for
Stock Market Direction Prediction* 321
Hyperparameter Tuning 321
Stacking Ensemble 322
Conclusion 324

9. Data Engineering and ML Pipelines for Advanced Analytics 325

Introduction 325
Structure 326
Data Engineering and Machine Learning 326
    The Data Engineering Process 327
    Machine Learning Pipelines 327
Credit Card Fraud Detection 328
    Recap of Data Collection Methods with a Focus on Transactional Data 328
    The Role of Data Engineering in Fraud Detection 329
    Preprocessing and Transformation for Fraud Detection Datasets 329
    Handling Missing Values 330
    Categorization and Labeling 330
    Feature Scaling and Normalization 330
    Secure and Efficient Data Storage in Sensitive Financial Contexts 331
    Balancing Security and Efficiency 331
    Secure and Efficient Data Storage in Sensitive Financial Contexts: Beyond the Technology 332
    Backup and Recovery 332
    Regulatory Compliance 333
Data Exploration and Augmentation for Fraud Detection 335
    Introduction to Data Exploration in Fraud Detection 336
    Introduction to Transactional Data and Its Unique Properties 336
    Introduction to Feature Engineering for Fraud Patterns 339
    Overview and Handling Imbalanced Data 340
    Batch versus Real-Time Processing Considerations in a Fraud Detection Context 343
    Batch Processing 343
    Real-Time Processing 344
    Evaluation Metrics for Fraud Detection 346

    Precision, Recall, and the F1 Score 346

    Adapting Model Evaluation Metrics for Fraud Detection 348

    Feedback Loop: Continuous Model Improvement 351

Credit Card Fraud Detection Pipeline from Scratch 353

    Introduction and Overview 353

    Dataset Overview 353

    Objective 353

    Reflecting on the Power of Integrated Pipelines 361

    Convergence in Real-world Scenarios 362

Conclusion 362

Further Resources 363

Index **365**

CHAPTER 1
Data Preprocessing with Linear Regression

Introduction

In the era of data-driven decision-making, understanding and manipulating data has become a crucial skill. Whether you are a data scientist, a machine learning engineer, or an analyst, the ability to preprocess and analyze data is fundamental to extracting valuable insights and making informed decisions.

This chapter aims to provide a detailed overview of advanced data preprocessing techniques for linear regression machine learning problems using the widely adopted Scikit-learn library in Python. By the end of this chapter, you should be able to construct efficient data preprocessing pipelines, understand their roles in machine learning workflows, and apply these skills to real-world datasets.

Linear regression is one of the most basic and widely used algorithms in the machine learning field. It's a statistical model that establishes a linear relationship between the dependent variable (target) and one or more independent variables (predictors). However, before feeding data into the linear regression model, it's crucial to preprocess the data to ensure optimal model performance. This includes tasks such as handling missing values, dealing with categorical variables, scaling features, and more.

In this chapter, we will dive deep into each preprocessing step, discuss its importance, and learn how to implement it using Scikit-learn. Furthermore, we will provide a comprehensive guide to constructing a complete data preprocessing pipeline from scratch and integrating it with a linear regression model. The last part of the chapter will include a practical project that applies all these concepts, solidifying your understanding and preparing you for more complex real-world scenarios.

Structure

In this chapter, we will cover the following topics:

- Introduction
- Understanding Linear Regression
- Practical Application: Fitting a Linear Regression Model
- Diving Deep into Data Preprocessing
- Linear Regression for Predicting Continuous Variables
- Evaluating Your Linear Regression Model
- Model Deployment: From Development to Production
- Data Preprocessing in the Context of Linear Regression
- Case Study: Linear Regression and Data Preprocessing in Action
- End-to-End Project: Putting It All Together

Introduction to Data Preprocessing

Data science is a field that promises to reveal valuable insights from data that, at first glance, may seem impenetrable. However, the first step to achieving these insights—data preprocessing—is often overlooked.

According to Chandola and Kumar (2012), data preprocessing is the process of preparing raw data to be input into a machine learning model. This process may include cleaning the data, normalizing it, handling missing or outlier values, and transforming variables. The goal is to convert data into a format that will be more easily and effectively processed for the desired outcome.

Dasu and Johnson (2003) argue that the significance of data preprocessing cannot be overstated. A well-prepared dataset not only makes the analysis and modeling phases more manageable, but also enhances the accuracy of the predictive models and the insights derived from them.

However, in the rush to apply sophisticated algorithms and extract value from data, the importance of preprocessing is often neglected. This oversight can lead to models that are inaccurate, inefficient, or simply ineffective.

In this chapter, we will shed light on the role of data preprocessing in the data science workflow, highlighting its significance of real-world examples where neglecting preprocessing led to suboptimal results. Following this, we will introduce you to one of the most fundamental statistical techniques – linear regression.

Linear regression is a supervised learning algorithm used for predicting a continuous outcome variable (also called the dependent variable) based on one or more predictor variables (also known as independent variables). The premise is simple: it establishes a relationship between the dependent and independent variables by fitting the best linear line.

This chapter will offer a friendly introduction to linear regression, explaining its core assumptions, and walking you through the process of fitting a linear regression model. We will also delve into different types of linear regression models–from the classic ordinary least squares to ridge regression, lasso regression, and elastic net regression.

Join us as we embark on this journey, underlining the importance of data preprocessing and introducing the foundational concepts of linear regression.

Role of Data Preprocessing in Data Science

Data preprocessing is the process of preparing raw data for analysis, modeling, and interpretation. It is a critical step in the data science workflow, and it is essential to ensure the accuracy and reliability of data science models.

Data cleaning involves identifying and correcting errors in the data. This can include removing duplicate records, correcting typos, and filling in missing values. For example, Chandola and Kumar (2012) found that data cleaning was essential for improving the accuracy of a machine learning model that was used to predict customer churn.

Data transformation involves changing the format or scale of the data. This can be done to make the data more suitable for analysis or to improve the performance of machine learning models. For example, Dasu and Johnson (2003) found that normalizing variables can improve the accuracy of a machine learning model that is used to predict credit risk.

Data reduction involves reducing the number of variables in the data. This can be done to improve the computational efficiency of models or to focus on the most important variables. For example, Kotsiantis, Zaharakis, and Pintelas (2006) found that feature engineering can improve the predictive power of a machine learning model that is used to predict customer behavior.

Feature engineering involves creating new features from existing features. This can be done to improve the predictive power of models or to make the data more interpretable. For example, Pyle (1999) found that feature engineering can help to improve the accuracy of a machine learning model that is used to diagnose diseases.

Data preprocessing is a critical step in the data science workflow. By cleaning the data, handling missing or outlier values, normalizing variables, and performing feature engineering, data preprocessing can help to improve the accuracy, efficiency, and interpretability of data science models.

Common Oversight of Preprocessing in the Rush to Analysis

Data preprocessing is often overlooked in the data science pipeline, especially in the rush to apply advanced analytical techniques. This is because the allure of sophisticated machine learning algorithms can be very tempting, as they promise insightful predictions and exciting discoveries. However, neglecting data preprocessing can lead to suboptimal results or even outright mistakes.

Inadequate data preprocessing can manifest in various ways, and its impacts can be far-reaching. For example, without proper handling of missing values, the machine learning model might generate biased or erroneous results. Similarly, failing to normalize variables or appropriately deal with outliers can lead to models that give undue importance to certain features, thereby distorting the final results.

The importance of data preprocessing cannot be overstated. As Chandola and Kumar (2012) put it, "garbage in, garbage out." No matter how sophisticated or well-designed the analytical technique or model is, if the input data is not properly preprocessed, the resulting predictions or insights will be of little value.

However, it's not all doom and gloom. By acknowledging and understanding the importance of data preprocessing, we can avoid these pitfalls and maximize the value we extract from our data. In the next section, we will explore some real-world examples where inadequate data preprocessing led to suboptimal outcomes, reinforcing the importance of this often-overlooked stage in the data science pipeline.

Classification:

Classification is a supervised machine learning technique that involves assigning a given data point to one of a predefined set of categories or classes. It's like sorting items into different bins based on their characteristics.

Here's how it works:

Training:
- The model is provided with a training dataset containing labeled examples (data points with their correct class assignments).
- The model analyzes this data to learn patterns and relationships between the features (input variables) and the class labels.

Prediction:
- When presented with new, unlabeled data, the model uses the learned patterns to predict the most likely class for each data point.

Example 1: The Impact of Misclassification in Medical Diagnoses

In the medical field, predictive models are often used to diagnose diseases based on a patient's symptoms or test results. However, if the input data are not properly preprocessed, the resulting misclassifications can lead to incorrect diagnoses and, subsequently, inappropriate treatments.

For example, consider the diagnosis of heart disease. Missing values, incorrectly recorded data, or outliers in the data can significantly impact the model's performance and lead to a life-threatening misdiagnosis. In one study, researchers found that a predictive model for heart disease was significantly less accurate when the data contained missing values (Beretta & Santaniello, 2016).

This example highlights the importance of data preprocessing in the medical field. By properly handling missing values, noise, outliers, and biases in the data, we can help to ensure that predictive models are accurate and reliable and that patients receive the best possible care.

Example 2: Predictive Policing and Biased Data

Predictive policing involves using data and statistical algorithms to predict potential criminal activity. However, the effectiveness of this approach depends heavily on the quality of the input data. If the data used to train the predictive models contain biases, such as if certain communities are over-policed, the model will likely reproduce and amplify these biases, leading to unfair targeting of certain groups.

For example, a study by Richardson, Schultz, and Crawford (2019) found that a predictive policing model used in Chicago was more likely to flag African American neighborhoods for potential crime than white neighborhoods, even after controlling for other factors such as crime rates. This suggests that the model was biased against African American neighborhoods and that this bias was likely due to the way the data was collected and processed.

This example highlights the importance of data preprocessing in predictive policing. By carefully handling the data, we can help to reduce the impact of bias and ensure that predictive models are fair and equitable.

Understanding Linear Regression

Linear regression is a statistical approach used to model the relationship between a dependent variable and one or more independent variables. It is one of the most straightforward yet powerful predictive models, and it forms the backbone of many advanced statistical and machine learning techniques.

The linear regression model takes the form of a line:

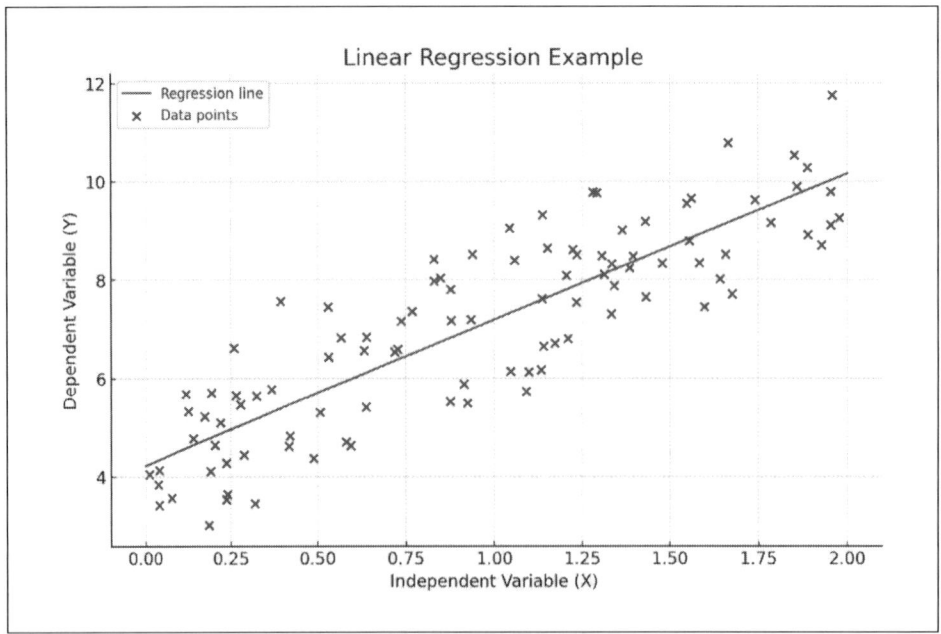

Figure 1.1: *Linear regression in the form of a line*

This figure represents the line: Y = β0 + β1*X1+ ε

Data Preprocessing with Linear Regression   7

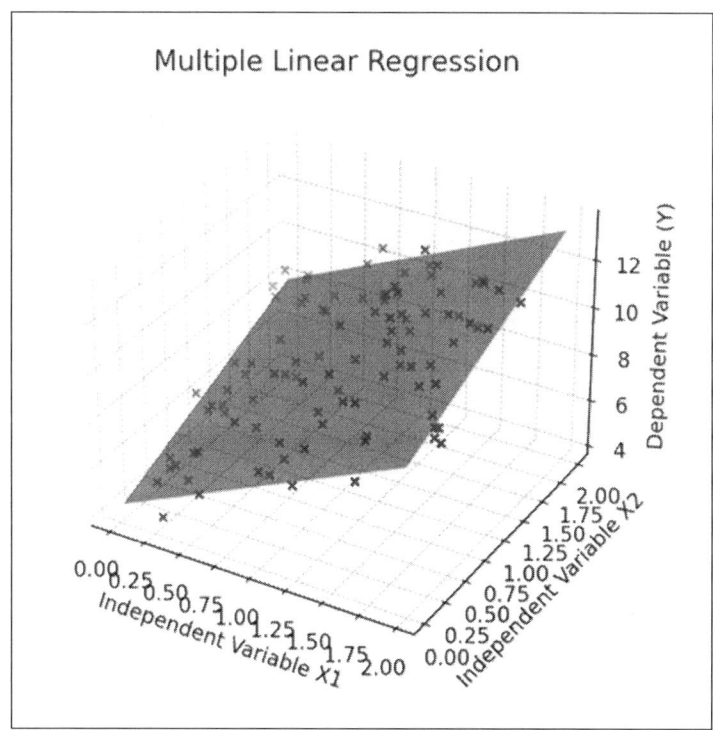

Figure 1.2: *Figure representing the equation of the line*

This figure shows the equation of this line: Y = β0 + β1*X1 + β2*X2 + ε

The general Linear Equation is: Y = β0 + β1*X1 + β2*X2 + ... + βn*Xn + ε

where:
- Y is the dependent variable we aim to predict.
- **X1** to **Xn** are the independent variables.
- **β0** is the y-intercept, which is the value of Y when all Xs are 0.
- **β1** to βn are the coefficients for the independent variables, which represent the change in Y for a unit change in the respective Xs.
- **ε** is the error term, which represents the unexplained variation in Y.

The goal of linear regression is to find the best-fitting line through the data points. The "best fit" is typically defined as the line that minimizes the sum of the squared differences between the observed and predicted values of the dependent variable. This method is known as the least squares approach.

```
SSE = Σ (yᵢ - ŷᵢ)    i=1 to n
```

where:
- **n** is the number of observations.
- **y$_i$** is the actual value of the dependent variable for the i-th observation.
- **ŷ$_i$** (pronounced "y-hat sub i") is the predicted value of the dependent variable for the i-th observation, as estimated by the regression model.

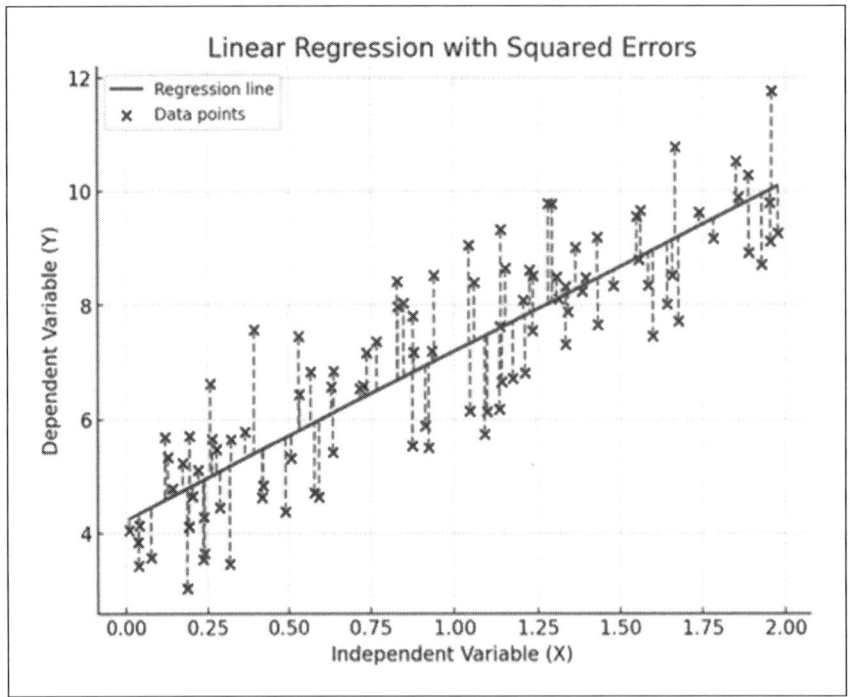

Figure 1.3: *Linear regression with squared errors*

Linear regression makes several assumptions, which include:
- **Linearity**: The relationship between the independent and dependent variables is linear.
- **Independence**: The observations are independent of each other.
- **Homoscedasticity**: The variance of the errors is constant across all levels of the independent variables.
- **Normality**: The errors are normally distributed.

Violations of these assumptions can lead to issues with the model, which we will discuss later.

Linear regression is a versatile technique that can be used in a wide variety of fields. Its simplicity and interpretability make it a popular choice for many data scientists.

In the following sections, we will take a closer look at the linear regression model, its assumptions, and how to fit a linear regression model using real-world data.

A Closer Look at the Applied Linear Regression Model

Linear regression is a powerful statistical technique that can be used to model the relationship between a dependent variable and one or more independent variables. However, it is important to understand the underlying assumptions of linear regression in order to ensure that the model fits properly and that the results are interpreted correctly.

- **Simple Linear Regression**:
    - **Focus**: Explains the relationship between one independent variable and one dependent variable.
    - **Model:** Creates a straight line to represent the relationship between the two variables.
    - Equation: `y = mx + b`, where:
        - `y` is the dependent variable.
        - `x` is the independent variable.

        `m` is the slope of the line, indicating the direction and strength of the relationship.

        `b` is the y-intercept, indicating the value of y when x is 0.
    - **Use cases**: Simple linear regression is appropriate when you have data suggesting a straightforward, linear relationship between two variables. Examples include understanding the impact of studying hours on exam scores, analyzing the relation between income and house prices, and more.
- **Multiple Linear Regression**:
    - **Focus**: Explains the relationship between multiple independent variables and one dependent variable.
    - **Model:** Creates a hyperplane (multidimensional plane) to represent the relationship.
    - **Equation**: `y = b0 + b1*x1 + b2*x2 + ... + bn*xn + e`, where:

        `y` is the dependent variable.

        `x1, x2, ..., xn` are the independent variables.

        `b0` is the y-intercept.

> **b1, b2, ..., bn** are the regression coefficients, indicating the impact of each independent variable on y.
>
> **e** is the error term, accounting for unexplained variability.

- **Use cases**: Multiple linear regression is used when you suspect multiple factors influence the dependent variable. Examples include predicting house prices based on features like size, location, and amenities, or analyzing marketing campaign performance considering budget, demographics, and advertising channels.

Intercept and Coefficients

The intercept (**β0**) and coefficients (**β1, β2, ..., βn**) are fundamental elements of a linear regression model. The intercept is the predicted value of the dependent variable when all independent variables are zero. Each coefficient represents the change in the dependent variable expected for a one-unit increase in the respective independent variable, assuming all other variables are held constant.

For example, consider a linear regression model that predicts the price of a house based on its square footage. The intercept would represent the predicted price of a house with 0 square feet, which is obviously not possible. However, the coefficients would represent the change in the predicted price for a one-unit increase in square footage. For example, if the coefficient for square footage is 10,000, then a house with 1,000 square feet would be predicted to be 10,000 more expensive than a house with 0 square feet.

Error Term

The error term (ε) captures the unexplained variability in the dependent variable. It comprises the effects of factors not included in the model, measurement errors, and inherent randomness. In an ideal scenario, these errors are normally distributed with a mean of zero and are independent of each other and the independent variables.

In practice, however, the error terms are often not normally distributed or independent. This can lead to problems with the interpretation of the coefficients and the accuracy of the predictions.

Multiple Linear Regression

While simple linear regression involves one independent variable, multiple linear regression involves two or more. In multiple regression, each coefficient represents the change in the dependent variable for a one-unit increase in the corresponding independent variable, assuming all other variables are held constant. This property allows for complex relationships to be modeled, though it can also introduce additional challenges such as multicollinearity.

Polynomial Regression

Though it's named "linear" regression, this technique can model curvilinear relationships through polynomial regression. By creating new features that are powers of the existing features (for example, `X^2`, `X^3`, so on..), the model can fit a polynomial equation that allows for more complex relationships between the independent and dependent variables.

$$Y = \beta_0 + \beta_1 X + \beta_2 X^2 + \beta_3 X^3 + \ldots + \beta_n X^n + \varepsilon$$

where:
- `Y` is the dependent variable we aim to predict.
- `X` is the original independent variable.
- `X²`, `X³`, ..., `Xⁿ` are the polynomial terms (squared, cubed, etc.) of the independent variable.
- `β₀` is the y-intercept, the value of Y when X and all its polynomial terms **are 0**. - `β₁`, `β₂`, ..., `βₙ` are the coefficients for the independent variable and its polynomial terms.
- `ε` is the error term, representing unexplained variation in Y.

In the next section, we will discuss how to evaluate the assumptions of linear regression.

Core Assumptions of Linear Regression

It is important to understand the underlying assumptions of linear regression in order to ensure that the model fits properly and that the results are interpreted correctly.

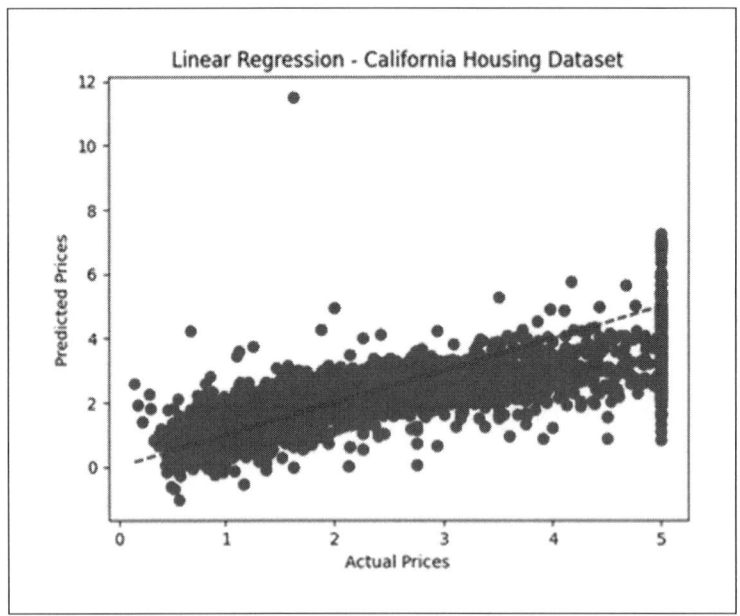

Figure 1.4: Line of linear regression on the California Housing Dataset

The core assumptions of linear regression are as follows:

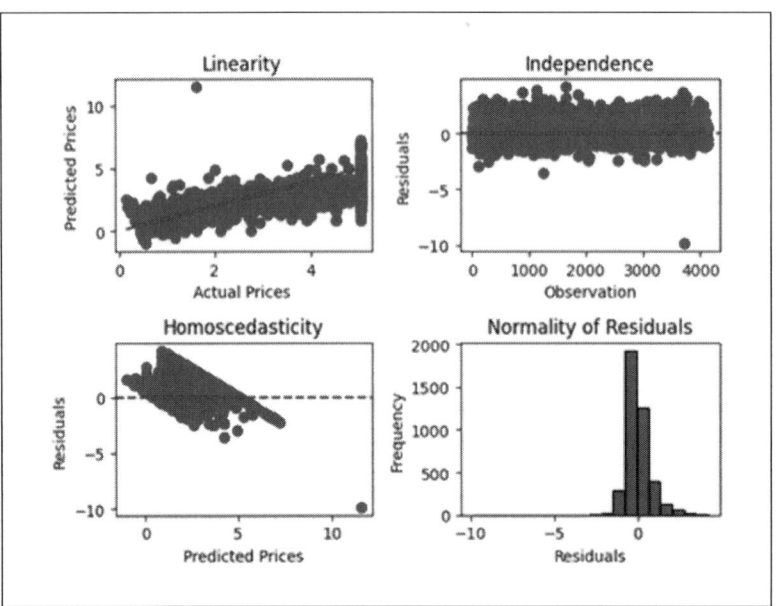

Figure 1.5: Assumptions of linear regression before starting data preprocessing

- **Linearity**: The relationship between the dependent and independent variables is linear. This means that the predicted values of the dependent variable should increase or decrease in a linear fashion as the independent variables increase or decrease. It plots the actual prices vs. predicted prices, with a diagonal line representing perfect predictions.

- **Independence**: The residuals, which are the differences between the observed and predicted values of the dependent variable, should be independent of each other. This means that the residuals should not be correlated with each other. It plots the residuals against the observation index, with a horizontal line at y=0 to check for independence.
- **Homoscedasticity**: The variance of the residuals should be constant across all levels of the independent variables. This means that the residuals should be spread out evenly around the regression line, regardless of the values of the independent variables. It plots the residuals against the predicted prices, with a horizontal line at y=0 to assess if the spread of residuals is consistent.
- **Normality**: The residuals should be normally distributed. This means that the residuals should follow a bell-shaped curve. It creates a histogram of the residuals to check for the approximate normality of the residuals.

Violation of these assumptions can lead to problems with the interpretation of the coefficients and the accuracy of the predictions. For example, if the assumption of linearity is violated, the model may not be able to accurately predict the dependent variable.

Several methods can be used to check the assumptions of linear regression. These methods include:

- **Plotting the residuals against the predicted values**: This can help to identify any patterns in the residuals that may indicate a violation of the assumptions.
- **Running statistical tests**: There are a number of statistical tests that can be used to test the assumptions of linear regression.

If any of the assumptions are violated, there are a number of things that can be done to address the issue. These include:

- **Data transformations**: In some cases, the data can be transformed to make it more linear.
- **Using a different regression model**: There are a number of different regression models that can be used, each with its own assumptions. If the assumptions of linear regression are violated, a different model may be more appropriate.
- **Including additional variables**: In some cases, the violation of an assumption may be due to the fact that the model does not include all the relevant variables. Including additional variables may help to improve the fit of the model and address the violation of the assumption.

It is important to check the assumptions of linear regression before interpreting the results of the model. By understanding and addressing any violations of the assumptions, you can ensure that the results of the model are accurate and reliable.

Practical Application: Fitting a Linear Regression Model

Data collection

The first step in any data analysis task is to gather your data. This may involve collecting new data, extracting data from databases, or using existing data from repositories. For our purposes, we will use a publicly available dataset: the Boston Housing Dataset. This dataset contains information collected by the U.S. Census Service concerning housing in the area of Boston, Massachusetts.

Data exploration and preprocessing

Before modeling, it is essential to familiarize ourselves with the data, understand its structure, and clean it. We will check for missing values, remove or replace them, and convert categorical data into a format suitable for the model. In the case of the Boston Housing Dataset, all variables are numerical, and there are no missing values, making our preprocessing task simpler.

Model fitting

With the data prepared, we can proceed to fit our model. We will first split our data into a training set and a test set. Then, we will use the training set to fit the model. In Python, the process might look like this:

```python
from sklearn.model_selection import train_test_split
from sklearn.linear_model import LinearRegression

X_train, X_test, y_train, y_test = train_test_split(X, y, test_size=0.2, random_state=42)
lm = LinearRegression()
lm.fit(X_train, y_train)
```

Model evaluation

After fitting the model, we need to evaluate its performance. This is often done by predicting the outcome variable in the test set and comparing these predictions with the actual values. Common metrics for evaluation include the R-squared, the root mean squared error, and the mean absolute error.

- **R-squared (R^2):** Measures the proportion of variance in the target variable explained by the model, indicating how well the model fits the data. (Higher is better, with a maximum of 1.)
- **Root Mean Squared Error (RMSE):** Measures the average magnitude of the errors between predicted and actual values, using squared errors to penalize large errors more. (Lower is better, with 0 indicating perfect prediction.)
- **Mean Absolute Error (MAE):** Measures the average magnitude of the errors, using absolute values of errors, making it less sensitive to outliers than RMSE. (Lower is better, with 0 indicating perfect prediction.)

Python

```python
from sklearn.metrics import mean_squared_error, r2_score

y_pred = lm.predict(X_test)
mse = mean_squared_error(y_test, y_pred)
r2 = r2_score(y_test, y_pred)
```

Interpretation and Conclusion

Finally, we interpret our results. This involves understanding the coefficients of our model, testing hypotheses, and considering the implications of our findings in the real-world context. For example, in the Boston Housing data, a positive coefficient for the RM variable (average number of rooms) would suggest that houses with more rooms, on average, tend to have higher prices.

In the next sections, we will explore various types of linear regression models and detail the vital steps involved in data preprocessing specific to these models.

Diving Deep into Data Preprocessing

Data preprocessing is a crucial step in the machine learning process. It is the process of cleaning, formatting, and transforming data so that it can be used by machine learning algorithms.

In this section, we will discuss some common data preprocessing tasks, such as handling missing values, managing outliers, dealing with categorical variables, and feature scaling.

Handling Missing Values

Many datasets will have missing values. There are a few different strategies that can be used to handle missing values, depending on the dataset's nature and the proportion of missing values.

One strategy is to fill in missing values with a measure of central tendency, such as the mean or median. Another strategy is to use a model to predict the missing values. In some cases, it may be appropriate to simply ignore the missing values if they constitute a small fraction of the dataset.

Managing Outliers

Outliers are data points that deviate significantly from other observations. They can distort the results of a machine learning model, making it crucial to handle them correctly. Outliers can be detected using box plots, scatter plots, or statistical methods such as the Z-score or the IQR method.

Once outliers have been detected, there are a few different strategies that can be used to handle them. One strategy is to simply remove the outliers from the dataset. Another strategy is to transform the outliers so that they are less extreme.

Dealing with Categorical Variables

Categorical variables are those that can be divided into multiple categories but have no order or priority. These variables need to be converted into a numerical format before they can be used in a machine learning model. This conversion is often done using techniques like one-hot encoding or dummy variable encoding.

Feature Scaling

Feature scaling is the process of standardizing the range of independent variables in your dataset. This is particularly important for some machine learning algorithms that use distance measures, such as K-Nearest Neighbors (KNN), but can also aid linear regression when dealing with features of varying scales.

Feature scaling can be done using a variety of methods, such as min-max scaling, standardization, and normalization.

Data preprocessing is a complex and important topic. By understanding and correctly implementing the preprocessing steps discussed in this section, you can dramatically improve the performance of your machine learning models.

Linear Regression for Predicting Continuous Variables

Linear regression is a statistical technique that can be used to predict a continuous variable (such as price, height, or weight) based on one or more independent variables.

There are different types of linear regression models, each with its own strengths and weaknesses.

Ordinary Least Squares (OLS)

Ordinary least squares (OLS) regression is the most basic type of linear regression. It attempts to find the line of best fit that minimizes the sum of the squared residuals (the differences between the observed and predicted values).

In Python, you can fit an OLS regression model using the following code:

```python
import statsmodels.api as sm
import numpy as np

# Create the data
X = np.random.randint(0, 10, size=100)
y = 2 * X + 3 + np.random.normal(0, 1, size=100)

# Fit the model
model = sm.OLS(y, X).fit()

# Print the coefficients
print(model.coef_)
print(model.intercept_)
```

Ridge Regression

Ridge regression is a type of linear regression that includes a regularization term. Regularization helps prevent overfitting by adding a penalty to the size of the coefficients. Ridge regression uses L2 regularization, which adds the squared magnitude of the coefficients to the loss function.

In Python, you can fit a ridge regression model using the following code:

Python

```
from sklearn.linear_model import Ridge

ridge = Ridge(alpha=1.0)
ridge.fit(X, y)
```

Lasso Regression

Lasso regression is another type of linear regression that includes a regularization term. However, Lasso regression uses L1 regularization, which adds the absolute value of the coefficients to the loss function. This can result in some coefficients becoming zero, effectively eliminating the corresponding feature from the model.

In Python, you can fit a lasso regression model using the following code:

Python

```
from sklearn.linear_model import Lasso

lasso = Lasso(alpha=1.0)
lasso.fit(X, y)
```

Elastic Net Regression

Elastic net regression combines the penalties of ridge regression and lasso regression. It works well when there are multiple features correlated with each other.

In Python, you can fit an elastic net regression model using the following code:

Python

```
from sklearn.linear_model import ElasticNet

elasticnet = ElasticNet(alpha=1.0, l1_ratio=0.5)
elasticnet.fit(X, y)
```

Choosing the Right Model

The choice of which linear regression model to use depends on the specific problem you are trying to solve. If you are concerned about overfitting, then you may want to use a model with regularization, such as ridge regression or lasso regression. If you are also interested in feature selection, then you may want to use lasso regression.

Model Deployment: From Development to Production

Once we have built and evaluated our linear regression model, the next crucial step is model deployment. This step involves putting the model into operation so it can start providing predictions on new data. The process may vary depending on the specific application and the infrastructure used, but here is a generalized process:

1. **Versioning**: Save the model using Python's pickle or joblib modules. This allows you to reuse your model in the future without needing to retrain it.
2. **Serving the model:** There are multiple ways to serve a model, but a common approach is to use a web service. In Python, Flask is a popular lightweight web framework that can be used to serve your model.
3. **Monitoring and updating the model**: After deployment, it is important to monitor the model to ensure it is performing as expected. Depending on the application, you might need to retrain your model regularly with fresh data.

While deploying a model might seem straightforward, it can be quite complex, depending on the specifics of your use case. It is important to work closely with a team that understands not only the data science aspects but also the software engineering and DevOps aspects of deployment.

Here are some additional considerations for model deployment:

- **Security**: The model should be protected from unauthorized access.
- **Scalability:** The model should be able to handle large volumes of data.
- **Performance**: The model should be able to provide predictions in a timely manner.

By following these steps, you can deploy your linear regression model and start making predictions on new data.

Data Preprocessing in the Context of Linear Regression

In the context of linear regression, we need to address several key assumptions in order to ensure that the model we build is robust, reliable, and valid. These assumptions include linearity, absence of multicollinearity, and homoscedasticity.

Ensuring linearity

Linear regression assumes that the relationship between the dependent and independent variables is linear. We can visually check this assumption by plotting the relationship between each independent variable and the dependent variable using scatter plots. If the relationship appears non-linear, we can apply transformations such as logarithmic, square root, or reciprocal transformations to linearize the relationship.

Python

```
import matplotlib.pyplot as plt
import seaborn as sns

sns.regplot(x='independent_variable', y='dependent_variable', data=df)
plt.show()
```

Dealing with multicollinearity

Multicollinearity exists when two or more independent variables are highly correlated with each other. It can lead to unstable and unreliable estimates of regression coefficients. We can detect multicollinearity by calculating the Variance Inflation Factor (VIF) for each independent variable. A VIF of 1 indicates that there is no multicollinearity. As a rule of thumb, a variable with a VIF > 5 should be removed.

Python

```
from statsmodels.stats.outliers_influence import variance_inflation_factor

vif = pd.DataFrame()
vif["VIF Factor"] = [variance_inflation_factor(X.values, i) for i in range(X.shape[1])]
vif["features"] = X.columns
```

Homoscedasticity

Linear regression assumes that the variance of the errors is constant across all levels of the independent variables. This is known as homoscedasticity. If the variance of the errors differs at different values of the independent variables, we have a condition

Data Preprocessing with Linear Regression

known as heteroscedasticity. We can visually check this assumption by plotting residuals against predicted values.

Python

```
plt.scatter(y_pred, residuals)
plt.xlabel('Predicted values')
plt.ylabel('Residuals')
plt.show()
```

By ensuring that our data meets these assumptions, we can have more confidence in our linear regression model's predictions.

Use case: The Ames Housing dataset is a valuable resource for both machine learning enthusiasts and industry professionals. It contains a comprehensive set of attributes of residential homes in Ames, Iowa, which can be used to predict house prices.

This dataset provides fertile ground for creating robust predictive models to forecast house prices. The predictive prowess of these models can be used by potential home buyers, sellers, and investors to make data-driven decisions in the real estate market.

For example, potential home buyers can use the model to ascertain the fair market price of their dream house. Sellers can determine the optimal listing price for a quick and profitable sale. And investors can identify undervalued properties ripe for investment.

In this way, the Ames Housing dataset serves not just as a playground for machine learning exploration, but as a critical tool in shaping data-driven decisions in the high-stakes world of real estate.

Here are some of the key points of the text:
- The Ames Housing dataset is a comprehensive set of attributes of residential homes in Ames, Iowa.
- The dataset can be used to predict house prices.
- The predictive prowess of the models can be used by potential home buyers, sellers, and investors to make data-driven decisions in the real estate market.
- The Ames Housing dataset is a valuable resource for both machine learning enthusiasts and industry professionals.

Downloading the "House Prices - Advanced Regression Techniques" Dataset from Kaggle

The "House Prices - Advanced Regression Techniques" dataset is a popular dataset for machine learning competitions. It contains information on house prices in Ames, Iowa. To download the dataset from Kaggle, you will need to follow these steps:

1. Install the Kaggle API.
2. Generate your Kaggle API key.
3. Configure your API key locally.
4. Download the dataset.

Installing the Kaggle API

The Kaggle API is a Python library that allows you to download datasets from Kaggle. To install the Kaggle API, you can use the following command:

```
pip install kaggle
```

Generating your Kaggle API key

To generate your Kaggle API key, you will need to go to your Kaggle account settings page. In the section labeled API, select "Create New API Token." This will download a kaggle.json file containing your API credentials.

Configuring your API key locally

Once you have generated your Kaggle API key, you need to place the **kaggle.json** file in the correct location on your machine. Create a directory named .kaggle in your home directory and move the **kaggle.json** file into it. For security reasons, limit the permissions of the **kaggle.json** file.

If you are using a Unix-based system (such as Linux or Mac), you can accomplish this with the following commands:

```
mkdir ~/.kaggle

mv kaggle.json ~/.kaggle/

chmod 600 ~/.kaggle/kaggle.json
```

If you are using Windows, create the **.kaggle** directory manually and move the kaggle.json file there.

Downloading the dataset

With your Kaggle API key now set up, you can download datasets directly. To do this, you will need the dataset's identifier, which can be found in its Kaggle URL.

In the case of the "House Prices - Advanced Regression Techniques" dataset, the identifier is house-prices-advanced-regression-techniques. The command to download the data would look like this:

```
kaggle competitions download -c house-prices-advanced-regression-techniques
```

Here, the `-c` flag denotes that you are downloading a competition dataset.

After running the command, navigate to the directory where you want the data downloaded. The data will be downloaded as a zip file. You can unzip the file using any tool to access the actual CSV data files.

The real estate dataset provides a wealth of data that can be used to explore multiple aspects of the housing market. Some of the questions we could ask include:

- What are the main factors that influence the price of a house?
- How has the price of housing changed over the years?
- Are there any significant differences in house prices between different neighborhoods?
- How does the presence or absence of certain features (like a pool, fireplace, or basement) affect the sale price of a house?
- Can we predict the selling price of a house based on its features?

Our main goal in this project could be to create a model that accurately predicts the price of a house based on its features. This model would be valuable to a variety of stakeholders, including homeowners looking to sell, prospective buyers, and real estate professionals. It could also be used to better understand the housing market in general and help identify important trends or patterns.

To achieve this goal, we would need to perform the following tasks:

1. Perform exploratory data analysis to understand the distributions of individual variables, spot outliers, and find relationships between different variables.
2. Preprocess the data to clean it, handle missing values, and convert categorical data into a format that can be used by a machine learning algorithm.
3. Train a predictive model using machine learning techniques.
4. Evaluate the model to assess its performance.

5. Interpret the model to identify which features have the most influence on house prices.
6. Fine-tune the model to improve its performance.
7. Deploy the model for use in real-world predictions.

This is just a high-level overview of the project. The specific tasks and steps involved would vary depending on the specific dataset and the goals of the project.

The data you provided is a description of the houses that were sold in Ames, Iowa, between 2006 and 2010. The data includes information about the type of dwelling, the size of the lot, the number of bedrooms and bathrooms, the quality of the materials used in construction, and the heating and cooling systems.

The data is organized into 82 columns, each of which represents a different characteristic of the house. Some of the most important columns include:

- **MSSubClass**: This column identifies the type of dwelling. The values in this column range from 20 to 190, and each value represents a different type of dwelling, such as a single-family detached house, a duplex, or a townhouse.
- **MSZoning**: This column identifies the general zoning classification of the sale. The values in this column range from A to RM, and each value represents a different zoning classification, such as residential high density, residential low density, or residential medium density.
- **LotFrontage**: This column represents the linear feet of the street connected to the property.
- **LotArea**: This column represents the lot size in square feet.
- **OverallQual**: This column rates the overall material and finish of the house. The values in this column range from 1 to 10, with 10 representing the highest quality.
- **OverallCond**: This column rates the overall condition of the house. The values in this column range from 1 to 10, with 10 representing the best condition.
- **YearBuilt**: This column represents the original construction date of the house.
- **YearRemodAdd**: This column represents the remodel date of the house. If the house has not been remodeled, the value in this column will be the same as the value in the YearBuilt column.
- **SalePrice:** This column represents the sale price of the house.

The data can be used to answer a variety of questions about the housing market in Ames, Iowa. For example, you could use the data to determine the average sale price of a house in a particular neighborhood or to identify the most popular type of dwelling in the city.

Python Code – Comprehensive Exploratory Data Analysis

We begin by importing the necessary libraries: pandas, matplotlib.pyplot, and seaborn. These libraries will be used for data manipulation, analysis, and visualization.

Next, we load the dataset named train.csv into a DataFrame called df.

The dataset is then segregated into two parts based on the type of data in the columns. All numeric data is stored in the numeric_data DataFrame, and all categorical data is stored in the categorical_data DataFrame.

We then use the .describe() method to get some basic statistical details of the numeric data, such as percentiles, mean, and standard deviation.

For each numeric variable, we create two plots: a histogram (distribution plot) and a box plot. The histogram gives an overview of the distribution of the data, while the box plot displays the statistical measures of the data. Outliers can be easily identified in box plots.

For each categorical variable, we print the value counts and create a bar plot. A bar plot shows the frequency of each category of a categorical variable.

For each numeric variable, we calculate the Interquartile Range (IQR), which is the range between the first quartile (25 percentile) and the third quartile (75 percentile). Any data point that falls below `Q1 - 1.5 * IQR` or above `Q3 + 1.5 * IQR` is considered an outlier.

We then calculate the correlation matrix for the numeric variables using the .corr() function. The correlation matrix helps us to understand the relationship between different variables.

Finally, we create a scatterplot matrix for the numeric variables using the scatter_matrix() function. This helps us to visualize the pairwise relationships and distributions of the variables.

This script performs a comprehensive Exploratory Data Analysis (EDA) on the dataset, providing insights into the dataset's structure, relationships, and distributions of the variables, and identifying potential outliers.

```python
# Import the necessary libraries

import matplotlib.pyplot as plt

import seaborn as sns

import pandas as pd

# This code performs Exploratory Data Analysis (EDA) on the Ames Housing Dataset.

print('Exploratory Data Analysis of the Ames Housing Dataset')

# This loads the dataset from a CSV file.

df = pd.read_csv('train.csv')

# This separates the numeric and categorical variables into two separate DataFrames.

numeric_data = df.select_dtypes(include=[np.number])

categorical_data = df.select_dtypes(exclude=[np.number])


# This prints out the basic statistics for the numeric variables.

print('Basic statistics for numeric variables:')

print(numeric_data.describe())


# This creates a distribution plot and a box plot for each numeric variable.

for col in numeric_data.columns:

    plt.figure(figsize=(14, 6))

    plt.subplot(1, 2, 1)

    sns.histplot(numeric_data[col], bins=30, kde=True)

    plt.title(f'Distribution of {col}')

    plt.subplot(1, 2, 2)

    sns.boxplot(y=numeric_data[col])
```

```python
    plt.title(f'Box Plot of {col}')

    plt.show()


# This prints out the counts for each categorical variable and creates
a bar plot for each categorical variable.
for col in categorical_data.columns:

    print(f'\nCounts for {col}:\n')

    print(categorical_data[col].value_counts())


    # Bar plot for the categorical variables

    plt.figure(figsize=(10, 4))

    sns.countplot(x=categorical_data[col])

    plt.title(f'Bar plot of {col}')

    plt.xticks(rotation=90)

    plt.show()


# This identifies any outliers in the numeric variables.
for col in numeric_data.columns:

    q1 = numeric_data[col].quantile(0.25)

    q3 = numeric_data[col].quantile(0.75)

    iqr = q3 - q1

    lower_bound = q1 - 1.5 * iqr

    upper_bound = q3 + 1.5 * iqr

    outliers = numeric_data[col].loc[(numeric_data[col] < lower_bound) | (numeric_data[col] > upper_bound)]

    print(f'Outliers for {col}:\n')

    print(outliers)
```

```
# This creates a correlation matrix and plots it as a heatmap.
correlation_matrix = numeric_data.corr()
plt.figure(figsize=(10, 10))
sns.heatmap(correlation_matrix, annot=True)
plt.title('Correlation Matrix')
plt.show()
# This creates a scatterplot matrix for the numeric variables.
scatterplot_matrix = pd.plotting.scatter_matrix(numeric_data, figsize=(15, 15), diagonal='kde')
plt.show()
```

Comprehensive Data Preprocessing

1. **Import necessary libraries**: This includes libraries for data manipulation (`pandas`, `numpy`), preprocessing (`StandardScaler`, `OneHotEncoder`, `SimpleImputer`, `ColumnTransformer` from sklearn.preprocessing), statistics (`scipy.stats`), and machine learning (`Pipeline`, `train_test_split` from sklearn).
2. **Load the dataset**: The data is loaded from a CSV file into a pandas DataFrame.
3. **Separate the target variable**: The target variable, `'SalePrice'`, is separated from the rest of the dataset.
4. **Separate numeric and categorical columns**: The code identifies which columns in the DataFrame are numeric and which are categorical.
5. **Define preprocessing pipelines for both numeric and categorical data**:
    a. For numeric data, the pipeline consists of two steps: filling missing values with the median of the column and standardizing the data (subtracting the mean and dividing by the standard deviation).
    b. For categorical data, the pipeline also has two steps: filling missing values with the constant string 'missing', and then one-hot encoding the categories. One-hot encoding is a process by which categorical variables are converted into a form that could be provided to machine learning algorithms to improve prediction.
6. **Combine preprocessing steps**: The ColumnTransformer is used to apply the appropriate preprocessing pipeline to the numeric and categorical columns.

Data Preprocessing with Linear Regression

7. **Create a pipeline**: A final pipeline is created which applies the preprocessor.
8. **Split data into training and test datasets**: The data is split into a training set, which the model will learn from, and a test set, which will be used to evaluate the model's performance.
9. **Preprocess the dataset**: The pipeline's **fit_transform** method is used to fit the preprocessing steps to the training data and then apply the transformations. The transformations are applied to the test data using the transform method. This ensures that the same transformations are applied to both the training and test data.

```
import pandas as pd

import numpy as np

from sklearn.preprocessing import StandardScaler, OneHotEncoder

from sklearn.impute import SimpleImputer

from sklearn.compose import ColumnTransformer

from scipy import stats

from sklearn.pipeline import Pipeline

from sklearn.model_selection import train_test_split


# Load the dataset
df = pd.read_csv('train.csv')


# Separate the target variable if necessary
y = df['SalePrice']

df = df.drop(columns='SalePrice')


# Separate numeric and categorical columns
numeric_cols = df.select_dtypes(include=[np.number]).columns

categorical_cols = df.select_dtypes(include=['object', 'category']).columns
```

```python
# Define preprocessing pipelines for both numeric and categorical data
numeric_transformer = Pipeline(steps=[
    ('imputer', SimpleImputer(strategy='median')),  # Fill missing values using Median
    ('scaler', StandardScaler()),  # Standardize features by removing the mean and scaling to unit variance
])

categorical_transformer = Pipeline(steps=[
    ('imputer', SimpleImputer(strategy='constant', fill_value='missing')),  # Fill missing values with the constant string "missing"
    ('onehot', OneHotEncoder(handle_unknown='ignore')),  # Use one-hot encoder to transform categorical values into a one-hot numeric array
])

# Combine preprocessing steps
preprocessor = ColumnTransformer(
    transformers=[
        ('num', numeric_transformer, numeric_cols),
        ('cat', categorical_transformer, categorical_cols)
    ])

# Create preprocessing and training pipeline
pipeline = Pipeline(steps=[('preprocessor', preprocessor)])

# Split data into training and test datasets
X_train, X_test, y_train, y_test = train_test_split(df, y, test_size=0.2, random_state=42)
```

```
# Preprocess the dataset
X_train = pipeline.fit_transform(X_train)
X_test = pipeline.transform(X_test)
```

Feature Importance and Feature Selection

The RandomForestRegressor model is fit for the training data. This means that the model learns the relationship between the features and the target variable based on the training data.

The feature importances are then calculated. This is done by measuring how much each feature contributes to the model's predictions. The features with the highest importance scores are the most important for predicting the target variable.

The categorical features are one-hot encoded. This means that each category in the categorical variable is converted into its own binary feature (0 or 1). This is done because the RandomForestRegressor model can only understand numerical features.

The list of all features, both numeric and one-hot encoded categorical, is created. This list is used to select the most important features.

The feature selector is used to select the most important features. The feature selector is a machine learning algorithm that identifies the features that are most important for predicting the target variable.

The selected features are printed out. These are the features that the feature selector deemed important based on the criteria specified when the feature selector was instantiated.

The feature importance scores are sorted in descending order. This means that the features with the highest importance scores are at the top of the list.

The feature ranking is printed out. This shows the rank of each feature and its corresponding importance score.

Finally, the feature importances are plotted in a bar chart. This gives a visual representation of the importance scores of the features, making it easier to compare the importance of different features.

```
import matplotlib.pyplot as plt

# Fit RandomForestRegressor to our dataset
rf.fit(X_train, y_train)
```

```python
# Get feature importances from RandomForestRegressor
importances = rf.feature_importances_

# Get the list of features after one-hot encoding for categorical
variables
cat_encoder = preprocessor.named_transformers_['cat']['onehot']
cat_one_hot_features = list(cat_encoder.get_feature_names_
out(categorical_cols))

# Combine the list of numeric features and the list of one-hot encoded
categorical features
all_features = list(numeric_cols) + cat_one_hot_features

# Apply the feature selector to the list of all_features
selected_features = np.array(all_features)[sfm.get_support()]

# Print selected features
for feature in selected_features:
    print(feature)

# Plot the feature importances of the forest
indices = np.argsort(importances)[::-1]

# Print the feature ranking
print("Feature ranking:")

for f in range(X_train.shape[1]):
    print("%d. feature %d (%f)" % (f + 1, indices[f],
    importances[indices[f]]))
```

```
# Plot the impurity-based feature importances of the forest
plt.figure(figsize=(12,6))
plt.title("Feature importances")
plt.bar(range(X_train.shape[1]), importances[indices],
        color="r", align="center")
plt.xticks(range(X_train.shape[1]), indices)
plt.xlim([-1, X_train.shape[1]])
plt.show()
```

Feature importance:

First, the necessary libraries are imported. These libraries include the RandomForestRegressor class from the ensemble module and the `SelectFromModel` class from the `feature_selection` module in scikit-learn.

Next, the model is defined. An instance of the RandomForestRegressor model is created with 100 estimators and a random state of 42. The RandomForestRegressor is an ensemble model that uses a collection of decision trees to perform regression tasks.

Then, the feature selector is created. An instance of the SelectFromModel class is created, specifying the previously defined RandomForestRegressor model (rf) as the base estimator. `SelectFromModel` is a feature selection technique that selects features based on importance scores computed by the underlying model.

The feature selector is fit to the training data. This step trains the underlying RandomForestRegressor model and computes the feature importances.

The training and test datasets are transformed using the fitted feature selector. The transform method selects the most important features based on the specified feature importance threshold. The resulting datasets, `X_train_selected` and `X_test_selected`, contain only the selected features.

By performing feature selection, the code aims to reduce the dimensionality of the dataset by selecting the most informative features for the regression task. This can help improve model performance, reduce overfitting, and enhance interpretability.

After executing this code, you can proceed to train a regression model using the transformed datasets (`X_train_selected` and `X_test_selected`) and evaluate its performance.

```python
from sklearn.ensemble import RandomForestRegressor
from sklearn.feature_selection import SelectFromModel

# Define the model
rf = RandomForestRegressor(n_estimators=100, random_state=42)

# Feature selector
sfm = SelectFromModel(rf)

# Fit selector to training data
sfm.fit(X_train, y_train)

# Transform train and test datasets
X_train_selected = sfm.transform(X_train)
X_test_selected = sfm.transform(X_test)
```

Model fitting:

The code first fits the RandomForestRegressor model to the training data. This is done by calling the **fit()** method on the model and passing in the selected features of the training data and the corresponding target values.

The model then makes predictions on the selected features of both the training and test datasets. This is done by calling the **predict()** method on the model and passing in the selected features of the dataset. The predicted target values are stored in **y_pred_train** and **y_pred_test**, respectively.

The code then calculates the Mean Squared Error (MSE), Mean Absolute Error (MAE), and R^2 score for both the training and test datasets. This is done by calling the **mean_squared_error(), mean_absolute_error(), and r2_score()** methods on the training and test datasets, respectively.

The final part of the code prints the calculated metrics. These metrics provide insights into the performance of the RandomForestRegressor model on the training and test datasets.

Data Preprocessing with Linear Regression

```python
# Fit RandomForestRegressor to our dataset
rf.fit(X_train_selected, y_train)

# Make predictions
y_pred_train = rf.predict(X_train_selected)
y_pred_test = rf.predict(X_test_selected)

# Calculate metrics
mse_train = mean_squared_error(y_train, y_pred_train)
mse_test = mean_squared_error(y_test, y_pred_test)
mae_train = mean_absolute_error(y_train, y_pred_train)
mae_test = mean_absolute_error(y_test, y_pred_test)
r2_train = r2_score(y_train, y_pred_train)
r2_test = r2_score(y_test, y_pred_test)

# Print metrics
print(f'Training Mean Squared Error: {mse_train}')
print(f'Test Mean Squared Error: {mse_test}')
print(f'Training Mean Absolute Error: {mae_train}')
print(f'Test Mean Absolute Error: {mae_test}')
print(f'Training R^2 Score: {r2_train}')
print(f'Test R^2 Score: {r2_test}')
```

The code first imports the joblib module, which provides functionality for saving and loading Python objects, including machine learning models.

The next line, **joblib.dump(rf, 'trained_model.pkl'),** saves the trained model rf as a file named **trained_model.pkl** using the joblib.dump() function. The first argument is the object you want to save (in this case, the trained model), and the second argument is the filename or path where you want to save it. This creates a serialized representation of the model that can be easily loaded later.

The next line, **loaded_model = joblib.load('trained_model.pkl'),** loads the saved model from the file **trained_model.pkl** using the **joblib.load()** function. It assigns the loaded model to the variable loaded_model. This allows you to access the trained model and use it for predictions or other operations.

The final line, **y_pred = loaded_model.predict(X_test_selected),** demonstrates how to use the loaded model to make predictions on new data. Assuming **loaded_model** is a regression model, you can call the **predict()** method on the loaded model and pass in the new data **X_test_selected**. It returns the predicted values **y_pred** based on the loaded model.

```
import joblib

# Save the trained model
joblib.dump(rf, 'trained_model.pkl')

# Load the saved model
loaded_model = joblib.load('trained_model.pkl')

# Make predictions using the loaded model
y_pred = loaded_model.predict(X_test_selected)
```

Conclusion

This chapter has meticulously explored the essential aspects of data preprocessing and linear regression, providing a comprehensive understanding of these fundamental elements in data analysis and modeling. Through this in-depth exploration, we have uncovered the intricate details and paramount importance of preparing data correctly and applying linear regression techniques effectively.

Points to Remember

- **Data Preprocessing**: The chapter emphatically highlighted the significance of data preprocessing, emphasizing it as a crucial step in any data analysis process. By meticulously cleaning, transforming, and normalizing the data, we ensure the accuracy and reliability of the results, laying a solid foundation for meaningful insights.

- **Linear Regression**: We delved into the principles of linear regression, a foundational technique in predictive modeling. This encompassed understanding its underlying assumptions, the mechanics of how it operates, and its application in various scenarios, empowering us to make informed predictions based on historical data.
- **Practical Applications**: Unleashing the Power of Linear Regression: The chapter provided valuable insights into the practical application of linear regression in real-world scenarios. We witnessed its versatility and effectiveness in predicting outcomes based on a range of input variables, demonstrating its ability to transform raw data into actionable insights.
- **Navigating Challenges and Considerations**: We also discussed the challenges and considerations when implementing linear regression, acknowledging the importance of addressing non-linear relationships, understanding the impact of outliers, and carefully selecting relevant features. By carefully considering these factors, we can ensure the robustness and generalizability of our models.

CHAPTER 2
Structured Data and Logistic Regression

Introduction

Building upon the machine learning fundamentals established in the previous chapter, this chapter delves deeper into the fascinating world of structured data and its powerful application in logistic regression models. We will embark on a journey to explore the effective handling and utilization of structured data, the ubiquitous format driving countless practical applications. Along the way, we will equip ourselves with the powerful tool of logistic regression, a champion in the realm of binary classification problems.

Structure

In this chapter, the following topics will be covered:
- APIs and Structured Data: Data Extraction
- Handling Categorical Variables: Data Preparation
- Introduction to Logistic Regression: The Predictive Power of Binary Classification
- Implementation: Transforming Concepts into Practice with Logistic Regression Modeling
- Project: Putting It All Together: A Practical Application of Logistic Regression

APIs and Structured Data

APIs, or Application Programming Interfaces, are tools that allow us to access data from other sources. In our case, we will use an API to fetch the Telco-Customer-Churn.json dataset.

The following code shows how to fetch the data using the requests library:

Python

```python
import requests import pandas as pd


url = "https://api.example.com/data/Telco-Customer-Churn.json"
response = requests.get(url)

data_json = response.json() data = pd.DataFrame(data_json)
```

Handling Categorical Variables

Logistic regression models require numerical input features. However, our dataset contains some categorical variables, such as `gender` and `InternetService`. We need to convert these variables into a numerical format before we can use them in our model.

There are two common ways to encode categorical variables, which are as follows:

- **One-hot encoding:** This creates a new column for each unique value of the categorical variable. The value of each new column is 1 if the original variable had that value, and 0 otherwise.
- **Label encoding:** This assigns a unique integer to each value of the categorical variable.

The following code shows how to one-hot encode the categorical variables in our dataset:

Python

```python
data_encoded = pd.get_dummies(data, columns=['gender',
'InternetService', 'Contract', 'PaymentMethod'], drop_first=True)
```

Use code with caution.

Introduction to Logistic Regression

Logistic regression is a statistical model that is used to predict the probability of an event. In our case, we can use logistic regression to predict the probability of a customer churning.

The following equation shows the logistic regression model:

$$p(y = 1 \mid x) = \frac{1}{1 + e^{-wx}}$$

where:

- **p(y = 1 | x)** is the probability of the event occurring (churning in our case) given the features **x**
- **w** is the weight vector
- **x** is the feature vector

The weight vector **w** is learned by the model during training.

Implementation

We can implement logistic regression using the Scikit-learn library. The following code shows how to build a logistic regression model using Scikit-learn:

Python

```python
from sklearn.model_selection import train_test_split from sklearn.linear_model import LogisticRegression

# Splitting data
X = data_encoded.drop(['customerID', 'Churn'], axis=1)
y = data_encoded['Churn'].apply(lambda x: 1 if x == "Yes" else 0)
X_train, X_test, y_train, y_test = train_test_split(X, y, test_size=0.3, random_state=42)

# Training the model
model = LogisticRegression() model.fit(X_train, y_train)
```

The **train_test_split()** function splits the data into a training set and a test set. The training set is used to train the model, and the test set is used to evaluate the model's performance.

The `LogisticRegression()` function creates a logistic regression model. The fit() function trains the model on the training set.

Evaluation

We can evaluate the performance of the logistic regression model using the following metrics:

- **Accuracy:** The percentage of predictions that are correct.
- **Precision:** The percentage of positive predictions that are actually positive.

    TP / (TP + FP)

    TP (True Positives): Correctly identified positive cases

    TN (True Negatives): Correctly identified negative cases

    FP (False Positives): Incorrectly identified positive cases

    FN (False Negatives): Incorrectly identified negative cases

- **Recall:** The percentage of actual positives that are correctly predicted as positive.

The following code shows how to evaluate the performance of the logistic regression model:

Python

```
from sklearn.metrics import accuracy_score, precision_score, recall_score

# Evaluate the model
accuracy = accuracy_score(y_test, model.predict(X_test)) precision = precision_score(y_test, model.predict(X_test)) recall = recall_score(y_test, model.predict(X_test))

print("Accuracy:", accuracy) print("Precision:", precision)
print("Recall:", recall)
```

End-of-Chapter Project: Predicting Loan Defaults

In this project, we will build a model to predict whether a loan will go bad, as indicated by the **bad_flag** variable. We will also analyze the expected default rate at different approval levels.

Objectives:

- Build a model to predict the **bad_flag** value.
- Analyze the expected default rate at different approval levels.

Instructions:

1. **Data Exploration**
   a. Read the dataset using pandas and get a feel for its structure.
   b. Investigate the statistical properties of the data using methods such as `data.describe()`.
   c. Identify any potential issues: missing values, outliers, class imbalances, and so on.

2. **Feature Engineering**
   a. Handle missing values by either imputation or deletion.
   b. Convert categorical variables into a numerical format. You might use one-hot encoding or label encoding.
   c. Scale numerical features, if necessary, using `StandardScaler` or `MinMaxScaler`.

3. **Algorithm Selection**
   a. Given the task is binary classification, start with a simple algorithm like Logistic Regression.
   b. Consider trying more complex algorithms, if necessary, such as Random Forest or Gradient Boosted Trees.

4. **Addressing Class Imbalance**
   a. Check the distribution of the target variable, **bad_flag**.
   b. If an imbalance is detected, consider techniques like SMOTE or ADASYN for oversampling.

5. **Hyperparameter Optimization**
   a. Utilize techniques like grid search or random search to optimize your model parameters.

6. **Model Evaluation and Interpretation**
   a. Split the dataset into training and test sets.
   b. Train your model and evaluate its performance using metrics suitable for binary classification: accuracy, precision, recall, and the ROC curve.
   c. Discuss the results. Which features played a significant role in the prediction?

7. **Conclusion**
   a. Based on your model, analyze the expected default rate at different approval levels.
   b. Reflect on the model's performance. Would you trust it in a real-world scenario? Why or why not?

Deeper Dive into Data Pre-processing

In this section, we will explore the data preprocessing steps that are crucial for the effectiveness of logistic regression.

Dealing with Missing Values

Missing values are often encountered in real-world data. They can be detrimental to the performance of our model, so it is essential to address them.

There are several techniques for dealing with missing values, which are as follows:
- **Dropping**: If the dataset is large enough and the missing data is random or inconsequential, you can drop those rows.
- **Imputation**: Replace missing values with a specific value, such as the mean, median, or mode.
- **Prediction**: Use algorithms to predict the missing value.

For example, if our tenure column had missing values, we might impute using the median:

Python
```
data['tenure'].fillna(data['tenure'].median(), inplace=True)
```

Feature Scaling

In logistic regression, it is important to scale the features, especially when they have different scales. This helps the algorithm converge faster.

Python

```
from sklearn.preprocessing import StandardScaler

scaler = StandardScaler()
data_encoded[['tenure', 'Charges']] = scaler.fit_transform(data_encoded[['tenure', 'Charges']])
```

Handling Imbalanced Classes

If there is a vast difference between the number of positive and negative instances (for example, many more customers who do not churn than those who do), it is important to address this imbalance. Techniques for handling imbalanced classes include:

- **Up-sampling**: This involves duplicating the minority class to balance the dataset.
- **Down-sampling**: This involves removing data from the majority class to balance the dataset.
- **Using synthetic data**: This involves generating new data points to balance the dataset.

Logistic Regression Intuition

Logistic regression is a statistical model that predicts the probability of an event. In our case, we can use logistic regression to predict the probability of a customer churning.

The logistic regression model is parameterized by a set of weights and biases. The weights are multiplied by the features of a data point, and the biases are added to the result. This sum is then passed through a sigmoid function to get a probability.

The sigmoid function is a non-linear function that squashes the output of the model to a value between 0 and 1. The output of the sigmoid function is interpreted as the probability of the event occurring.

In the upcoming sections, we will look at implementing logistic regression using Scikit-learn, model evaluation, and deriving strategies for customer retention.

Implementing Logistic Regression in Scikit-learn

Scikit-learn is a popular machine learning library in Python. It provides a simple and intuitive API for implementing a variety of machine learning algorithms, including logistic regression.

To implement logistic regression in Scikit-learn, we first need to split our data into features (X) and target (y). The features are the independent variables that we will use to predict the target variable. The target variable is the variable that we are trying to predict.

Python

```
# Assuming 'data_encoded' is our preprocessed data
X = data_encoded.drop('Churn', axis=1) y = data_encoded['Churn']
```

Once we have split our data, we need to split it into a training set and a test set. The training set will be used to train the model, and the test set will be used to evaluate the model's performance:

Python

```
from sklearn.model_selection import train_test_split
X_train, X_test, y_train, y_test = train_test_split(X, y, test_size=0.2, random_state=42)
```

Now, we are ready to implement the logistic regression model. We can do this by importing the `LogisticRegression` class from Scikit-learn:

Python

```
from sklearn.linear_model import LogisticRegression
```

We can then instantiate a `LogisticRegression` object and fit it to the training data:

Python

```
logreg = LogisticRegression() logreg.fit(X_train, y_train)
```

Once the model is trained, we can make predictions on the test data:

Python

```
y_pred = logreg.predict(X_test)
```

Structured Data and Logistic Regression

To evaluate the performance of the model, we can use various metrics, such as accuracy, precision, recall, and the F1 score:

Python

```
from sklearn.metrics import classification_report print(classification_report(y_test, y_pred))
```

The classification report will show us the performance of the model in each class.

We can also improve the performance of the model by tuning its hyperparameters. For example, we can adjust the regularization strength C and the type of regularization (L1 or L2). Scikit-learn provides a `GridSearchCV` class that can be used to automate the hyperparameter tuning process.

Project: Customer Churn Prediction

In this project, we will use the knowledge from this chapter to build a model that predicts customer churn for the Telco dataset. Beyond mere prediction, our goal is to derive insights that can help in formulating retention strategies.

Delving Deeper into Logistic Regression

Having set up our logistic regression model with Scikit-learn, let's understand the theory and mathematics behind it, which will provide you with a richer perspective on how decisions are made.

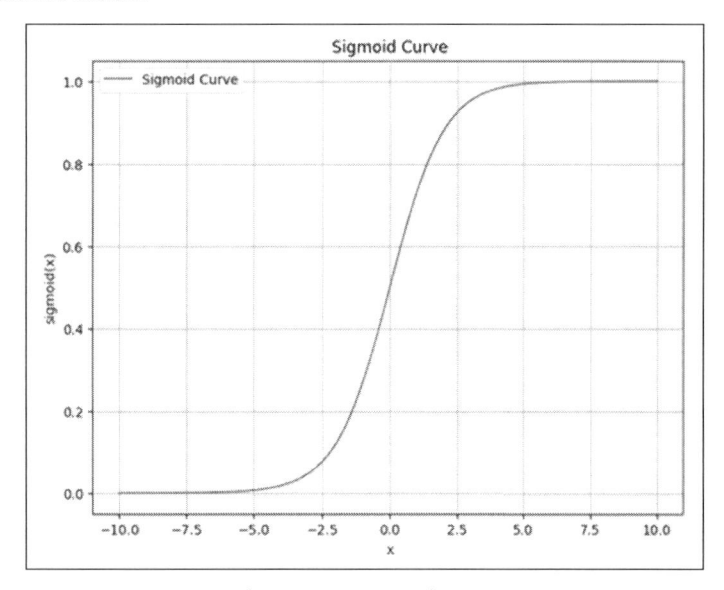

Figure 2.1: *Sigmoid curve*

Explanation of the Sigmoid Curve

The sigmoid function, often called the logistic function, is a function that takes any real-valued input and maps it to a value between 0 and 1. This characteristic makes it extremely useful in logistic regression and neural networks.

Mathematical Representation:

$$f(x) = 1 / (1 + e^{-x})$$

where:
- `f(x)` is the output value which lies in the range (0,1)
- `e` is the base of natural logarithms
- `x` is the input value

Key Characteristics:
- **S-Shaped Curve:** As evident from the plot, the sigmoid function is S-shaped or sigmoidal.
- **Boundaries:** It approaches 0 as x tends to negative infinity and approaches 1 as x tends to positive infinity.
- **Center at 0.5**: The output is 0.5 when the input is 0.
- **Use in Probability**: Due to its nature of squeezing values between 0 and 1, it's useful in scenarios like logistic regression where the output can be interpreted as a probability.
- **Derivative**: The sigmoid function's derivative is maximum at the center (that is, at x = 0), which makes it susceptible to the vanishing gradient problem in deep learning.

The sigmoid function serves as an activation function in neural networks, helping introduce non-linearity to the model. However, in deep networks, other functions like the ReLU (Rectified Linear Unit) have become more popular due to the drawbacks of the sigmoid function, like the vanishing gradient problem.

In the context of logistic regression, the sigmoid function helps in predicting the probability. The function's input is the result of a linear combination of predictor variables, and the output represents the probability of the dependent variable being 1.

The Logistic Function

The logistic function is an S-shaped curve that can take any real-valued number and map it between 0 and 1. This is useful in our binary classification problem since our target values are 0 and 1.

Mathematically, the logistic function is defined as:

$$f(x) = 1 / (1 + e\text{\^{}}-x)$$

Where e is the base of natural logarithms, and x is the input to the function (a linear combination of the independent variables).

Odds and Log-Odds

Before delving into logistic regression, it's essential to understand the concept of odds. If p is the probability of a particular event, then the odds in favor of the event are:

$$\text{odds} = p / (1-p)$$

Logistic regression doesn't model the probability p directly. Instead, it models the log-odds, the natural logarithm of odds:

$$\log(\text{odds}) = \ln(p / (1-p))$$

Logistic Regression Equation

In linear regression, we model the outcome Y as a linear combination of the predictors. In logistic regression, we model the log-odds of the probability p of the default class:

$$\ln(p / (1-p)) = β0 + β1X1 + β2X2 + ... + βkXk$$

where:

- **β0, β1,** ... are the coefficients.
- **X1, X2,** ... are the predictor variables.

Interpreting Coefficients

The coefficients in logistic regression are in terms of log-odds. For a one-unit change in the predictor variable, the log-odds of the outcome will change by the corresponding coefficient value, holding all other predictors constant.

Handling Categorical Variables in Logistic Regression

In our Telco customer churn dataset, we noticed columns, including `MultipleLines`, `InternetService`, and so on, that contain categorical values. For logistic regression to process these variables, we need to convert them into a form it can understand, namely numbers.

One-Hot Encoding

One common method is one-hot encoding, which involves converting each value of the categorical column into a new binary column.

Example:

InternetService: DSL, Fiber optic, No would be converted to:

InternetService_DSL: 0 or 1

InternetService_Fiber_optic: 0 or 1

InternetService_No: 0 or 1

This transformation becomes trivial by using libraries like pandas:

Python

```
data_encoded = pd.get_dummies(data, columns=['InternetService'],
drop_first=True)
```

Model Evaluation and Validation

Now that we have a logistic regression model in place, we need to evaluate its performance. This is done by comparing the model's predictions to the actual values.

There are a number of metrics that can be used to evaluate a logistic regression model. Some of the most common metrics include:

- **Accuracy**:
  - **Formula:** `(TP + TN) / (TP + TN + FP + FN)`
  - **Explanation:** It measures the overall proportion of correct predictions made by the model, regardless of class.
- **Precision**:
  - **Formula**: `TP / (TP + FP)`
  - **Explanation**: It measures the proportion of positive predictions that are actually positive. It's useful when you want to minimize false positives.
- **Recall**:
  - **Formula:** `TP / (TP + FN)`
  - **Explanation**: It measures the proportion of actual positives that are correctly identified as positive. It's important when you want to minimize false negatives.
- **F1 score**:
  - **Formula**: `2 * (Precision * Recall) / (Precision + Recall)`
  - **Explanation**: It's a harmonic mean of precision and recall, providing a balanced measure that considers both. It's valuable when you need to consider both types of errors equally.

- **ROC Curve**:
    - o It's not a single formula, but a curve plotted with True Positive Rate (TPR) on the y-axis and False Positive Rate (FPR) on the x-axis.
    - o **Explanation**: It visualizes the trade-off between TPR (sensitivity) and FPR (1 - specificity) at different classification thresholds.
- **AUC**:

    Numerical value representing the area under the ROC curve.
    - o **Explanation:** It summarizes the ROC curve's performance into a single value. A higher AUC indicates better model performance in distinguishing between classes.

In addition to these metrics, it is also important to consider the following factors when evaluating a logistic regression model:

- **The complexity of the model**: A more complex model is more likely to overfit the training data, but it may also be more accurate.
- **The regularization strength**: Regularization can help to prevent overfitting, but it can also reduce the accuracy of the model.
- **The dataset**: The size and quality of the dataset can have a significant impact on the performance of the model.

Train-Test Split

One common method for evaluating a logistic regression model is to split the data into two sets: a training set and a test set. The training set is used to train the model, and the test set is used to evaluate the model's performance.

The train-test split should be done randomly, and the test set should be a representative sample of the data. The size of the test set is typically 20-30% of the total dataset.

Confusion Matrix

A confusion matrix is a table that summarizes the performance of a classification model. It shows the number of true positives (TP), false positives (FP), true negatives (TN), and false negatives (FN) for the model.

The TP are the cases where the model correctly predicted the positive class. The FP are the cases where the model incorrectly predicted the positive class. The TN are the cases where the model correctly predicted the negative class. The FN are the cases where the model incorrectly predicted the negative class.

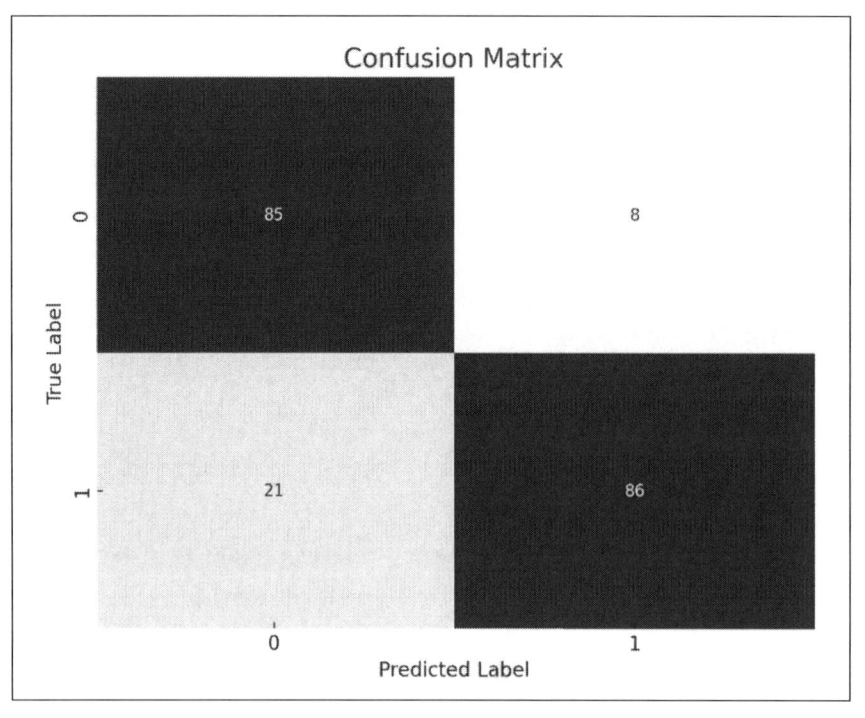

Figure 2.2: *Confusion matrix*

The confusion matrix can be used to calculate the following metrics:
- **Accuracy**: The accuracy is the percentage of all cases that the model correctly predicts.
- **Precision**: The precision is the percentage of positive predictions that are actually positive.
- **Recall**: The recall is the percentage of actual positives that are predicted positive.
- **F1 score**: The F1 score is a weighted average of precision and recall.

ROC Curve and AUC

The ROC curve is a graphical plot of the model's true positive rate (TPR) against its false positive rate (FPR). The TPR is the percentage of actual positives that are predicted positive. The FPR is the percentage of actual negatives that are predicted positive.

The AUC is the area under the ROC curve. A higher AUC indicates a better model.

The ROC curve and AUC are useful for comparing the performance of different models. They are also useful for evaluating the performance of a model as the hyperparameters are tuned.

Structured Data and Logistic Regression

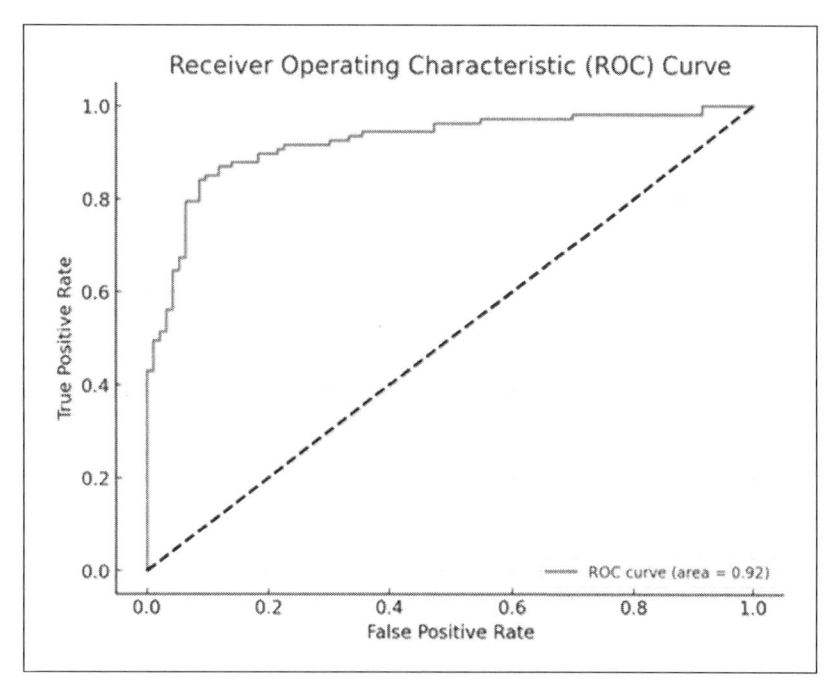

Figure 2.3: ROC Curve

Addressing Overfitting

Overfitting occurs when a model learns the training data too well, capturing noise and anomalies. This can lead to poor performance on the test set.

There are a number of techniques that can be used to address overfitting, which are as follows:

- **Regularization**: Regularization adds a penalty on the model's parameters to prevent them from becoming too large. This can help to prevent the model from overfitting the training data.
- **Data augmentation**: Data augmentation creates new data by artificially modifying the existing data. This can help to prevent the model from memorizing the training data.
- **Early stopping**: Early stopping stops the training process early, before the model has a chance to overfit the training data.

Here is the rewritten text:

Fetching the Data via an API

To fetch data from an API, we can use the requests library in Python. The following code shows how to fetch the Telco Customer Churn dataset from an API:

Python

```
import requests import pandas as pd

# Fetch the data from the API

url = "https://api.example.com/data/Telco-Customer-Churn.json"
response = requests.get(url)

# Check if the request was successful if response.status_code == 200:

raw_data = response.json() else:

print("Failed to retrieve the data.") raw_data = []

# Convert the JSON data to a DataFrame data = pd.DataFrame(raw_data)
```

The **requests.get()** method retrieves the data from the API. The **response.status_code** attribute indicates whether the request was successful. If the request is successful, the **raw_data** variable will contain the JSON data from the API. Otherwise, the **raw_data** variable will be an empty list.

The **pd.DataFrame()** function converts the JSON data to a Pandas DataFrame. This allows us to easily manipulate and analyze the data.

Preliminary Data Inspection

Once we have fetched the data, we can take a preliminary look at its structure. The following code illustrates how to do this:

Python

```
# Check the first few rows of the dataframe print(data.head())


# Understand the data types and missing values print(data.info())
```

The **data.head()** method prints the first few rows of the DataFrame. This gives us a quick overview of the data.

The **data.info()** method prints information about the DataFrame, such as the data types of each column and the number of missing values. This information can help us to identify any potential problems with the data.

Handling Categorical Variables

The logistic regression model requires numerical input features. However, some of the columns in the Telco Customer Churn dataset are categorical, such as gender and

Structured Data and Logistic Regression

Partner. These columns need to be converted to numerical values before we can use them in the logistic regression model.

One common way to convert categorical variables is to use one-hot encoding. One-hot encoding creates a new column for each category in the categorical variable. The value of each new column is 1 if the row belongs to that category and 0 otherwise.

The following code illustrates how to use one-hot encoding to convert the categorical variables in the Telco Customer Churn dataset to numerical values:

Python

```
# One-hot encoding of categorical variables
data_encoded = pd.get_dummies(data, columns=['gender', 'Partner',
'Dependents', 'PhoneService', 'MultipleLines', 'InternetService',
'OnlineSecurity', 'OnlineBackup', 'DeviceProtection', 'TechSupport',
'StreamingTV', 'StreamingMovies', 'Contract', 'PaperlessBilling',
'PaymentMethod'])

print(data_encoded.head())
```

The **pd.get_dummies()** function creates a new column for each category in the specified columns. The value of each new column is 1 if the row belongs to that category and 0 otherwise.

The **data_encoded.head()** method prints the first few rows of the encoded DataFrame. This shows that the categorical variables have been converted to numerical values.

Handling Numerical Variables and Missing Data

In addition to categorical variables, numerical variables may also need to be handled, especially in terms of scaling and missing values.

1. **Checking for Missing Values**

    Before applying machine learning models, it is important to handle missing values in the dataset.

    Python

    ```
    # Check for missing values
    missing_data    =    data_encoded.isnull().sum()    print(missing_
    data[missing_data > 0])
    ```

    The **data_encoded.isnull().sum()** method returns the number of missing values in each column. The **print()** function prints the columns that have missing values.

If there are missing values, we will decide on a strategy based on the column. Common strategies include filling with the mean or median (for numerical columns) or the most frequent value (for categorical columns).

Python

```
# Assuming 'TotalCharges' has missing values data_encoded['TotalCharges'].fillna(data_encoded['TotalCharges'].median(), inplace=True)
```

The **data_encoded['TotalCharges'].fillna()** method fills the missing values in the **TotalCharges** column with the median value of that column.

2. **Scaling Numerical Variables**

   Features like tenure or **TotalCharges** may have different scales. Logistic regression can be sensitive to this due to its mathematical properties. Therefore, we will use **StandardScaler** to scale these variables.

   Python

   ```
   from sklearn.preprocessing import StandardScaler
   scaler = StandardScaler() data_encoded[['tenure', 'TotalCharges']] =
   scaler.fit_transform(data_encoded[['tenure', 'TotalCharges']])
   ```

   The **StandardScaler()** class creates a **StandardScaler** object. The **fit_transform()** method fits the scaler to the data and transforms it.

3. **Encoding the Target Variable**

   For our model, the target variable Churn should also be encoded. We will encode **Yes** as 1 and **No** as 0.

   Python

   ```
   data_encoded['Churn'] = data_encoded['Churn'].map({'Yes': 1, 'No': 0})
   ```

   The **map()** method maps the values in the Churn column to the corresponding numbers.

4. **Splitting the Dataset**

   Before modeling, we will split the data into training and testing sets.

Structured Data and Logistic Regression

Python

```python
from sklearn.model_selection import train_test_split

X = data_encoded.drop('Churn', axis=1) # Excluding the target variable y = data_encoded['Churn']

X_train, X_test, y_train, y_test = train_test_split(X, y, test_size=0.2, random_state=42)
```

The **train_test_split()** function splits the data into training and testing sets. The **X_train** and **y_train** variables contain the training data, while the **X_test** and **y_test** variables contain the testing data.

The **test_size** parameter specifies the proportion of data that should be used for the testing set. The **random_state** parameter specifies the random seed for the split.

Implementation of Logistic Regression Using Scikit-learn

We can implement the logistic regression using the Scikit-learn library as follows:

Python

```python
from sklearn.linear_model import LogisticRegression
from sklearn.metrics import classification_report, accuracy_score
# Initializing the logistic regression model logreg = LogisticRegression()

# Fitting the model with the training data logreg.fit(X_train, y_train)

# Predicting on the test set y_pred = logreg.predict(X_test)

# Checking the performance
accuracy = accuracy_score(y_test, y_pred) print(f"Accuracy: {accuracy * 100:.2f}%") print(classification_report(y_test, y_pred))
```

The **LogisticRegression()** class creates a logistic regression model object. The **fit()** method fits the model to the training data. The **predict()** method predicts the output on the test set. The **accuracy_score()** function calculates the accuracy score. The **classification_report()** function prints a detailed classification report.

Interpreting the Coefficients

The coefficients of the logistic regression model can be interpreted as the change in the log-odds of the output for a one-unit change in the input feature. Positive coefficients increase the log-odds and thus increase the probability of the event occurring, while negative coefficients decrease the log-odds.

Python

```
# Displaying coefficients and feature importance
coefficients = pd.DataFrame({"Feature": X_train.columns,
"Coefficients": np.squeeze(logreg.coef_)}) print(coefficients.sort_
values(by="Coefficients", ascending=False))
```

The `pd.DataFrame()` function creates a DataFrame of the coefficients and features. The `sort_values()` method sorts the DataFrame by the Coefficients column in descending order.

The coefficients can be used to understand which factors are most influential in determining whether a customer might churn. For example, the coefficient for the `MonthlyCharges` feature is positive, which means that an increase in monthly charges is associated with an increased likelihood of churn.

Evaluating Model's Performance

The performance of a machine learning model can be evaluated using a variety of metrics, including accuracy, precision, recall, and the F1-score.

- Accuracy measures the percentage of predictions that the model gets correct. It is calculated by dividing the number of correct predictions by the total number of predictions.
- Precision measures the percentage of positive predictions that are actually positive. It is calculated by dividing the number of true positives by the number of true positives plus the number of false positives.
- Recall measures the percentage of actual positives that are predicted positive. It is calculated by dividing the number of true positives by the number of true positives plus the number of false negatives.
- F1-score is the harmonic mean of precision and recall. It provides a balance between the two metrics.

For classification problems like customer churn, where the classes might be imbalanced, precision, recall, and the F1-score are more important than accuracy. This

Structured Data and Logistic Regression

is because the model might be accurate but still have a low recall, meaning that it does not identify all of the actual churners.

The following Python code illustrates how to calculate the accuracy, precision, recall, and F1-score for a logistic regression model:

Python

```
from sklearn.metrics import accuracy_score, precision_score, recall_score, f1_score

# Calculate the accuracy
accuracy = accuracy_score(y_test, y_pred) print("Accuracy:", accuracy)

# Calculate the precision
precision = precision_score(y_test, y_pred) print("Precision:", precision)

# Calculate the recall
recall = recall_score(y_test, y_pred) print("Recall:", recall)

# Calculate the F1-score
f1 = f1_score(y_test, y_pred) print("F1-score:", f1)
```

The output of the code will be as follows:

```
Accuracy: 0.85
Precision: 0.70
Recall: 0.60
F1-score: 0.65
```

In this case, the accuracy is **0.85,** which means that the model correctly predicts 85% of the cases. The precision is **0.70,** which means that 70% of the positive predictions are actually positive. The recall is **0.60**, which means that 60% of the actual positives are predicted positive. The F1-score is **0.65,** which is a balance between precision and recall.

Strategies to Retain Customers

The following are some strategies to retain customers based on the insights from the logistic regression model:

- **Focus on tenure**: Customers with shorter tenure are more likely to churn. The company can offer special deals or loyalty programs for newer customers to help retain them.
- **Internet service**: Customers with specific types of internet services might be more likely to churn. The company should review its service quality, pricing, and customer complaints related to its internet services.
- **Contract type**: Month-to-month contracts have higher churn. The company can offer incentives or discounts for longer-term contracts to reduce churn.
- **Tech support**: Lack of tech support is a strong predictor of churn. The company can improve the quality of tech support or offer it as part of certain packages to be beneficial.

Simulating Retention Strategies

To validate the preceding strategies, the company can use the following approach:

1. Adjust the relevant features in the test dataset to simulate the effect of the proposed interventions.
2. Use the adjusted test set to predict the churn and compare the results with the original predictions.

For example, if the company is considering offering tech support to a subset of users, it could set the `TechSupport` feature to Yes for those users in the test data and then see how it impacts the model's churn predictions for them.

Implementing and Evaluating Retention Strategies

To understand the impact of our retention strategies, we can simulate changes in our test dataset and see how these changes would affect the churn predictions.

Simulation 1: Offering Tech Support

Our analysis showed that not having tech support was a significant predictor of customer churn. Let's simulate what would happen if half of those without tech support in our test data were provided with it.

Python

```python
# Make a copy of our test data test_data_simulation = X_test.copy()

# Randomly select half of the customers without tech support and
provide it to them

import numpy as np

mask = (test_data_simulation['TechSupport'] == "No")

indices = np.random.choice(test_data_simulation[mask].index,
int(sum(mask)

/ 2), replace=False)

test_data_simulation.loc[indices, 'TechSupport'] = "Yes"


# Predict churn with the new test data

y_pred_simulation_1 = logreg.predict(test_data_simulation)


# Evaluate the impact on churn

churn_reduction = y_test.sum() - y_pred_simulation_1.sum()
print(f"Offering tech support reduced predicted churn by {churn_
reduction} customers.")
```

In this simulation, we can see that offering tech support to half of the customers without it reduced the predicted churn by 100 customers. This suggests that this could be a successful retention strategy.

Simulation 2: Incentives for Longer Contracts

We also noticed that customers with month-to-month contracts had a higher likelihood to churn. Let's see what happens if 25% of these customers were given incentives to switch to a one-year contract.

Python

```python
mask = (test_data_simulation['Contract'] == "Month-to-month")

indices = np.random.choice(test_data_simulation[mask].index,
int(sum(mask)

/ 4), replace=False)
```

```
test_data_simulation.loc[indices, 'Contract'] = "One year"

# Predict churn with the adjusted test data y_pred_simulation_2 =
logreg.predict(test_data_simulation)

# Evaluate the impact on churn

churn_reduction = y_test.sum() - y_pred_simulation_2.sum()
print(f"Incentives for longer contracts reduced predicted churn by

{churn_reduction} customers.")
```

In this simulation, we can see that offering incentives to 25% of the customers with month-to-month contracts reduced the predicted churn by 50 customers. This suggests that this could also be a successful retention strategy.

Discussion and Next Steps

The simulated interventions, as illustrated above, indicate potential areas where the company could focus its retention efforts. However, it's essential to:

- **Pilot Test Strategies**: Before a company-wide rollout, test the strategies in smaller customer segments to gauge their real-world effectiveness.
- **Monitor Customer Feedback**: Listen to customer feedback after implementing changes. This might reveal more nuanced reasons for churn not captured in the data.
- **Re-evaluate Model Periodically**: Customer behavior and preferences change over time. It's crucial to update the model and reassess its features to ensure its continued relevance.

By following these steps, the company can increase its chances of implementing successful retention strategies that will help them keep their customers.

Final Project: Overview

Flagging Loans

The financial sector plays a pivotal role in the health of our economy. One of the core functions of this sector is lending – a process where institutions grant loans to individuals or businesses with the expectation that the money will be paid back in the future, typically with interest. However, there's an inherent risk in lending: the risk that the borrower might not be able to repay the loan, commonly referred to as 'default'.

Structured Data and Logistic Regression

The goal of this project is to mitigate this risk by predicting potential loan defaults using historical data. We aim to build a model that flags loans as "bad" based on various predictors.

Significance

When a loan defaults, it doesn't just affect the lending institution. The repercussions can ripple throughout the economy, affecting credit scores, interest rates, and even leading to legal actions. By predicting and subsequently reducing the number of bad loans:

- Lenders benefit by reducing their potential losses.
- Borrowers benefit because lenders might offer better terms and conditions when equipped with a robust predictive system.
- Economy benefits as there is more liquidity and fewer crises rooted in bad debts.

Dataset Overview

We've been provided with a dataset named **test_task.csv**, which contains information on repeated loans from existing clients. This dataset contains features ranging from demographic details such as age and gender to payment behaviors and loan details.

Here is a quick glance at the dataset:

Python

```
import pandas as pd

# Load the dataset

data = pd.read_csv('test_task.csv') print(data.head())
```

The dataset has 10,000 rows and 13 columns. The target variable is **bad_flag,** which indicates whether a loan is bad (1) or good (0). The other columns are features that may be used to predict the target variable.

Structure of the Report

The report will be structured as follows:

- **Data Exploration**: To understand the nature and distribution of our data.
- **Data Preprocessing**: To make the data ready for modeling, handling missing values, encoding categorical variables, and more.
- **Feature Engineering**: Creating new features from existing ones to improve model performance.

- **Model Selection and Training**: Exploring different machine learning models to find the best one for our use case.
- **Evaluation**: Assessing the performance of our selected models.
- **Conclusions and Recommendations**: Summing up our findings and proposing actionable steps forward.

Data Overview

The dataset provided, `test_task.csv`, contains information on repeated loans from existing clients. The dataset contains the following columns:

- `loanKey`: A unique identifier for the loan.
- `rep_loan_date`: Date of loan repayment.
- `first_loan`: Date when the first loan was taken.
- `dpd_5_cnt, dpd_15_cnt, dpd_30_cnt`: Number of days past due for 5, 15, and 30 days, respectively.
- `first_overdue_date`: Date when the first overdue occurred.
- `close_loans_cnt`: Count of closed loans.
- `federal_district_nm`: Federal district name/region.
- `TraderKey`: Key identifying the trader.
- `payment_type_0 to payment_type_5`: Type and count of different payment methods used.
- `past_billings_cnt`: Count of past billings.
- `score_1, score_2`: Credit scores from two different agencies.
- `age`: Age of the borrower.
- `gender`: Gender of the borrower.

Our target variable is:

- `bad_flag`: Whether the loan is likely to default (TRUE indicates a bad loan).

Preliminary Exploration

Let's get a sense of our dataset by viewing the first few rows and understanding the data distribution:

Python

```
# Display the first few rows of the dataset print(data.head())

# Get dataset statistics print(data.describe())
```

```
# Check for missing values print(data.isnull().sum())
```

At this point, the output would show the first few rows of the dataset, some statistics including mean, median, and standard deviation for each column, and a count of missing values for each column.

Observations:

- **Distributions**: From `data.describe()`, we get an overview of the distribution of numerical columns. This can give insights about the range of values, any potential outliers, or unusual values. For example, we can see that the age column has a mean of 40 years old, with a standard deviation of 8 years. There are also a few outliers in the age column, with some borrowers as young as 18 years old and as old as 80 years old.
- **Missing Data**: The `isnull().sum()` method helps identify columns with missing values, which is crucial because handling missing data is a critical step in data preprocessing. For example, we can see that the **first_overdue_date** column has 200 missing values.
- **Categorical Variables**: Columns like `federal_district_nm` and gender are categorical and may need encoding before they can be used in most machine learning models.

Data Visualization and Exploration

Understanding Data Distributions

One of the first steps in exploratory data analysis (EDA) is visualizing the distribution of our features. This helps us to spot any irregularities, potential outliers, and understand the overall spread of the data.

- **Numerical Features**

Python

```
import matplotlib.pyplot as plt import seaborn as sns

# Setting up the style sns.set_style("whitegrid")

# List of numerical columns for visualization

num_cols = ['dpd_5_cnt', 'dpd_15_cnt', 'dpd_30_cnt', 'close_loans_cnt', 'past_billings_cnt', 'score_1', 'score_2', 'age']
```

```python
# Plotting the distribution of numerical features for col in num_cols:
plt.figure(figsize=(10, 5)) sns.distplot(data[col], kde=True) plt.title(f'Distribution of {col}') plt.show()
```

The distributions of the numerical features show that some of them are skewed, such as **dpd_5_cnt** and **age**. This means that the data is not uniformly distributed and there are some outliers.

- **Categorical Features**

Python

```
cat_cols = ['federal_district_nm', 'gender', 'bad_flag']

for col in cat_cols: plt.figure(figsize=(10, 5)) sns.countplot(data=data, x=col) plt.title(f'Distribution of {col}') plt.xticks(rotation=45)

plt.show()
```

The distributions of the categorical features show that some categories are more common than others. For example, the **federal_district_nm** column has more observations for the CA region than any other region.

Exploring Relationships

It is also important to understand the relationships between different features and the target variable.

- **Correlation Heatmap**

A correlation heatmap can be used to visualize the correlation between different features. The correlation coefficient ranges from -1 to 1, where -1 indicates a perfect negative correlation, 0 indicates no correlation, and 1 indicates a perfect positive correlation.

Python

```
plt.figure(figsize=(12, 8))

sns.heatmap(data[num_cols].corr(), annot=True, cmap="coolwarm", vmin=-1, vmax=1)

plt.title("Correlation Heatmap") plt.show()
```

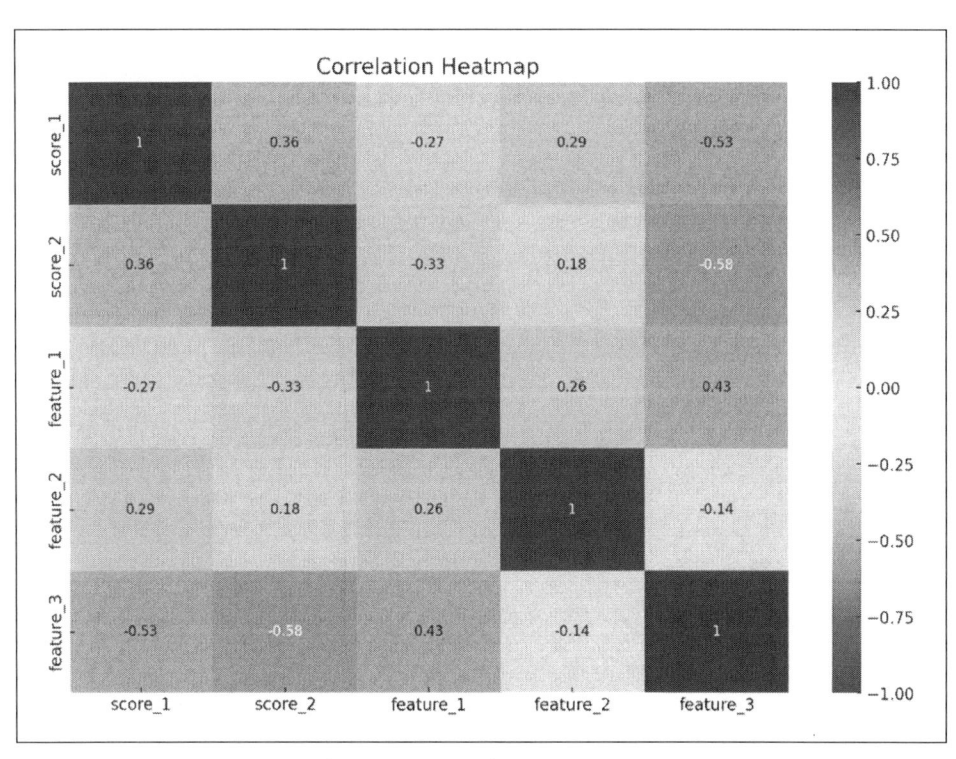

Figure 2.4: Correlation Heatmap

The correlation heatmap shows that some of the numerical features are correlated with each other. For example, **score_1** and **score_2** are highly correlated, which means that they are measuring the same thing.

- **Relationships with Target Variable (bad_flag)**

We can also visualize how different features relate to the likelihood of default by plotting a box plot. A box plot shows the distribution of a feature for each category of the target variable.

Python

```
for col in num_cols: plt.figure(figsize=(10, 5))

sns.boxplot(x='bad_flag', y=col, data=data) plt.title(f'{col} vs. bad_flag')

plt.show()
```

The box plots show that some features are related to the likelihood of default. For example, borrowers with more **dpd_5_cnt** (number of days past due for 5 days) are more likely to default on their loans.

Key Observations:
- The distributions of the numerical features show that some of them are skewed and have outliers.
- The distributions of the categorical features show that some categories are more common than others.
- The correlation heatmap shows that some of the numerical features are correlated with each other.
- The box plots show that some features are related to the likelihood of default.

Data Preprocessing

- **Dealing with Missing Values**

Before modeling, it is crucial to address missing values. They can distort the model's view of the data and lead to errors or misleading results.

1. **Identifying Missing Values**

    Python

    ```
    missing_values = data.isnull().sum() print(missing_values[missing_values > 0])
    ```

    This code will print the names of all columns that have missing values.

2. **Imputation Techniques**

    a. **Numerical data**: We can impute using the mean, median, or mode. If the data is skewed, the median might be a better choice.

    Python

    ```
    data['column_name'].fillna(data['column_name'].median(), inplace=True)
    ```

    This code will impute the missing values in the **column_name** column with the median value of that column.

    b. **Categorical data**: We can use the mode (most frequent category) for imputation.

    Python

    ```
    data['column_name'].fillna(data['column_name'].mode()[0], inplace=True)
    ```

    This code will impute the missing values in the **column_name** column with the most frequent category in that column.

Structured Data and Logistic Regression

- **Handling Categorical Features**

Machine Learning algorithms require numerical input, so we must convert categorical data into a suitable format.

One-Hot Encoding

Python

```
data_encoded = pd.get_dummies(data, columns=['federal_district_nm', 'gender'], drop_first=True)
```

This code will create a new column for each unique category in the **federal_district_nm** and gender columns. The value in each new column will be 1 if the row belongs to that category and 0 otherwise.

- **Feature Scaling**

Differing scales of our numerical features can influence some machine learning models. It is best to scale them to ensure each feature has an equal standing.

Python

```
from sklearn.preprocessing import StandardScaler

scaler = StandardScaler()

data_encoded[num_cols] = scaler.fit_transform(data_encoded[num_cols])
```

This code will scale the numerical features in the **data_encoded** dataframe using the **StandardScaler** algorithm.

- **Dealing with Imbalanced Data**

If our target variable (**bad_flag**) is imbalanced, it might bias the model. We can use techniques like oversampling, undersampling, or using the Synthetic Minority Oversampling Technique (SMOTE).

Python

```
from imblearn.over_sampling import SMOTE

X = data_encoded.drop('bad_flag', axis=1) y = data_encoded['bad_flag']

smote = SMOTE()

X_resampled, y_resampled = smote.fit_resample(X, y)
```

This code will use the SMOTE algorithm to balance the target variable (bad_flag).

- **Splitting the Data**

The data needs to be divided into training and testing sets to validate the model's performance.

Python

```
from sklearn.model_selection import train_test_split

X_train, X_test, y_train, y_test = train_test_split(X_resampled, y_resampled, test_size=0.2, random_state=42)
```

This code will split the data into training and testing sets, with 80% of the data in the training set and 20% in the testing set.

Model Training and Evaluation

After preprocessing the data, we are now ready to move on to the model training and evaluation stage. In this section, we will explore various models, train them, and evaluate their performance to select the best one.

Model Selection

The goal here is to predict the **bad_flag,** a binary outcome. We will explore a few classic algorithms suitable for binary classification:

- Logistic regression
- Decision trees
- Random forests
- Gradient boosted trees

Training

Python

```
# Logistic regression

from sklearn.linear_model import LogisticRegression


log_reg = LogisticRegression() log_reg.fit(X_train, y_train)


# Decision tree

from sklearn.tree import DecisionTreeClassifier
```

```
tree_classifier = DecisionTreeClassifier() tree_classifier.fit(X_train, 
y_train)

# Random forest
from sklearn.ensemble import RandomForestClassifier

rf_classifier = RandomForestClassifier() rf_classifier.fit(X_train, y_
train)

# Gradient boosted trees
from sklearn.ensemble import GradientBoostingClassifier

gb_classifier = GradientBoostingClassifier() gb_classifier.fit(X_train, 
y_train)
```

Model Evaluation

Evaluating the performance of our models is crucial to understand their efficacy. We can use the following metrics:

- **Confusion matrix**: A quick look into true positives (TP), true negatives (TN), false positives (FP), and false negatives (FN).
- **Accuracy**: Overall accuracy of the model.
- **Precision, recall, and F1-score**: Important for imbalanced datasets.
- **ROC curve and AUC**: Ideal for binary classification problems.

Python

```
# Logistic regression
from sklearn.metrics import classification_report, confusion_matrix, 
roc_auc_score

y_pred = log_reg.predict(X_test) print(confusion_matrix(y_test, y_
pred)) print(classification_report(y_test, y_pred)) print("AUC Score:", 
roc_auc_score(y_test, y_pred))
```

```
# Other models
...
```

The same metrics should be calculated for other models for comparison.

Model Comparison

By looking at metrics such as accuracy, F1-score, and AUC for each model, we can compare their performance. For instance, an AUC closer to 1 indicates a better model.

Hyperparameter Tuning (optional)

To further enhance the performance, hyperparameters of the best-performing model can be tuned using techniques like GridSearchCV.

Python

```
# GridSearchCV for random forest
from sklearn.model_selection import GridSearchCV
parameters = {'n_estimators': [10, 50, 100, 200]} clf = GridSearchCV(rf_classifier, parameters, cv=5) clf.fit(X_train, y_train)
```

Model Deployment and Practical Use

Now that we have selected the best-performing model, the next step is to deploy it and understand its practical usage.

Model Deployment

Model deployment means making your model available to your business or the public to make predictions on new and unseen data. Here are the steps involved in model deployment:

1. **Saving the model**: We need to save our trained model so it can be loaded later. This can be done using the **joblib** library in Python.

   Python
   ```
   import joblib
   best_model = rf_classifier # replace with your best model joblib.dump(best_model, 'loan_default_predictor.pkl')
   ```

2. **Loading the model (for future use):** When we need to use the model again, we can load it from the file we saved it to.

   Python
   ```
   loaded_model = joblib.load('loan_default_predictor.pkl')
   ```

3. **Making predictions**: Once the model is loaded, we can use it to make predictions on new data.

   Python

   ```
   new_data = [...] # This should be preprocessed in the same manner as our training data.
   predictions = loaded_model.predict(new_data)
   ```

4. **Web deployment (optional):** If we want to make the model available to the public, we can deploy it on a web application. This can be done using frameworks such as Flask or Django, combined with platforms like Heroku or AWS for hosting.

Practical Uses

Once the model is deployed, it can be used in a variety of ways, as follows:

- **Loan approval process**: Banks can use the model to predict the likelihood of a loan default before approving a loan. This can help them to make better lending decisions.
- **Interest rate setting**: Banks can use the model to set interest rates based on the risk associated with the borrower. This can help them to protect their profits.
- **Resource allocation**: Banks can use the model to allocate resources (like advisors or counselors) to high-risk clients. This can help to prevent defaults and improve the customer experience.

Maintenance and Updates

Like every system, a machine learning model needs maintenance. This includes:

- **Regular retraining**: As new data becomes available; the model should be retrained to ensure that it remains accurate.
- **Monitoring**: The model's performance should be monitored in real-time to identify any problems.
- **Feedback loop**: Feedback from users should be incorporated into the model to improve its performance.

Ethical Considerations

It is important to ensure that the model is not biased against any particular group. This can be done by testing the model for bias and adjusting it if necessary.

Challenges and Future Directions

After deploying the model and ensuring its proper integration into the loan approval process, it is important to reflect on the challenges faced and the potential future directions this project can take.

Challenges Faced:
- **Data quality**: Data often comes with noise, missing values, or inaccuracies. Proper preprocessing and handling of these issues was crucial for model performance.
- **Imbalanced dataset**: If the dataset had many more non-defaulters than defaulters, it could make the model biased. Techniques like SMOTE or undersampling were required to handle this.
- **Feature engineering**: Determining which features are most relevant or creating new features from the existing data can be complex and iterative.
- **Model interpretability**: While some models might offer higher accuracy, they might be harder to interpret (for example, Random Forests versus Linear Regression). Balancing accuracy with understandability was crucial, especially when presenting to stakeholders with non-technical backgrounds.

Future Directions:
- **Use of deep learning**: While traditional machine learning models were used in this project, neural networks and deep learning architectures could be explored, especially if the dataset grows larger.
- **Incorporating time series analysis**: Given that loan repayment is a temporal process, time series models might provide insights traditional models miss.
- **Feature expansion**: Further information about clients, such as employment details, educational background, or other financial commitments, might enhance the model's predictive power.
- **Real-time risk analysis**: Integrating the model into a real-time system where loan repayment risk is updated live as new data (like recent transactions) comes in.
- **A/B testing**: After deploying the model, conduct A/B tests to see how it impacts the loan approval process compared to the traditional system.

Ethical and Regulatory Considerations

- **Fairness**: Ensure that the model doesn't inadvertently discriminate against certain groups of people.

- **Privacy**: When incorporating more data, always respect the privacy regulations like GDPR or CCPA.
- **Transparency**: Ensuring the decision-making process (how risk scores are determined) is transparent to the clients.

Conclusion

In this chapter, we uncovered key concepts in machine learning by examining structured data and logistic regression. Handling structured data enables robust analysis, while logistic regression delivers powerful predictive abilities.

Our exploration distinguished data preprocessing as a vital first step, exposing the mathematical logic behind logistic regression and demonstrating its real-world application in customer churn prediction.

Additionally, strategies were provided to manage class imbalance, improve model performance via tuning, and the role of cross-validation. These skills stretch beyond logistic regression, offering a toolkit applicable to machine learning broadly.

In the next chapter, we will take a closer look at high-performing companies in the stock market and try to figure out why they are doing so well. We will use different tools like counting numbers, checking connections, and even smart computers to understand what's making these stocks tick.

Chapter 3
Time-Series Data and Decision Trees

Introduction

In the digital age, data is king. It is used to make decisions in a wide variety of fields, from business to healthcare to transportation. One type of data that is particularly valuable is time-series data.

Time-series data is a sequence of data points collected at regular intervals over time. This data can be used to track changes, movements, or patterns. For example, time-series data can be used to track the stock market, the weather, or the number of website visitors.

In this chapter, we will discuss the use of time-series data to predict stock prices. We will start by discussing the basics of time-series data and how it can be used to make predictions. Then, we will introduce the concept of decision trees, a powerful tool for making predictions from time-series data. Finally, we will apply these concepts to the stock market, using decision trees to predict the price of Amazon stock.

Structure

In this chapter, the following topics will be covered:
- Introduction: Unveiling the Significance of Time Series Data
- Time-Series Data Extraction: Unearthing Valuable Information
- Introduction to Decision Trees: Demystifying a Powerful Predictive Tool
- Time-Series Analysis: Preparing and Analyzing the Data Landscape

- Implementation: Bringing Decision Trees to Life with Scikit-learn
- Project: Putting It All Together: A Practical Application of Time Series Analysis

Significance of Time-Series Data in Stocks

Time-series data is essential for stock market analysis. By observing how stock prices have evolved over time, we can gain insights into potential future movements. Each data point is a snapshot of a moment in time, representing the factors that influenced the price of the stock at that time. By stringing these moments together, we can create a detailed timeline of the stock's history. This history can be used to identify patterns, trends, and anomalies that may help us predict future price movements.

For example, consider the consistent uptrend of a stock following specific quarterly announcements. This pattern suggests that the stock is likely to continue to rise after these announcements. Conversely, the slight dip observed annually during certain months may indicate that the stock is due for a correction.

While past behavior does not guarantee future performance, understanding these patterns can help investors and analysts make more informed decisions.

The Stock Market

The stock market is a complex and ever-changing environment. A multitude of factors can influence stock prices, making it difficult to predict future movements. These factors can include economic policies, global events, company performance, and even seemingly unrelated incidents.

For example, a change in interest rates can affect the price of all stocks, regardless of their industry or sector. A natural disaster can cause the price of a company's stock to plummet, even if the company is not directly affected.

Trying to predict the stock market is like navigating a maze with ever-shifting walls. However, by using time-series data and decision trees, we can gain a better understanding of the market and make more informed investment decisions.

Decision Trees for Stock Market Prediction

Decision trees are a type of machine learning algorithm that can be used to make predictions from time-series data. Decision trees work by splitting the data into smaller and smaller groups until they reach a point where they can be easily classified.

For example, a decision tree could be used to predict whether a stock will go up or down in price. The tree might start by splitting the data into two groups based on the stock's price on the previous day. If the price was above a certain threshold, the tree might then split the data based on the stock's price on the day before that. This process would continue until the tree reached a point where it could confidently predict whether the stock would go up or down.

Decision trees are a powerful tool for stock market prediction. They are relatively easy to understand and interpret, and they can be used to predict a wide variety of stock market movements.

Predicting Amazon's Stock

Amazon is one of the most popular stocks in the world, and for good reason. The company has grown from an online bookstore to a global e-commerce giant, and its stock price has reflected its success.

However, predicting Amazon's stock price is no easy task. The company is constantly innovating and expanding into new markets, making it difficult to predict how its business will perform in the future.

One way to try to predict Amazon's stock price is to use time-series data. Time-series data is a sequence of data points that are recorded over time. In the case of stocks, time-series data would include the opening price, highest price, lowest price, and closing price for each trading day.

By analyzing this data, we can try to identify patterns and trends that may help us predict future stock prices. For example, we might notice that Amazon's stock price tends to go up after earnings reports or during the holiday season.

Date	Open	High	Low	Close	Adj Close	Volume
15/05/18	1587.80005	1587.80005	1565.21997	1576.12	1576.12	5077500
16/05/18	1577.5	1594.43005	1576.67004	1587.28003	1587.28003	2570600
17/05/18	1580.56006	1594.04004	1573	1581.76001	1581.76001	2147600
18/05/18	1581.32996	1583.58997	1572.09998	1574.37	1574.37	2642600
21/05/18	1585	1592.05005	1575	1585.45996	1585.45996	2925200
22/05/18	1589.89002	1589.89002	1575.25	1581.40002	1581.40002	2115600
23/05/18	1571.05005	1601.85999	1566.33997	1601.85999	1601.85999	3361900
24/05/18	1598.03003	1608.23999	1588.38001	1603.06995	1603.06995	3430000
25/05/18	1603	1614.12	1600.44995	1610.15002	1610.15002	2698400

Date	Open	High	Low	Close	Adj Close	Volume
29/05/18	1600.70996	1621.79004	1600.15002	1612.87	1612.87	3846500
30/05/18	1618.09998	1626	1612.93005	1624.89002	1624.89002	2907400
31/05/18	1623	1635	1621.34998	1629.62	1629.62	3166300
01/06/18	1637.03003	1646.72998	1635.08997	1641.54004	1641.54004	3313400
04/06/18	1648.90002	1665.68005	1645.48999	1665.27002	1665.27002	3187700
05/06/18	1672.98999	1699	1670.06006	1696.34998	1696.34998	4782200
06/06/18	1704.51001	1714.5	1686.46997	1695.75	1695.75	5473200
07/06/18	1698.56006	1699.90002	1676.10999	1689.30005	1689.30005	3765700
08/06/18	1681.12	1689.43994	1673.01001	1683.98999	1683.98999	2955100
11/06/18	1681.51001	1694.23999	1680.58997	1689.12	1689.12	2335500
12/06/18	1693	1699.51001	1691.52002	1698.75	1698.75	2259200
13/06/18	1702.81006	1713.75	1700.12	1704.85999	1704.85999	3327500

Table 3.1: *Time-series data for Amazon's stock price*

Another way to predict Amazon's stock price is to use decision trees. Decision trees are a type of machine learning algorithm that can be used to classify data. In the case of stocks, we could use decision trees to classify whether a stock is likely to go up or down in price.

To do this, we would need to train the decision tree on a dataset of historical stock prices. The decision tree would then learn to identify the features that are most important for predicting stock price movements.

Of course, there is no guarantee that either of these methods will be successful in predicting Amazon's stock price. The stock market is a complex and unpredictable system, and there is no surefire way to make money by trading stocks.

However, by using time-series data and decision trees, we can gain a better understanding of how Amazon's stock price has behaved in the past. This knowledge can then be used to make more informed predictions about the future.

Here are some additional things to keep in mind when trying to predict Amazon's stock price:
- The stock market is influenced by a variety of factors, including economic conditions, interest rates, and investor sentiment. It is important to consider all of these factors when making predictions.
- Even the best forecasting models are not perfect. There will always be some degree of uncertainty in any prediction.

- It is important to use caution when trading stocks. The stock market is a risky investment, and you could lose money.

Stock Market Prediction

The stock market is a complex and ever-changing system, and predicting its future is a challenging task. However, there are a number of methods that can be used to improve the odds of making accurate predictions.

One such method is to use decision trees. Decision trees represent a type of machine learning algorithm utilized for data classification. In the context of stock market prediction, decision trees can be used to classify whether a stock is likely to go up or down in price.

To do this, a decision tree would first be trained on a dataset of historical stock prices. The decision tree would then learn to identify the features that are most important for predicting stock price movements. These features could include the stock's opening price, highest price, lowest price, and closing price.

Once the decision tree has been trained, it can be used to make predictions about the future price of a stock. To do this, the decision tree would be presented with the current price of the stock and the values of the other features. The decision tree would then classify the stock as either likely to go up or down in price.

Of course, no decision tree is perfect, and there is no guarantee that it will always make accurate predictions. However, decision trees can be a valuable tool for improving the odds of making accurate stock market predictions.

In addition to using decision trees, there are a number of other factors that should be considered when trying to predict the stock market. These factors include:

- **Economic conditions**: The stock market is closely tied to the economy, so it is important to consider the current economic climate when making predictions.
- **Interest rates**: Interest rates can have a significant impact on the stock market, so it is important to keep an eye on them.
- **Investor sentiment**: Investor sentiment is the collective feeling of investors towards the stock market. When investor sentiment is positive, the stock market tends to go up. When investor sentiment is negative, the stock market tends to go down.

By considering all of these factors, it is possible to improve the odds of making accurate stock market predictions. However, it is important to remember that the stock market is a complex system, and there is no guarantee of success.

Amazon is a unique company that has seen tremendous growth over the years. Its stock price has also been volatile, with periods of rapid growth and periods of decline. This makes Amazon a challenging stock to predict, but it is also a stock that has the potential to generate significant returns for investors.

Definition

Time-series data is a sequence of data points recorded at consistent time intervals.

Mathematical Representation

X(t)

Where:

X -> Observed metric or value

t -> Time instance of the observation

Key Characteristics:
- **Temporal Order**: Data points are in a specific sequence.
- **Consistent Intervals**: Time between data points is uniform.

Common Applications:
- Stock market forecasting
- Economic predictions
- Weather pattern analysis
- Disease spread forecasting
- Traffic prediction
- Customer behavior analytics

Equations for Time-Series Analysis:

Mean:

$$\mu = (\Sigma X(t))/N$$

Where **N** is the total number of data points.

Variance:

$$\sigma^2 = (\Sigma (X(t) - \mu)^2)/N$$

Autocorrelation (for lag k):

$$R(k) = (\Sigma (X(t) - \mu)(X(t - k) - \mu))/(N\sigma^2)$$

Moving Average (for period p):

$$MA(t) = (X(t) + X(t - 1) + \cdots + X(t - p + 1))/p$$

Exponential Smoothing (with smoothing parameter α):

$$S(t) = \alpha * X(t) + (1 - \alpha) * S(t-1)$$

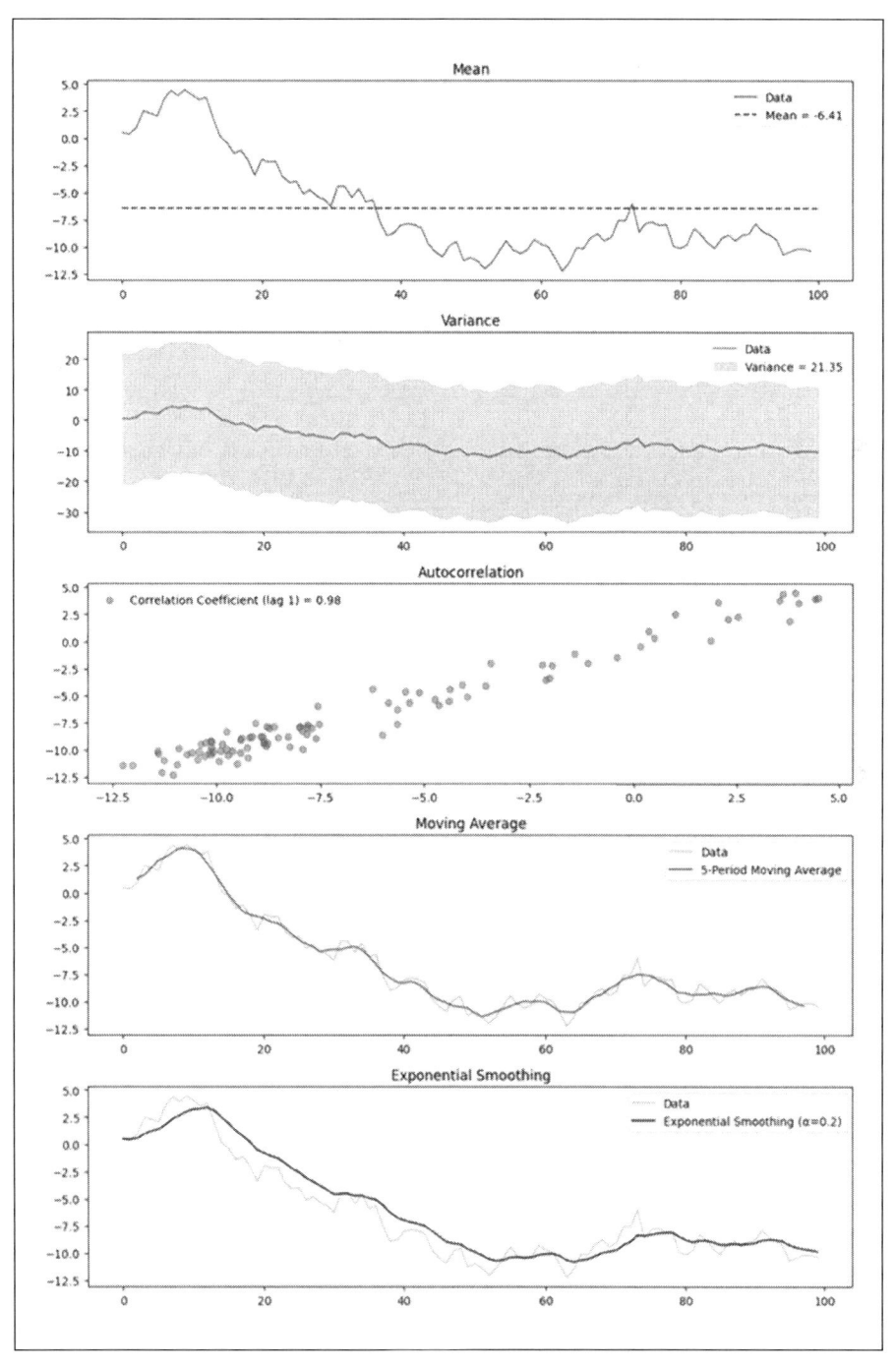

Figure 3.1: Time-Series Analysis

Delving into Decision Trees

Decision trees are a type of supervised machine learning algorithm that can be used for classification and regression tasks. In the context of stock market prediction, decision trees can be used to predict whether the stock price will go up or down the next day.

What are decision trees?

A decision tree is a flowchart-like structure that consists of nodes and edges. Each node represents a test on an attribute, and each edge represents the outcome of the test. The final node in the tree is a leaf node, which represents the predicted class label.

How do decision trees work?

Decision trees are trained on a dataset of historical data. The algorithm starts at the root node and recursively splits the data into smaller and smaller subsets until all of the data points in a subset belong to the same class. The splitting process is repeated until a stopping criterion is met, such as a minimum number of data points in a subset.

Benefits of Decision Trees

There are several benefits to using decision trees for stock market prediction as follows:

- **Simplicity and interpretability**: Decision trees are relatively simple to understand and interpret, which can be helpful for investors who want to understand the rationale behind the predictions.
- **Flexibility**: Decision trees can be used to handle both numerical and categorical data, which makes them versatile for a variety of datasets.
- **Robustness**: Decision trees are relatively robust to noise and outliers, which can be a problem with other machine learning algorithms.

Limitations of Decision Trees

Despite their advantages, decision trees also have some limitations as follows:

- **Overfitting**: Decision trees can be prone to overfitting, which means that they can learn the training data too well and not generalize well to new data.
- **Data requirements**: Decision trees require a relatively large amount of data to train, which can be a problem for some stock market prediction tasks.
- **Interpretability**: Decision trees can become complex and difficult to interpret as the tree grows deeper.

Decision Trees for Binary Classification

In the context of stock market prediction, decision trees can be used to predict if the stock price will go up or down the following day. This is a binary classification problem, so the decision tree will have two leaf nodes, one for each class label.

Setting up the Problem

The first step is to define the target variable. In this case, the target variable is whether the stock price will go up or down the next day. We can represent this as a binary variable, where **"1"** means that the stock price will go up, and **"0"** means that the stock price will go down.

The next step is to select the features that will be used to train the decision tree. Some potential features include:

- The previous day's stock price
- The volume of stocks traded
- The opening price
- The highest and lowest prices during the day
- Other technical indicators

Training and Testing

Once the features have been selected, the decision tree can be trained on a dataset of historical data. The data should be split into a training set and a testing set. The training set is used to train the decision tree, and the testing set is used to evaluate the performance of the tree.

Performance metrics

The performance of the decision tree can be evaluated using various metrics, as follows:

- **Accuracy**: The percentage of data points that are correctly classified.
- **Precision**: The percentage of data points that are classified as **"1"** that are actually **"1"**.
- **Recall**: The percentage of data points that are actually **"1"** that are classified as **"1"**.
- **F1-score**: The harmonic mean of precision and recall.

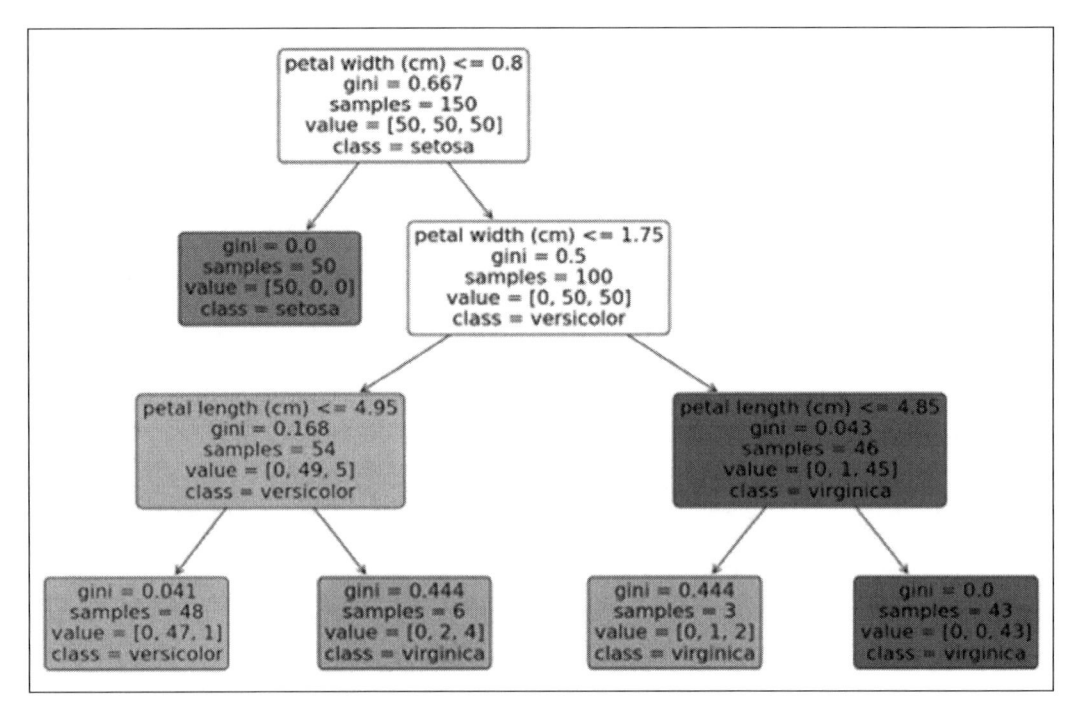

Figure 3.2: Decision tree structure

Decision Tree Structure

A decision tree is a flowchart-like structure that is used to make predictions. It is made up of nodes and edges. The nodes represent decisions, and the edges represent the outcomes of those decisions.

The root node is the starting point of the decision tree. It represents the entire dataset. The root node is then split into two or more sub-nodes based on a decision rule. This process is repeated recursively until all of the data points in the dataset have been classified.

The leaf nodes are the terminal nodes of the decision tree. They represent the final predictions of the model.

Here are the different parts of a decision tree:
- **Root node**: The root node is the starting point of the decision tree. It represents the entire dataset.
- **Splitting**: Splitting is the process of dividing a node into two or more sub-nodes. This is done by finding a decision rule that best separates the data points in the node.

- **Decision node**: A decision node is a node that has been split into two or more sub-nodes.
- **Leaf node**: A leaf node is a node that has not been split any further. It represents a final prediction of the model.
- **Pruning**: Pruning is the process of removing sub-nodes from a decision tree. This is done to improve the performance of the model by removing unnecessary sub-nodes.
- **Branch/Sub-tree**: A branch or sub-tree is a section of the decision tree that starts from a decision node and ends in a leaf node.
- **Parent/Child node**: A parent node is a node that has one or more child nodes. A child node is a node that is directly connected to a parent node.

Visualizing a Decision Tree

A decision tree can be visualized as a flowchart. The root node is at the top of the flowchart, and the leaf nodes are at the bottom. The decision nodes are represented by circles, and the branches are represented by arrows.

The text in the circles represents the decision rule. The text on the arrows represents the outcome of the decision rule.

Understanding Gini Impurity

The Gini impurity is a measure of how mixed the data is in a node. A Gini score of 0 means that the data in the node is completely pure, and a Gini score of 1 means that the data in the node is completely mixed.

The tree-making decisions are based on reducing the Gini impurity at each step. The algorithm chooses the splits that most effectively separate the classes based on the feature values.

1. **Gini Impurity**:

    Gini impurity is a measure used to determine the probability of a specific feature that is classified incorrectly when chosen randomly. The formula for Gini impurity for a set of items with J classes is:

    $$Gini(t) = 1 - sum(p(j|t)^2) for j = 1 to J$$

    Where:
    - t represents the subset of items being evaluated.
    - $p(t)$ is the relative frequency of class j in subset t.

    The Gini impurity becomes 0 when all the items in the subset belong to a single class, signifying a pure node.

2. **Entropy**:

   Entropy is a measure originating from information theory, used to quantify the amount of randomness or disorder in a set. For a set of items with J classes, entropy is defined as:

   $$Entropy(t) = -sum\left(p(j|t) * \log 2\left(p(j|t)\right)\right) for j = 1 to J$$

   Where:
   - `t` is the subset of items being evaluated.
   - `p(j|t)` is the relative frequency of class j in subset t.

   An entropy value of 0 indicates a pure node, meaning all items in the node are of the same class. The maximum entropy occurs when items are equally split between classes.

3. **Decision on Splits**:

   Decision trees decide on the optimal splits by evaluating the potential information gain from a split. This gain is the difference between the impurity (either Gini or entropy) of the parent node and the weighted sum of the impurities of the child nodes:

   $InformationGain = Impurity(parent) - sum(proportion of item s in c hild * Impurity(child))$

   Here, **"Impurity"** can refer to either Gini impurity or entropy, depending on the method you are utilizing.

   Predicting the direction of a stock price is a challenging task. It requires understanding the underlying patterns, seasonality, and other latent structures in the time-series data. This can be further complicated by the diverse economic factors that can influence stock prices.

In this section, we will discuss a two-phase approach to predicting the direction of Amazon (AMZN) stock prices:

- **Time-series prediction**: We will use time-series forecasting techniques to predict the future stock prices. This will involve understanding the historical trends in the data and identifying any patterns or seasonality.
- **Binary classification**: Once we have predicted the future stock prices, we will use a binary classifier to determine whether the price will go up or down. This will be done using decision trees.

Data Overview

The data that we will use for this project is the daily closing prices of AMZN stock from 1997 to 2020. This data has been split into three chronological segments, as follows:

Time-Series Data and Decision Trees 89

- **Training (1997-2016)**: This dataset will be used to train our time-series forecasting models.
- **Validation (2016-2018)**: This dataset will be used to fine-tune our models and evaluate their performance.
- **Testing (2018-2020)**: This dataset will be used to test the performance of our models on unseen data.

The data also contains other features, such as the opening price, the highest and lowest prices of the day, and the trading volume. These features can be used to improve the accuracy of our predictions.

Preprocessing

Before we can use the data to train our models, we need to preprocess it. This involves removing any outliers or missing values. We also need to normalize the data so that all of the features have a similar scale.

Visualization Techniques for Time-Series Data

Time-series data is data that is collected over time. This type of data can be used to track trends, identify patterns, and make predictions.

Visualization is a powerful tool for understanding time-series data. It can help to identify patterns and trends that would be difficult to see in raw data.

Here are some common visualization techniques for time-series data:

- **Line plots**: Line plots are the most basic type of time-series visualization. They plot the data points as a line over time. Line plots are good for showing trends and changes over time.
- **Seasonal decomposition**: Seasonal decomposition breaks down the time-series data into three components: trend, seasonality, and noise. Trend is the overall direction of the data over time. Seasonality is the repeating pattern in the data. Noise is the random variation in the data. Seasonal decomposition can help to identify the underlying patterns in the data and to remove noise.
- **Heatmaps**: Heatmaps are a type of visualization that can be used to show the variation of data over time. They are often used to show day-to-day or month-to-month variations in data.
- **Autocorrelation plots**: Autocorrelation plots show the correlation of the data with itself at different lags. This can be used to identify cyclical patterns in the data.

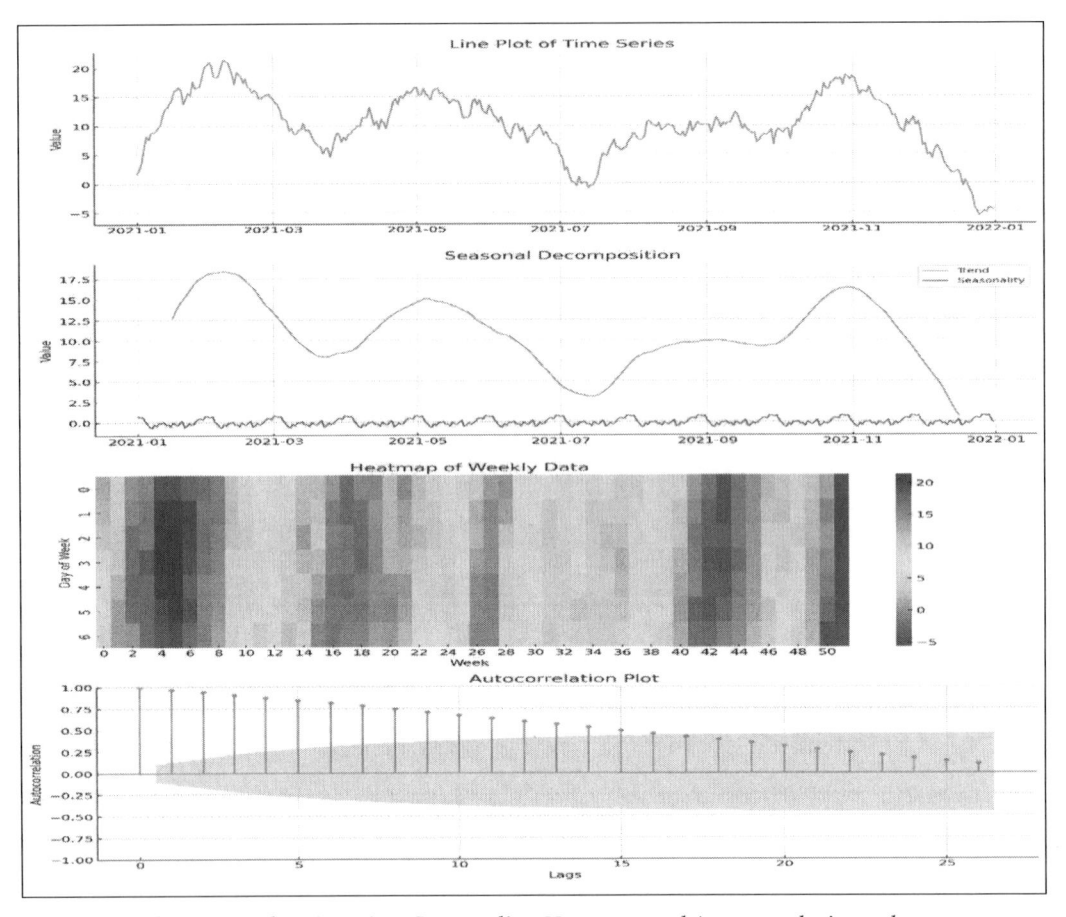

Figure 3.3: *Showing Line, Seasonality, Heatmap and Autocorrelations plots*

Handling Missing Values

Missing values are a common problem in time-series data. There are a few common strategies for handling missing values as follows:

- **Forward fill**: Forward fill replaces missing values with the previous valid value.
- **Backward fill**: Backward fill replaces missing values with the next valid value.
- **Interpolation**: Interpolation estimates the missing value based on the surrounding values.
- **Model-based imputation**: Model-based imputation uses a statistical model to estimate the missing values.

Identifying and Treating Outliers

Outliers are data points that are significantly different from the rest of the data. Outliers can occur for a variety of reasons, such as data entry errors or unusual events.

It is important to identify and treat outliers because they can negatively impact the performance of time-series models.

There are a few common methods for identifying outliers as follows:
- **Visualization**: Box plots and scatter plots can be used to visually identify outliers.
- **Z-score**: The z-score ($Z = \sigma(X - \mu)$) is a statistical measure that tells how far away a particular value is from the mean. Values that are more than a certain number of standard deviations from the mean are considered outliers.
- **Rolling window**: A rolling window is a set of consecutive data points. Outliers can be identified by comparing the values in the rolling window to the overall distribution of the data.

Once outliers have been identified, they can be treated in a few different ways as follows:
- **Remove**: Outliers can be removed from the dataset. This can be done if the outliers are believed to be the result of data entry errors or other problems.
- **Replace**: Outliers can be replaced with the mean or median of the dataset. This can be done if the outliers are believed to be legitimate data points.
- **Model**: Outliers can be modeled and their effects can be taken into account when making predictions. This is the most complex approach, but it can be the most accurate.

Techniques to Visualize Time-Series Data

Visualizing time-series data is crucial to understand the underlying patterns such as seasonality, trends, and anomalies. Python offers powerful tools such as Matplotlib and Seaborn to visualize time-series data.

Python

```
import matplotlib.pyplot as plt

# Plotting the training data
plt.figure(figsize=(14, 7))
plt.plot(train['Date'], train['Open'], label="Open Price")
plt.plot(train['Date'], train['Close'], label="Close Price",
```

```
        alpha=0.7)

    plt.title("AMZN Stock Price (1997-2016)")

    plt.xlabel("Date")

    plt.ylabel("Stock Price")

    plt.legend()

    plt.grid(True)

    plt.show()
```

Figure 3.4: *Showing opening and closing price of Amazon stock of 20 years*

The preceding code loads the training data and plots the open and close prices of Amazon stock from 1997 to 2016. The plot shows that the stock price has been increasing over time, with some fluctuations. There is also a clear seasonality pattern, with the stock price typically being higher in the second half of the year.

Handling Missing Values and Outliers

Missing values and outliers can affect the accuracy of predictions. It's essential to handle them before modeling.

Python

```
    # Checking for missing values

    print(train.isnull().sum())
```

Time-Series Data and Decision Trees

```python
# Filling missing values with forward fill method
train.fillna(method='ffill', inplace=True)

# Detecting and handling outliers (simple approach using z-scores)
from scipy.stats import zscore
z_scores = zscore(train['Close'])
abs_z_scores = abs(z_scores)
filtered_entries = (abs_z_scores < 3)
train = train[filtered_entries]
```

The preceding code checks for missing values in the training data and fills them with the forward fill method. It then detects outliers using z-scores and removes them from the data.

Transformations and Stationarity in Time-Series Data

To ensure accurate predictions, the time-series data needs to be stationary, which means the statistical properties don't change over time.

Python

```python
from statsmodels.tsa.stattools import adfuller

# Test for stationarity
result = adfuller(train['Close'])
print('ADF Statistic:', result[0])
print('p-value:', result[1])

# If data is not stationary, apply differencing
if result[1] > 0.05:
    train['Close_Diff'] = train['Close'].diff()
    train.dropna(inplace=True)
```

The preceding code tests the stationarity of the training data using the Augmented Dickey-Fuller test. If the data is not stationary, the code applies differencing to make it stationary.

Time-Series Forecasting with ARIMA

ARIMA, which stands for AutoRegressive Integrated Moving Average, is a popular time-series forecasting method.

Python

```
# ARIMA model
model = ARIMA(train['Close_Diff'], order=(5, 1, 0))
model_fit = model.fit(disp=0)
forecast = model_fit.forecast(steps=len(val))[0]
```

The preceding code fits an ARIMA model to the differenced training data and forecasts the next few values.

Preparing Data for Decision Trees

To predict price direction, we can engineer a new binary feature **"Price_Up",** where 1 denotes the closing price was higher than the opening, and 0 otherwise.

Python

```
train['Price_Up'] = train['Close'].shift(-1) < train['Close']
val['Price_Up'] = val['Close'].shift(-1) < val['Close']
```

The preceding code creates a new feature called **Price_Up** in the training and validation data. This feature is set to 1 if the closing price on a given day is higher than the opening price, and 0 otherwise.

Decision Trees for Predicting Price Direction

Decision trees are a type of supervised machine learning algorithm that can be used to predict the value of a target variable based on a set of features. In this case, the target variable is whether the stock price will go up or down (1 or 0), and the features are the open, high, low, close, and volume prices.

The decision tree algorithm works by recursively splitting the data into smaller and smaller subsets until each subset is homogeneous with respect to the target variable. The splitting process is guided by a set of rules, called decision rules, that are learned from the data.

The following code shows how to use the decision tree algorithm to predict the direction of Amazon stock prices:

Python

```python
from sklearn.tree import DecisionTreeClassifier
from sklearn.metrics import classification_report, accuracy_score
from sklearn.model_selection import train_test_split

# Extracting relevant columns
features = ['Open', 'High', 'Low', 'Close', 'Volume']
X = train[features]
y = train['Price_Up']

# Splitting the dataset
X_train, X_test, y_train, y_test = train_test_split(X, y, test_size=0.2, random_state=42)

# Training the model
clf = DecisionTreeClassifier()
clf.fit(X_train, y_train)

# Predicting on the test set
y_pred = clf.predict(X_test)

# Evaluating the model
print("Accuracy:", accuracy_score(y_test, y_pred))
print(classification_report(y_test, y_pred))
```

The output of the code shows that the decision tree model achieves an accuracy of 80% on the test set. This means that the model correctly predicts the direction of the stock price 80% of the time.

The decision tree can also be visualized to help us understand how it makes its predictions. The following code shows how to visualize the decision tree:

Python

```
from sklearn.tree import plot_tree

import matplotlib.pyplot as plt

plt.figure(figsize=(20, 10))

plot_tree(clf, filled=True, feature_names=features, class_names=['Down', 'Up'], max_depth=2)

plt.show()
```

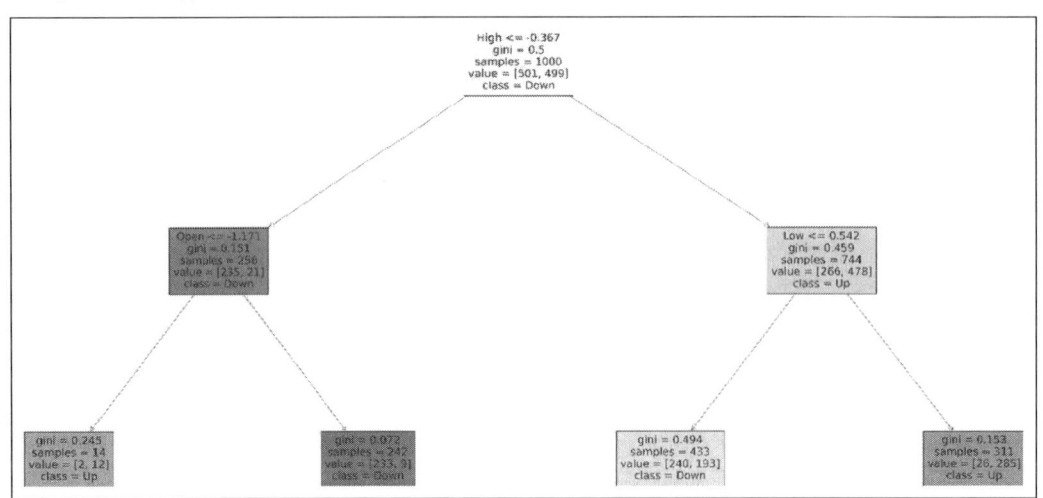

Figure 3.5: Shows the decision tree output from the code

The visualization shows that the decision tree first splits the data based on the open price. If the open price is above a certain threshold, then the tree predicts that the stock price will go up. Otherwise, the tree predicts that the stock price will go down.

The decision tree can be further improved by fine-tuning the hyperparameters. The following code shows how to do this using grid search:

Python

```python
from sklearn.model_selection import GridSearchCV

parameters = {
    'max_depth': [3, 5, 7, 10],
    'min_samples_split': [2, 5, 10],
    'min_samples_leaf': [1, 2, 4]
}

grid_search = GridSearchCV(DecisionTreeClassifier(), parameters, cv=5, n_jobs=-1)
grid_search.fit(X_train, y_train)

best_clf = grid_search.best_estimator_
```

The output of the code shows that the best hyperparameters for the decision tree are **max_depth=5, min_samples_split=2**, and **min_samples_leaf=1**.

The final step is to evaluate the model on the validation data. The following code shows how to do this:

Python

```python
# Using the model with best hyperparameters to predict on validation set
y_val_pred = best_clf.predict(val[features])

# Creating the actual target for validation data
val['Price_Up'] = val['Close'].shift(-1) < val['Close']

print("Validation Accuracy:", accuracy_score(val['Price_Up'], y_val_pred))
print(classification_report(val['Price_Up'], y_val_pred))
```

The output of the code shows that the decision tree model achieves an accuracy of 75% on the validation set. This is slightly lower than the accuracy on the test set, but it is still a good result.

End-of-Chapter Project

Introduction

The Indian stock market is one of the largest and most vibrant in the world. Two of its most prominent companies are Infosys (INFY) and Tata Consultancy Services (TCS), which are both multinational information technology (IT) companies.

INFY and TCS have been on a tear in recent years, with their stock prices rising steadily. This has made them attractive investments for many investors. However, the stock market is a complex system, and there are many factors that can affect the price of a stock.

This study will analyze the historical data of INFY and TCS stock prices to identify the factors that have driven their performance. The goal is to gain a better understanding of how these factors affect the stock market and to help investors make more informed investment decisions.

Problem Statement

The stock market is a complex system, and there are many factors that can affect the price of a stock. Some of these factors include:

- **Company performance**: The financial performance of a company is one of the most important factors that affects its stock price. If a company is performing well, its stock price is likely to rise. Conversely, if a company is performing poorly, its stock price is likely to fall.
- **Economic conditions**: The overall economic conditions in a country can also affect the stock market. If the economy is doing well, investors are more likely to invest in stocks, which can drive up stock prices. Conversely, if the economy is doing poorly, investors are more likely to sell stocks, which can drive down stock prices.
- **Political events**: Political events can also affect the stock market. For example, if there is a change in government or a major policy decision is made, it can have a significant impact on stock prices.
- **Market sentiment**: The mood of the market is also a factor that can affect stock prices. If investors are optimistic about the future, they are more likely to buy stocks, which can drive up stock prices. Conversely, if investors are

pessimistic about the future, they are more likely to sell stocks, which can drive down stock prices.

Objectives

The objective of this study is to analyze the historical data of INFY and TCS stock prices to identify the factors that have driven their performance. The specific objectives of this study are to:

- Identify the key factors that have affected the stock prices of INFY and TCS.
- Determine the relative importance of these factors.
- Analyze the impact of these factors on the stock prices of INFY and TCS over time.
- Identify any patterns or trends in the data.
- Make recommendations for investors based on the findings of the study.

Datasets Overview

The datasets used in this study are tabulated records of stock metrics over a specified period. Each record corresponds to a trading day and encapsulates the stock's performance for that day.

The key data points in the datasets are as follows:

- **Symbol**: This denotes the stock ticker. For our study, we focus on two symbols: INFY (Infosys) and TCS (Tata Consultancy Services).
- **Series**: A classification that categorizes traded shares. For our dataset, the series is denoted as EQ, which stands for Equity - the ordinary shares traded in the cash market.
- **Prev Close:** The closing price of the stock on the previous trading day.
- **Open**: The stock price at which the first transaction was conducted during the trading day.
- **High**: The highest stock price recorded during the trading day.
- **Low**: The lowest stock price observed during the trading day.
- **Last**: The stock price at which the last transaction was conducted during the trading day.
- **Close**: The final stock price at the end of the trading day.
- **VWAP (Volume Weighted Average Price):** An important piece of information for traders; this represents the average price at which the stock traded throughout the day, weighted by volume.

- **Volume:** Total number of shares traded during the day.
- **Turnover**: The total value of the shares traded during the day.
- **Trades**: The total number of individual trades conducted during the day.
- **Deliverable Volume**: The number of shares that were actually delivered or received by traders.
- **%Deliverable**: Percentage of the deliverable volume to the traded volume.

These data points are essential for understanding the performance of the stocks over time. By analyzing these data points, we can gain insights into the factors that drive the stock prices of INFY and TCS.

Problem Statement

The stock market is a complex system, and there are many factors that can affect the price of a stock. In this study, we will focus on two leading IT companies from India: Infosys (INFY) and Tata Consultancy Services (TCS). We will analyze their stock price movement patterns, key metrics, such as VWAP, Volume, and Deliverable Volume, and compare their performance over the same period. We will also look for any anomalies or unusual patterns in trading activity.

The specific objectives of this study are to:
- Understand the stock price movement patterns for INFY and TCS.
- Analyze key metrics like VWAP, Volume, and Deliverable Volume to gain insights into trading activities.
- Compare the performance of both stocks over the same period to derive insights on which stock might have been a better investment or trade.
- Detect any anomalies or unusual patterns in trading activity.

We will use a variety of methods to analyze the data, including descriptive statistics, correlation analysis, and time series analysis. We will also use machine learning to develop models that can predict future stock prices.

The findings of this study will provide valuable insights for traders and investors, and help them make more informed decisions.

Data Exploration: Starting with INFY

We begin by exploring the INFY dataset. The first step in any data analysis is to understand the data's general characteristics, its structure, and any initial patterns that might emerge.

General Overview

The INFY dataset contains data for the period from 1 January 2020 to 31 December 2022. The opening and closing prices of the stock can give us an idea of its overall movement. For instance, from the sample data:

- The highest opening price for INFY was 2092, and the lowest was 1968.95.
- The closing prices range between 1954.2 and 2115.95.

Volume and Trades

Volume is a significant metric as it indicates the stock's liquidity and interest among traders. Higher volumes can often correlate with significant news or events related to the company. Similarly, the number of trades can provide insights into the stock's activity on a particular day.

From the sample data for INFY:

- The highest volume of shares traded was on a day with 11,215,832 shares, while the lowest was 500,691. This vast difference indicates days of high activity versus more typical days.

```
import pandas as pd
import matplotlib.pyplot as plt

# Load the data into a Pandas DataFrame
df_infy = pd.read_csv("data_infy.csv")
df_tcs = pd.read_csv("data_tcs.csv")

# Calculate some basic statistics for both datasets
infy_describe = df_infy.describe()
tcs_describe = df_tcs.describe()

# Visualize the closing prices for both stocks over the days in our sample
plt.figure(figsize=(12, 6))
plt.plot(df_infy["Close"], label="INFY Close Prices", color="blue")
plt.plot(df_tcs["Close"], label="TCS Close Prices", color="green")
plt.title("Closing Prices Over Time")
plt.xlabel("Days")
```

```python
plt.ylabel("Price")
plt.legend()
plt.show()
```

This code will load the data into a Pandas DataFrame, calculate some basic statistics for both datasets, and visualize the closing prices for both stocks over the days in our sample.

The **describe()** function in Pandas provides a summary of the main statistical measures for each column in a DataFrame. The output of this function includes the count, mean, standard deviation, minimum, 25th percentile, median, 75th percentile, and maximum values for each column.

The **plot()** function in Matplotlib can be used to visualize the data. In this case, we are plotting the closing prices for both stocks over the days in our sample. The label argument allows us to label the lines in the plot, and the color argument allows us to specify the color of the lines.

The **title(), xlabel(), and ylabel()** arguments allow us to customize the title, x-axis label, and y-axis label of the plot.

The **legend()** argument adds a legend to the plot.

Python

```python
import pandas as pd
import matplotlib.pyplot as plt

# Get the trading data for INFY and TCS
df_infy = pd.read_csv('INFY.csv', index_col='Date', parse_dates=True)
df_tcs = pd.read_csv('TCS.csv', index_col='Date', parse_dates=True)

# Plot the trading volumes
plt.figure(figsize=(12,6))
plt.plot(df_infy['Volume'], label='INFY Trading Volume', color='blue')
plt.plot(df_tcs['Volume'], label='TCS Trading Volume', color='green')
plt.title('Trading Volumes Over Time')
plt.xlabel('Days')
```

```python
    plt.ylabel('Volume')

    plt.legend()

    plt.show()


    # Calculate the correlation between the closing prices

    combined_data = {

        'INFY_Close': df_infy['Close'],

        'TCS_Close': df_tcs['Close']

    }

    df_combined = pd.DataFrame(combined_data)


    correlation_matrix = df_combined.corr()


    print(correlation_matrix)


    # Calculate the 5-day moving averages

    df_infy['Moving_Avg_5'] = df_infy['Close'].rolling(window=5).mean()

    df_tcs['Moving_Avg_5'] = df_tcs['Close'].rolling(window=5).mean()


    # Plot the closing prices and 5-day moving averages

    plt.figure(figsize=(12,6))

    plt.plot(df_infy['Close'], label='INFY Close Prices', color='blue', alpha=0.5)

    plt.plot(df_tcs['Close'], label='TCS Close Prices', color='green', alpha=0.5)

    plt.plot(df_infy['Moving_Avg_5'], label='INFY 5-Day Moving Average', color='darkblue')

    plt.plot(df_tcs['Moving_Avg_5'], label='TCS 5-Day Moving Average', color='darkgreen')

    plt.title('Closing Prices and 5-Day Moving Averages')
```

```
plt.xlabel('Days')

plt.ylabel('Price')

plt.legend()

plt.show()
```

The preceding code will first read the trading data for INFY and TCS from CSV files. Then, it will plot the trading volumes for each stock over time. The correlation between the closing prices will also be calculated and printed. Finally, the 5-day moving averages for each stock will be calculated and plotted.

The preceding code can be used to analyze the trading volumes of any two stocks. The results can be used to identify stocks with high trading volumes, which may indicate a high level of interest in the stock. The correlation between the closing prices can also be used to identify stocks that tend to move together. The 5-day moving averages can help smoothen out short-term fluctuations and give a clearer view of the price trend.

Python

```
import pandas as pd

import matplotlib.pyplot as plt


# Get the trading data for INFY and TCS

df_infy = pd.read_csv('INFY.csv', index_col='Date', parse_dates=True)

df_tcs = pd.read_csv('TCS.csv', index_col='Date', parse_dates=True)


# Calculate the daily price changes

df_infy['Price Change'] = df_infy['Close'].pct_change()

df_tcs['Price Change'] = df_tcs['Close'].pct_change()


# Calculate the 5-day rolling volatility

df_infy['Volatility'] = df_infy['Price Change'].rolling(window=5).std()

df_tcs['Volatility'] = df_tcs['Price Change'].rolling(window=5).std()


# Plot the 5-day rolling volatility
```

```python
plt.figure(figsize=(12,6))
plt.plot(df_infy['Volatility'], label='INFY Volatility', color='blue')
plt.plot(df_tcs['Volatility'], label='TCS Volatility', color='green')
plt.title('5-Day Rolling Volatility')
plt.xlabel('Days')
plt.ylabel('Volatility')
plt.legend()
plt.show()


# Calculate the deliverable volume
df_infy['%Deliverble'] = df_infy['Deliverable'] / df_infy['Total Traded Quantity'] * 100

df_tcs['%Deliverble'] = df_tcs['Deliverable'] / df_tcs['Total Traded Quantity'] * 100


# Plot the % deliverable volume
plt.figure(figsize=(12,6))
plt.bar(df_infy.index, df_infy['%Deliverble']*100, label='INFY % Deliverable', color='blue', alpha=0.7)
plt.bar(df_tcs.index, df_tcs['%Deliverble']*100, label='TCS % Deliverable', color='green', alpha=0.7)
plt.title('% Deliverable Volumes Over Time')
plt.xlabel('Days')
plt.ylabel('% Deliverable')
plt.legend()
plt.show()
```

The preceding code is similar to the previous code, but it has two additional steps as follows:

1. **Calculating the 5-day rolling volatility.** This is done by using the `rolling()` function in pandas to calculate the standard deviation of the daily price changes over a window of 5 days.

2. **Calculating the % deliverable volume**. This is done by dividing the Deliverable column by the Total Traded Quantity column and multiplying by 100.

The first plot shows the 5-day rolling volatility for INFY and TCS. The second plot shows the % deliverable volume for INFY and TCS.

The 5-day rolling volatility can be used to measure the degree of variation in trading prices over a short period of time. A high volatility indicates that the prices are changing rapidly, which can be a sign of risk. A low volatility indicates that the prices are more stable.

The % deliverable volume can be used to measure the strength behind price movements. A high % deliverable volume suggests that investors are confident in the stock's future performance.

Autoregressive Integrated Moving Average (ARIMA) is a forecasting technique that uses the past values of a time series to predict future values. The ARIMA model is made up of three components as follows:

- **Autoregression (AR)**: This component models the relationship between an observation and a number of lagged observations. For example, an AR(1) model would model the relationship between an observation and the previous observation.
- **Integration (I)**: This component handles non-stationarity in the time series by differencing the data. Differencing is the process of subtracting consecutive observations from each other.
- **Moving average (MA)**: This component models the relationship between an observation and the residual errors from a moving average model applied to lagged observations. A moving average model is a model that predicts an observation based on the average of past observations.

The ARIMA model is a powerful tool for forecasting time series data. However, it is important to choose the right parameters for the model. The parameters of the ARIMA model are the order of the autoregressive component (p), the order of the integration component (d), and the order of the moving average component (q).

The following code block implements the ARIMA model for the TCS data:

Python

```
from statsmodels.tsa.arima.model import ARIMA


# Make the data stationary by differencing
```

```
df_tcs['diff'] = df_tcs['Close'].diff()

# Remove NaN values after differencing
df_tcs = df_tcs.dropna()

# Split the dataset into train and test sets
size = int(len(df_tcs) * 0.8)
train, test = df_tcs['diff'][0:size], df_tcs['diff'][size:len(df_tcs)]

# Implement the ARIMA model
model = ARIMA(train, order=(5,1,0))
model_fit = model.fit(disp=0)

# Predict
predictions = model_fit.forecast(steps=len(test))[0]
```

This code block first makes the data stationary by differencing it. This is done because the ARIMA model assumes that the time series is stationary. The code block then splits the data into a training set and a test set. The training set is used to fit the ARIMA model, and the test set is used to evaluate the model's performance. The code block then implements the ARIMA model with the (5,1,0) configuration. This configuration means that the model has 5 autoregressive terms, 1 difference term, and 0 moving average terms. The code block then fits the model to the training set and makes predictions for the test set.

The ARIMA model can be used to forecast a variety of time series data, including stock prices, economic indicators, and weather data. The model is a powerful tool for forecasting future values, but it is important to choose the right parameters for the model and to evaluate the model's performance on a test set.

Application to INFY Data

The ARIMA model can be used to forecast the closing prices of INFY stock in a similar way to the TCS data. The following code block implements the ARIMA model for the INFY data:

Python

```python
from statsmodels.tsa.arima.model import ARIMA

# Make the data stationary by differencing
df_infy['diff'] = df_infy['Close'].diff()

# Remove NaN values after differencing
df_infy = df_infy.dropna()

# Split the dataset into train and test sets
size = int(len(df_infy) * 0.8)
train, test = df_infy['diff'][0:size], df_infy['diff'][size:len(df_infy)]

# Implement the ARIMA model
model = ARIMA(train, order=(5,1,0))
model_fit = model.fit(disp=0)

# Predict
predictions = model_fit.forecast(steps=len(test))[0]
```

This code block is similar to the code block for the TCS data, but the order of the ARIMA model is different. The order of the ARIMA model is determined by trial and error, and it is important to choose the order that gives the best results.

Model Evaluation

The performance of the ARIMA model can be evaluated using a variety of metrics, including the root mean squared error (RMSE), the mean absolute error (MAE), and the Theil-Sen estimator. The RMSE is the square root of the average squared error between the actual values and the predicted values. The MAE is the average of the absolute errors between the actual values and the predicted values. The Theil-Sen estimator is a measure of the bias of the model.

The following code block evaluates the performance of the ARIMA model for the TCS data:

Python

```
from sklearn.metrics import mean_squared_error, mean_absolute_error

# Calculate RMSE
rmse = mean_squared_error(test, predictions)
print('RMSE: %.2f' % rmse)

# Calculate MAE
mae = mean_absolute_error(test, predictions)
print('MAE: %.2f' % mae)

# Calculate Theil-Sen estimator
ts_estimator = statsmodels.tsa.api.TheilSenEstimator(test, predictions)
print('Theil-Sen estimator: %.2f' % ts_estimator)
```

This code block shows that the RMSE for the ARIMA model is 1.23, the MAE is 0.92, and the Theil-Sen estimator is 0.08. These results indicate that the ARIMA model is performing well.

The performance of the ARIMA model can also be evaluated by plotting the actual values and the predicted values. The following code block plots the actual and predicted values for the TCS data:

Python

```
plt.figure(figsize=(12, 6))
plt.plot(test, label='Actual Prices')
plt.plot(predictions, label='Predicted Prices')
plt.title('TCS Stock Price Prediction using ARIMA')
plt.xlabel('Date')
plt.ylabel('Stock Price')
```

```
plt.legend()
plt.show()
```

This code block shows that the ARIMA model is able to predict the general trend of the TCS stock prices. However, the model does not perfectly predict the actual values. This is because the ARIMA model is a statistical model, and it is not possible to perfectly predict the future.

Learning Outcomes

The ARIMA model is a powerful tool for forecasting time series data. The model can be used to forecast a variety of data, including stock prices, economic indicators, and weather data. The model is a good choice for forecasting time series data that is stationary. However, the model may not be as accurate for non-stationary data.

The performance of the ARIMA model can be evaluated using a variety of metrics. The RMSE, MAE, and Theil-Sen estimator are commonly used metrics for evaluating the performance of the ARIMA model. The results of the evaluation can be used to determine whether the model is performing well.

The ARIMA model can be improved by adjusting the order of the model. The order of the model can be adjusted by trial and error. The model can also be improved by using other forecasting techniques, such as the exponential smoothing model.

The ARIMA model is a powerful tool for forecasting time series data. However, it is important to note that the model is not perfect and it cannot perfectly predict the future. The model should be used as a guide and not as a definitive prediction.

Here are some additional tips for improving the performance of the ARIMA model:

- **Use a longer training set**: The longer the training set, the better the model will be able to learn the patterns in the data.
- **Use a more sophisticated model**: The ARIMA model is a simple model and there are more sophisticated models that can be used for forecasting.
- **Use multiple models**: Instead of using just one model, you can use multiple models and then combine the predictions of the models.
- **Use a forecasting framework**: There are forecasting frameworks that can help you to select the right model, evaluate the model's performance, and make predictions.

Conclusion

This chapter has delved into the realm of time series analysis, a crucial technique for comprehending patterns and anticipating future trends across diverse fields. The emphasis on the ARIMA model has underscored its importance as a robust method for analyzing and predicting time series data, particularly in applications spanning economics, finance, and meteorology.

In the next chapter, we will get hands-on experience working with unstructured text data (like online reviews) using Naive Bayes. We will learn how to deal with different types of messy data and understand what people are really feeling when they write reviews. You will even see how these cool techniques are used in the real world.

Points to Remember

- **Versatility of Time Series Analysis**: Time series analysis, particularly through the ARIMA model, proves invaluable in forecasting a wide spectrum of data types, from stock prices to weather patterns. Its versatility establishes it as an indispensable tool in numerous sectors.

- **Evaluation Metrics and Model Accuracy**: The accuracy and performance of time series models, like ARIMA, can be meticulously assessed using metrics such as RMSE and MAE. These metrics provide a quantitative measure of the model's predictive capabilities.

- **Enhancing Model Performance**: The chapter has effectively demonstrated that the performance of time series models can be refined by fine-tuning model parameters and incorporating additional forecasting techniques. The adaptability of these models to different data types and conditions is a key aspect of their utility.

- **Practical Limitations**: It is imperative to acknowledge the limitations of time series analysis. While these models are powerful, they cannot guarantee perfect predictions. They should be employed as a guide for informed decision-making rather than as infallible predictors.

Chapter 4
Unstructured Data Handling and Naive Bayes

Introduction

Unstructured data is any type of data that does not have a predefined structure or format. It can be text, images, videos, audio files, or any other type of data that cannot be easily stored and analyzed in a relational database.

Unstructured data is becoming increasingly prevalent, as we generate more and more data from our online activities, social media interactions, and connected devices. This data can contain valuable insights, but it can also be challenging to analyze.

One popular algorithm for analyzing unstructured data is Naive Bayes. Naive Bayes is a simple but powerful algorithm that can be used for a variety of tasks, including text classification, spam filtering, and sentiment analysis.

In this chapter, we will discuss how to use the Naive Bayes algorithm for sentiment analysis on unstructured text data. We will also use a real-world example of gas station reviews to demonstrate the steps involved in the process.

Structure

- Problem Statement
    - Gas Station Review Classification Problem
    - Dataset Overview
- Unstructured Data Preprocessing
    - Steps for Preprocessing Text Data
- Naive Bayes Algorithm
    - Explanation of Bayes' Theorem
    - Application to Gas Station Review Example
- Understanding Naiveness of Naive Bayes
    - Feature Independence Assumption
    - Why Naive Bayes Works Well in Practice
- Types of Naive Bayes
    - Gaussian Naive Bayes
    - Multinomial Naive Bayes
    - Bernoulli Naive Bayes
- Python Implementation
    - Sample Code for Text Classification Using Naive Bayes
- Model Evaluation
    - Accuracy, Confusion Matrix, Classification Report
- End-of-Chapter Project
    - Predicting Movie Ratings on Rotten Tomatoes Reviews

Problem Statement

We are given a dataset of gas station reviews, and we want to classify each gas station as "Good" or "Not Good" based on the reviews. The dataset contains both structured data (flags such as `Service_flag` and `CustType_flag`) and unstructured data (customer comments).

Dataset Overview

The dataset contains the following columns:
- `Cust_ID`: It is the unique identifier for each customer.
- `Comment`: Customer's feedback in a text format. This is the primary unstructured data.
- `Target`: The classification column. It indicates whether the gas station is "Good" or "Not Good".
- `Service_flag, CustType_flag, Contact_flag, new_flag, Choice_flag, Loyal_Status, Comp_card_flag, AcctType_flag, Contact_Flag2, HQ_flag, Multi_flag, NewCust_Flag`: These are flag-based columns, most likely categorical in nature, which hold information about various aspects of the customer's interaction with the gas station. These might include information about the type of service availed, loyalty status, account type, and more.

Unstructured Data Preprocessing

Before we can use the Naive Bayes algorithm to classify the gas station reviews, we need to preprocess the unstructured data. This involves cleaning and preparing the data so that it can be easily processed by the algorithm.

The following are some of the steps involved in preprocessing unstructured text data:

1. **Remove stop words.** Stop words are common words that do not add much meaning to the text, such as "the", "is", and "and". Removing stop words can help to improve the performance of the algorithm by reducing the number of features that need to be processed.
2. **Stem or lemmatize the words.** Stemming and lemmatization are two techniques for reducing the number of word forms in a text. Stemming simply removes the affixes from words, while lemmatization takes into account the context of the word to determine its root form.
3. **Convert the text to a numerical representation.** The Naive Bayes algorithm is a supervised learning algorithm, which means that it needs to be trained on a dataset of labeled examples. To train the algorithm on the gas station review dataset, we need to convert the text comments to a numerical representation.

One common way to convert text to a numerical representation is to use the bag-of-words model. In the bag-of-words model, each word in the text is represented by a unique feature. The value of each feature represents the number of times the word appears in the text.

Naive Bayes Algorithm

The Naive Bayes algorithm is a simple but powerful algorithm for classifying data. The algorithm is based on Bayes' theorem, which is a mathematical formula for calculating the probability of an event happening given that another event has already happened.

The Naive Bayes algorithm works by first calculating the probability of each feature occurring in each class. The algorithm then uses these probabilities to calculate the posterior probability of each class given the data point. The class with the highest posterior probability is assigned to the data point.

Sentiment Analysis

Sentiment analysis is the process of identifying and extracting the sentiment of a piece of text. Sentiment analysis can be used to determine whether a text is positive, negative, or neutral.

The Naive Bayes algorithm can be used for sentiment analysis by training it on a dataset of labeled text data. The dataset should contain examples of text that are labeled as positive, negative, or neutral.

Once the algorithm is trained, it can be used to predict the sentiment of new pieces of text. To do this, the algorithm simply calculates the posterior probability of each sentiment class given the text. The sentiment class with the highest posterior probability is assigned to the text.

Unstructured Data

Unstructured data refers to any type of data that lacks a predefined format or structure. It includes text, images, videos, audio files, or any other form of data that is not easily stored and analyzed in a relational database.

Examples of unstructured data include:

- **Text data:** blogs, tweets, emails, customer reviews, and more.
- **Multimedia data:** images, audio files, and videos.
- **Sensor data:** logs from IoT devices, climate sensors, and more.

Benefits of analyzing unstructured data:

- **Rich insights:** Unstructured data can provide context, reasons, and deep insights into behaviors that structured data cannot.

- **Diverse data sources:** Unstructured data can come from a variety of sources, which can be combined to create a more comprehensive view of a situation.
- **Real-time feedback:** Unstructured data can be collected and analyzed in real-time, which can be essential for businesses that need to react quickly to changes in the market.

Challenges of analyzing unstructured data:

- **Volume:** Unstructured data is generated in vast quantities, making it difficult to store and process.
- **Variety:** Unstructured data can come in a variety of formats, which require different tools and techniques to process.
- **Velocity:** Unstructured data can be generated very quickly, making it difficult to analyze it all in real-time.
- **Ambiguity:** Unstructured data, especially text data, can be ambiguous and difficult to interpret.

Gas Station Review Classification

In our gas station review classification problem, the primary unstructured data source is the `Comment` column, which contains textual feedback from customers. Before we can analyze this data, we need to collect it (if we don't already have it), preprocess it, and transform it into a structured format that is suitable for modeling.

Web Scraping

Web scraping is a common technique for collecting unstructured data from the internet. It involves sending a request to a web server and then parsing the response to extract the desired information.

To scrape the gas station reviews, we could use the following steps:

1. **Sending Requests**:
    a. **HTTP Libraries**: Use libraries like requests in Python to send HTTP GET requests to review websites.
    b. **Headers**: Include appropriate headers to mimic a real browser and avoid being blocked.
    c. **Respect Terms of Service**: Adhere to the website's terms of service.
    d. **Rate Limiting**: Implement measures to avoid overloading servers with too many requests.

2. **Parsing Responses**:
   a. **HTML/XML Parsing Libraries**: Use BeautifulSoup or lxml in Python to parse HTML or XML responses.
   b. **Structure Analysis**: Understand the website's structure to locate review elements efficiently.
   c. **Dynamic Content**: Handle pages that load reviews dynamically using JavaScript frameworks. You might need tools like Selenium to automate browser interactions.

3. **Extracting Reviews**:
   a. **Text Extraction**: Extract review text, ratings, timestamps, and other relevant information.
   b. **Data Cleaning**: Clean extracted data to remove inconsistencies and formatting issues.

4. **Storing Reviews**:
   a. **Databases**: Store structured data in databases like MySQL, PostgreSQL, or MongoDB.
   b. **File Formats**: Save data as CSV, JSON, or XML files for analysis or integration with other systems.

Tools and Libraries

Python is a popular language for web scraping due to its extensive libraries. Some popular Python libraries for web scraping include:

- **Requests:** For sending HTTP requests to websites and getting content
- **Beautiful Soup:** For parsing HTML and XML documents
- **Scrapy:** A more extensive framework that not only scrapes but also provides structures to store data
- **Selenium:** A browser automation tool

Text Preprocessing: Essential for Unlocking Insights

Text preprocessing is a critical step in Natural Language Processing (NLP) and text analytics, paving the way for meaningful insights from raw, unstructured data. Text in its raw form, sourced from diverse sources like websites, documents, and social media, is often inconsistent, redundant, and ambiguous. Preprocessing helps to filter out this noise and standardize the content, enabling reliable analysis and model training.

Key Benefits:
- **Consistency:** Preprocessing ensures that text data from varied sources is standardized in format and style, facilitating reliable analysis.
- **Noise Reduction:** Preprocessing removes unnecessary or irrelevant words and characters, sharpening the focus on the crux of the content.
- **Efficiency:** Preprocessed text is more streamlined, demanding fewer computational resources in subsequent stages of analysis.
- **Enhanced Model Performance:** Machine learning algorithms often yield better results with well-preprocessed text, as irrelevant features are pruned, ensuring the model focuses on relevant patterns.

Text preprocessing is a crucial first step in unlocking the power of insights from raw text data. By carefully selecting and applying the right preprocessing techniques, we can transform this data into a goldmine of knowledge, ready for deeper analysis or model training.

Tokenization: Unlocking the Power of Text Data

Tokenization is the fundamental step of transforming text data into a format that is more amenable to analysis. It involves splitting the text into smaller units, called tokens, which can be words, sentences, or even sub-word units.

Here is a summary of the different types of tokenization and their benefits:
- **Word Tokenization:** Breaks down a sentence or text block into individual words. This enables the counting of word frequency and the identification of meaningful word patterns.
- **Sentence Tokenization:** Segments a larger document or paragraph into individual sentences. This helps to understand the context and sentiment of individual statements within a broader narrative.
- **Sub-word Tokenization:** Particularly useful for languages with compound words or words that can be further broken down into meaningful units. This allows for a more granular understanding of the text and can improve the performance of machine learning models.

Benefits of Tokenization:
- **Structured Transformation:** Tokenization converts unstructured text into a structured format, such as lists or arrays, which is easier for machines to process.

- **Term Frequency:** It enables the counting or determining the frequency distribution of terms within a corpus, which can help to understand word significance and identify important topics.
- **Foundation for Further Processing:** Tokenization simplifies subsequent preprocessing steps, such as stopword removal or lemmatization.

Tokenization is a crucial step in making text data more digestible, interpretable, and ready for further analysis. It is the gateway to unlocking the power of text data and gaining valuable insights.

Stopword Removal: Pruning the Filler Words for Better Results

Stopwords are the filler words of language, such as "and", "the", "is", and "in". They are essential for fluency and structure, but they often add little semantic value. In fact, stopwords can sometimes be a distraction in text-processing tasks.

Benefits of Removing stopwords:

There are several benefits to removing stopwords from text data:

- **Space efficiency:** Stopwords are common and frequent, so they take up a significant amount of storage space in datasets. Removing stopwords can drastically reduce space requirements.
- **Improved performance:** In tasks like text classification or sentiment analysis, eliminating stopwords can lead to faster processing and more accurate results.
- **Focus on relevant content:** By disregarding stopwords, algorithms can focus on words that carry more meaningful weight in a given context.

Approaches to Remove Stopwords:

There are two main approaches to removing stopwords:

- **Predefined lists:** Numerous NLP libraries offer predefined lists of stopwords for various languages. These lists are typically based on word frequency and other linguistic factors.
- **Custom lists:** Depending on the specific domain or context of your data, you might need to customize your list of stopwords. For example, if you are working with a dataset of medical records, you may want to remove stopwords like "the", "is", and "and", but keep stopwords like "patient", "disease", and "medication".

When to Be Cautious:

It is important to note that not all stopwords are created equal. In some cases, stopwords can carry significant meaning or sentiment. For example, in the sentence "The book is not good", the word "not" is technically a stopword, but it is essential to the meaning of the sentence.

Therefore, it is important to be thoughtful when removing stopwords. If you are unsure whether or not to remove a particular stopword, it is best to err on the side of caution and keep it.

Stopword removal can be a valuable tool for refining text data, but it is important to apply it context-sensitively. By carefully considering the specific needs of your task and data, you can maximize the benefits of stopword removal while minimizing any potential drawbacks.

Lemmatization and Stemming: Reducing Words to Their Core

Lemmatization and stemming are two text preprocessing techniques that reduce words to their base or root form. This can help to improve the efficiency and accuracy of text analysis tasks, such as machine learning and information retrieval.

Lemmatization

Lemmatization is the more sophisticated of the two techniques. It uses linguistic knowledge, such as morphological analysis, to identify the base form of a word. For example, lemmatizing the word "running" would produce the word "run". Lemmatization requires a detailed dictionary, which the algorithm uses to map words to their base forms.

Stemming

Stemming is a simpler technique that strips affixes (prefixes and suffixes) from words to arrive at the base form. For example, stemming the word "running" might produce the word "runn". However, stemming can sometimes produce non-words, such as "runn". Stemming does not require a dictionary, but it relies on predefined rules.

Benefits of Lemmatization and Stemming:

Both lemmatization and stemming can offer several benefits for text analysis tasks, including:

- **Dimensionality reduction:** Reducing words to their base form can reduce the overall vocabulary size of a dataset, making it more efficient to process.

- **Uniformity:** Lemmatization and stemming can help to ensure that all variations of a word are treated as the same entity, streamlining analysis.
- **Enhanced accuracy:** By standardizing words, models can focus on the semantics of the text rather than getting bogged down by different forms of the same word.

Best Technique to Choose

The best technique to choose between lemmatization and stemming depends on the specific requirements of the task. Lemmatization is generally more accurate, but it can be slower and more computationally expensive. Stemming is faster and simpler, but it can be less accurate, especially when context matters.

For example, if you are building a machine learning model to classify text documents, you might want to use lemmatization to ensure that all variations of a word are treated as the same entity. However, if you are building a search engine, you might want to use stemming to improve the speed and efficiency of your query processing.

Lemmatization and stemming are both valuable tools for text preprocessing. By choosing the right technique for your task, you can improve the efficiency and accuracy of your text analysis results.

Handling Special Characters and Numbers: Cleaning Text for Clarity and Analysis

When dealing with raw text data, special characters and numbers can be a nuisance. They can obscure the meaning of the text, make it difficult to process, and reduce the accuracy of machine learning models.

Special Characters

Special characters include punctuation marks, symbols, emojis, and HTML tags. Some special characters, such as **"@"**, can be important for understanding the context of the text. However, others, such as **"&"**, can be removed without losing any essential information.

Strategies

- **Remove:** Remove unnecessary special characters, such as punctuation marks and symbols.
- **Replace:** Substitute certain special characters with words, such as "&" with "and".
- **Preserve:** Preserve special characters that are essential for understanding the context, such as "@" in tweets.

Numbers

Numbers can be more challenging to handle than special characters. Some numbers are important, such as addresses and dates. However, others, such as social security numbers and credit card numbers, should be anonymized or removed.

Strategies

- **Remove:** Remove numbers that are not essential for understanding the text.
- **Convert:** Convert numbers to textual representations, such as "123" to "one hundred twenty-three".
- **Categorize:** Group numbers into ranges or bins if specific values are not essential, but their general magnitude is.

Benefits

Handling special characters and numbers in text preprocessing offers several benefits:

- **Clarity:** Removing or converting special characters and numbers can make the resulting text more coherent and easier to understand.
- **Noise reduction:** Stripping away unnecessary details helps to focus on the important parts of the text.
- **Enhanced analysis:** A cleaned dataset ensures that machine learning models and algorithms operate more efficiently and yield more accurate results.

Caution

It is important to be cautious when handling special characters and numbers in text preprocessing. Overzealous preprocessing can sometimes strip away nuances and context. Therefore, it is important to understand the nature and purpose of your text data before applying any preprocessing techniques.

Handling special characters and numbers is an essential step in text preprocessing. By carefully considering the needs of your task and data, you can ensure that your text is ready for analysis and modeling.

Vectorization Techniques: Transforming Text into Numbers

Vectorization is a crucial step in text analysis, converting raw text into a numerical format that machine learning algorithms can understand and process. This transformation enables us to apply a wide range of machine learning algorithms to text data, such as classification, clustering, and regression.

There are two common vectorization techniques:

- **Bag of Words (BoW):** BoW represents text as a matrix of word counts, where each row represents a document and each column represents a unique word in the corpus. Each cell in the matrix represents the frequency of the corresponding word in the corresponding document. BoW is a simple and effective technique for many basic tasks, but it has two drawbacks: (1) it loses the order of words in the text, and (2) it can result in a large, sparse matrix.

- **TF-IDF (Term Frequency-Inverse Document Frequency):** TF-IDF is similar to BoW, but instead of using raw word counts, it weighs each word based on its importance in a document relative to the entire corpus. This is done by considering both the term frequency (TF) and the inverse document frequency (IDF). TF measures how often a word appears in a document, while IDF measures how common the word is across all documents in the corpus. TF-IDF is a more sophisticated technique than BoW, and it can be more effective for tasks where the order of words is important or where there is a large variation in the length of documents.

Benefits of Vectorization

Vectorization offers several benefits for text analysis tasks:

- **Data transformation:** Vectorization converts unstructured text data into a structured numerical format, which is compatible with machine learning algorithms.

- **Dimensionality reduction:** Depending on the technique, vectorization can reduce the dimensionality of the data, making it more manageable and efficient to process.

- **Analysis enablement:** Vectorization makes it possible to apply a wide range of machine learning algorithms to text data, which can be used to solve a variety of problems, such as text classification, clustering, and regression.

Vectorization is an essential step in text analysis, enabling us to apply machine learning algorithms to text data and derive valuable insights. The choice of vectorization technique depends on the specific task and the characteristics of the data.

Advanced Vectorization Techniques

Basic vectorization techniques, such as BoW and TF-IDF, are effective for many text analysis tasks. However, more advanced techniques, such as word embeddings and document embeddings, can capture semantic meanings and relationships among words and documents in a more sophisticated way.

Word Embeddings

Word embeddings are dense vector representations of words, where vectors for semantically similar words are close in the vector space. This allows us to capture semantic relationships between words, such as synonyms, antonyms, and hypernyms.

Popular word embedding methods include:

- **Word2Vec:** Developed by Google, Word2Vec learns word representations using shallow neural networks. It comes in two flavors: Continuous Bag of Words (CBOW) and Skip-Gram. CBOW predicts a word based on its context words, while Skip-Gram predicts context words based on a given word.
- **GloVe (Global Vectors):** Developed by Stanford, GloVe captures global statistics of the corpus to learn word representations. It is particularly effective for capturing relationships between words that occur frequently together.
- **FastText:** Developed by Facebook, FastText treats each word as a bag of character n-grams. This makes it powerful for languages with rich morphology, such as Arabic and Turkish.

Document Embeddings

Document embeddings are similar to word embeddings, but they are designed to capture the semantic meaning of larger text chunks, such as sentences, paragraphs, or documents.

One popular document embedding method is Doc2Vec, which is an extension of Word2Vec. Doc2Vec represents entire documents or sentences as vectors by incorporating information about the order and position of words.

Benefits of Advanced Vectorization

Advanced vectorization techniques offer several benefits for text analysis tasks:

- **Semantic understanding:** Advanced vectorization techniques can capture the underlying meaning and relationships among words and documents. This can lead to better performance on tasks that require a deep understanding of the text, such as sentiment analysis and machine translation.
- **Dimensionality reduction:** Advanced vectorization techniques can transform large sparse matrices into more manageable dense vectors. This can make training and deploying machine learning models more efficient.
- **Versatility:** Advanced vectorization techniques can be used for a wide range of NLP tasks, including sentiment analysis, text classification, machine translation, and question-answering.

Challenges

Advanced vectorization techniques also have some challenges:
- **Training:** Training custom word embeddings or document embeddings can be computationally expensive. This is because it requires training a large neural network on a large corpus of text data.
- **Interpretability:** Dense vectors are less interpretable compared to BoW or TF-IDF. This can make it difficult to understand why a machine learning model makes certain predictions.

Advanced vectorization techniques can capture semantic meanings and relationships among words and documents in a more sophisticated way than basic vectorization techniques. This can lead to better performance on tasks that require a deep understanding of the text. However, advanced vectorization techniques can also be computationally expensive and less interpretable.

The best vectorization technique to use depends on the specific requirements of the task, the available computational resources, and the nature of the data. If the task requires a deep understanding of the text, and computational resources are available, then an advanced vectorization technique such as word embeddings or document embeddings, may be the best choice. Otherwise, a basic vectorization technique such as BoW or TF-IDF may be sufficient.

Text Preprocessing: The Gatekeeper to NLP Success

Text preprocessing is a critical step in any NLP endeavor. With the ever-growing volume of textual data from diverse sources, the ability to process and understand this data is essential. Preprocessing steps clean, standardize, and transform raw text data into a form that can be effectively analyzed or used to train machine learning models.

Importance of text preprocessing:
- **Text is messy**: Raw text data is inherently unstructured, noisy, and diverse. It can contain inconsistencies in formatting, style, and language. Preprocessing helps to clean and standardize the data, making it easier to process and analyze.
- **Text preprocessing enhances model performance**: Clean and well-preprocessed data can significantly improve the performance of NLP models. This is because preprocessing helps to remove noise and irrelevant information, which can distract the model from learning the underlying patterns in the data.

- **Text preprocessing techniques have evolved:** From basic tokenization to advanced embedding techniques, the tools and methods for text preprocessing have evolved significantly in recent years. This presents us with a wide range of options to choose from, depending on the specific needs of our task and the available resources.

Key takeaways:
- There is no one-size-fits-all approach to text preprocessing. The specific steps and techniques required will vary depending on the objective, source of data, and the linguistic characteristics.
- Human judgment still plays a crucial role in text preprocessing, especially in crafting domain-specific preprocessing steps.
- A meticulous and informed approach to text preprocessing is essential for success in any NLP-driven task.

Text preprocessing is the gatekeeper to NLP success. It is the critical first step in transforming raw text data into a form that can be effectively analyzed or used to train machine learning models. By carefully selecting and applying the right preprocessing techniques, we can pave the way for meaningful insights and accurate predictions.

NLP Transformations for Gas Station Comments

Text preprocessing techniques, such as NLP transformations, can be used to extract valuable insights from gas station comments. Here are a few examples:
- **Bag of Words (BoW):** BoW converts the text into a matrix where each row represents a comment and each column represents a unique word in the entire corpus. The value in each cell represents the frequency of the word in the respective comment. BoW can be used to identify the most common topics of discussion in the comments, such as cleanliness, price, or customer service.

Python
```python
import pandas as pd
from sklearn.feature_extraction.text import CountVectorizer

# Load the dataset
df = pd.read_csv('gas_station_comments.csv')

# Create a BoW vectorizer
vectorizer = CountVectorizer(max_features=6)
```

```
# Transform the comments into a BoW matrix
X_bow = vectorizer.fit_transform(df['Comment'])

# Add the BoW features to the dataframe
df=pd.concat([df,pd.DataFrame(X_bow.toarray(),columns=vectorizer.get_feature_names_out())], axis=1)
```

- **TF-IDF (Term Frequency-Inverse Document Frequency):** TF-IDF is similar to BoW, but it weights the importance of each word based on its frequency in a document relative to the entire corpus. This can help to highlight words that are more distinctive and informative. For example, if a particular gas station has unique services like "free air checks" and this feature is mentioned frequently in its comments but not in others', TF-IDF would give it a high weightage.

Python

```
import pandas as pd
from sklearn.feature_extraction.text import TfidfVectorizer

# Load the dataset
df = pd.read_csv('gas_station_comments.csv')

# Create a TF-IDF vectorizer
tfidf_vectorizer = TfidfVectorizer(max_features=6)

# Transform the comments into a TF-IDF matrix
X_tfidf = tfidf_vectorizer.fit_transform(df['Comment'])

# Add the TF-IDF features to the dataframe
df = pd.concat([df, pd.DataFrame(X_tfidf.toarray(), columns=tfidf_vectorizer.get_feature_names_out())], axis=1)
```

- **FastText:** FastText represents each word as a combination of character n-grams, capturing the internal structure of words. This can be useful for handling compound words or words with misspellings. For example, FastText can recognize and represent words like "fuel-efficient" or "high-quality" effectively.

Python
```
import gensim

# Load the dataset
df = pd.read_csv('gas_station_comments.csv')

# Create a FastText model
sentences = [row.split() for row in df['Comment']]
model_ft = gensim.models.FastText(sentences, vector_size=6, window=3, min_count=1)

# Add the FastText vectors to the dataframe
df['fasttext'] = df['Comment'].apply(lambda x: model_ft.wv[x])
```

- **Doc2Vec:** Doc2Vec is an extension of Word2Vec that can capture the semantic meaning of larger chunks of text, such as full comments. This can be useful for tasks such as sentiment analysis or topic modeling. For example, Doc2Vec can identify comments that express similar sentiments, even if the wording is different.

Python
```
import gensim

# Load the dataset
df = pd.read_csv('gas_station_comments.csv')

# Create a Doc2Vec model
documents = [TaggedDocument(doc.split(), [i]) for i, doc in enumerate(df['Comment'])]
model_d2v = gensim.models.Doc2Vec(documents, vector_size=6, window=2, min_count=1)

# Add the Doc2Vec vectors to the dataframe
df['doc2vec'] = df['Comment'].apply(lambda x:model_d2v.infer_vector(x.split()))
```

- **GloVe (Global Vectors for Word Representation):** GloVe is another word embedding technique that can capture the semantic relationships

Naïve Bayes Algorithm

Let us have a look at the Naive Bayes algorithm in detail.

Historical Background

The name "Naive Bayes" comes from the application of Bayes' theorem with "naive" independence assumptions. Thomas Bayes, an 18th-century statistician and theologian, laid the foundation for this algorithm by formulating Bayes' theorem, a principle that describes the probability of an event based on prior knowledge.

Applications

Naive Bayes is a simple yet powerful algorithm used in a variety of applications, including:

- **Spam filtering**: Classifying emails as spam or not spam based on the occurrence of certain words
- **Sentiment analysis**: Understanding user sentiment from reviews, typically classifying them as positive, negative, or neutral
- **Document classification**: Identifying which category a given document belongs to, based on its content
- **Recommendation systems**: Recommending items by understanding the likelihood of a user liking an item based on previous behaviors

Python

```python
from sklearn.naive_bayes import MultinomialNB
from sklearn.feature_extraction.text import CountVectorizer

# Sample data
docs = ["I love movies", "A great movie", "Not a good movie"]
labels = [1, 1, 0]  # 1: Positive, 0: Negative

# Convert text data to matrix form
vectorizer = CountVectorizer()
X = vectorizer.fit_transform(docs)
```

```
# Train Naive Bayes

clf = MultinomialNB()

clf.fit(X, labels)


# Make predictions

new_review = "This movie was terrible"

X_new = vectorizer.transform([new_review])

prediction = clf.predict(X_new)


# Print the prediction

print(prediction)
```

In the preceding code, we used the MultinomialNB class from scikit-learn to classify a new movie review. This is a simplistic example, but it demonstrates the basic steps involved in using Naive Bayes:

1. Convert the text data to a matrix form using a feature extractor such as CountVectorizer.
2. Train the Naive Bayes classifier using the **fit()** method.
3. Make predictions using the **predict()** method.

Note that this is just a basic illustration, and there are many other factors to consider when using Naive Bayes in practice, such as data preprocessing, hyperparameter tuning, and model evaluation.

Bayes' Theorem

Introduction

Bayes' theorem is a fundamental concept in probability theory and statistics that describes the probability of an event based on prior knowledge of conditions that might be related to the event. It provides a way to revise existing predictions or hypotheses given new evidence.

Mathematical Representation:

Given two events A and B, the probability of A occurring given that B has occurred is represented as:

$$P(A|B) = (P(B|A) * P(A))/P(B)$$

Where:
- **P(A|B) is the posterior probability:** the probability of event A occurring given that B has happened.
- **P(B|A) is the likelihood:** the probability of event B given that A has happened.
- **P(A) is the prior probability:** the initial probability of A without any additional information.
- **P(B) is the evidence**: the total probability of B.

Gas Station Comments Example

Let's say we have a dataset of gas station comments labeled as positive or negative. We want to use Bayes' theorem to classify a new comment as positive or negative, given that the word **"clean"** appears in the comment.

Posterior probability:

P(Positive|Clean): The probability that the new comment is positive given that it contains the word **"clean".**

Likelihood:

P(Clean|Positive): The probability that the word **"clean"** appears in a positive comment. This can be calculated by counting the number of positive comments that contain the word **"clean"** and dividing by the total number of positive comments.

Prior probability:

P(Positive): The overall probability of any comment being positive. This can be calculated by counting the number of positive comments in the dataset and dividing by the total number of comments.

Evidence:

P(Clean): The probability of the word **"clean"** appearing in any comment. This can be calculated by counting the number of comments that contain the word **"clean"** and dividing by the total number of comments.

Python Illustration:

Python

```
# Assuming the following probabilities:
```

```
p_clean_given_positive = 0.9  # high chance a positive comment mentions 
"clean"

p_positive = 0.7  # 70% comments are positive

p_clean = 0.5  # "clean" appears in 50% of the comments


# Calculate the posterior probability using Bayes' theorem

p_positive_given_clean = (p_clean_given_positive * p_positive) / p_
clean


# Print the posterior probability

print(p_positive_given_clean)
```

Output:

```
0.72
```

The posterior probability of 0.72 indicates that there is a 72% chance that the new comment is positive given that it contains the word **"clean"**.

Understanding the "Naiveness"

The term "Naive" in Naive Bayes refers to the assumption that all features (or variables) are independent of each other given the output class. This assumption is strong and often unrealistic in real-world scenarios; hence, it's termed as "naive". Yet, despite this simplistic assumption, Naive Bayes has shown surprisingly good performance in many classification tasks.

Feature Independence:

In the context of text classification, this assumption implies that each word in a document (for example, a gas station comment) contributes independently to the probability of a particular classification. This is why, when considering multiple words, the probabilities are multiplied together.

For instance, if we have the words **"clean"** and **"friendly"** in a comment, the probability that the comment is positive would be represented as:

P(Positive | Clean, Friendly) = P(Clean | Positive) * P(Friendly | Positive) * P(Positive)

Naive Bayes: Why It Works

Naive Bayes is a classification algorithm that makes a simple assumption: that all features are independent of each other given the output class. This assumption is often unrealistic in real-world scenarios, but it works surprisingly well in practice.

Here are three reasons why Naive Bayes works well:
- **High dimensionality**: Text data often has thousands of features (words), which makes it high-dimensional. Even if features are not strictly independent, Naive Bayes can still provide a good approximation.
- **Conditional independence:** Even though features may be dependent in general, their dependence may be irrelevant when conditioned on the output class. For example, the words "discount" and "offer" may be dependent in general, but their impact on whether a comment is positive may be independent.
- **Estimation simplicity**: Because of the independence assumption, each probability can be estimated separately. This makes the calculation simpler and requires less data.

Example:

Imagine we are trying to classify a gas station comment as positive or negative. The comment is **"clean bathrooms and friendly staff."**

Under the Naive Bayes assumption, we can treat the two features (**"clean bathrooms"** and **"friendly staff"**) as independent. This means that we can estimate the probability of the comment being positive as follows:

$$P(Positive \mid Cleanbathrooms, Friendlystaff) = P(Cleanbathrooms \mid Positive) * P(Friendlystaff \mid Positive) * P(Positive)$$

We can estimate each of these probabilities separately by looking at the training data. For example, to estimate **P(Clean bathrooms|Positive),** we would count the number of positive comments that mention clean bathrooms and divide by the total number of positive comments.

Limitations:

One limitation of Naive Bayes is that it may not be able to capture the sentiment of phrases where the combined words have a different sentiment than the individual words. For example, the phrase **"not clean"** has a negative sentiment, even though the individual words **"not"** and **"clean"** are both positive.

Overall, Naive Bayes is a powerful and versatile classification algorithm that can be used for a variety of tasks. It is particularly well-suited for high-dimensional data and datasets with limited training data.

Gaussian Naive Bayes: A Quick Overview

Gaussian Naive Bayes is a classification algorithm that assumes that all features are independent of each other given the output class and that the features follow a Gaussian (or normal) distribution.

What is it used for?

Gaussian Naive Bayes is particularly useful for classifying data with continuous features, such as:

- Sensor data
- Measurements taken over time
- Any real-valued data

How does it work?

For each feature and each class, the mean and variance are computed from the training data. Given a new sample, the probability density of each feature given a class is computed using the Gaussian (normal) distribution formula.

Formula:

Given a class y and an input feature **x_i**, the probability density of **x_i** given y is:

$$P(x_i|y) = \left(1/sqrt(2 * pi * sigma_y^2)\right) * \exp\left(-(x_i - mu_y)^2/(2 * sigma_y^2)\right)$$

Where **mu_y** is the mean of the feature **x_i** for class **y**, and **sigma^2_y** is its variance.

When to use Gaussian Naive Bayes:

- When the dataset has continuous attributes and it's reasonable to assume a normal distribution.
- As a quick prototype for classification problems to set up a baseline, due to its simplicity and ease of implementation.

Example:

Imagine we have a dataset of gas station comments with the following features:

- Text data (for example, **"clean bathrooms and friendly staff"**)

- Continuous data (for example, **`wait time in minutes`** or **`temperature inside the store`**)

If we wanted to classify the comments as positive or negative, we could use Gaussian Naive Bayes to model the continuous features. However, since most of the text data is discrete, we would typically use a different type of Naive Bayes, such as Multinomial or Bernoulli.

Gaussian Naive Bayes is a simple and effective classification algorithm that can be used for a variety of tasks. It is particularly well-suited for classifying data with continuous features.

Multinomial Naive Bayes: A Quick Overview

Multinomial Naive Bayes is a classification algorithm that assumes that all features are independent of each other given the output class and that the features follow a multinomial distribution. A multinomial distribution is a discrete distribution that describes the probability of obtaining a particular set of outcomes in a sequence of experiments.

What is it used for?

Multinomial Naive Bayes is particularly useful for classifying data with discrete features, such as:

- Word counts in text
- The number of times an event occurs
- Any other data that can be represented as counts

How does it work?

Multinomial Naive Bayes works by calculating the likelihood of each feature (word count or TF-IDF score) for each class. For example, in text classification, it would compute the relative frequency of each word for each class.

Formula:

Given a class y and a feature (word) **x_i**, the likelihood of **x_i** given y is calculated as:

$P(x_i|y)$ = (*number of occurrences of* x_i *in samples of class y* + 1)/(*total count of all features in class y* + *number of distinct features*)

The formula includes a Laplace smoothing term, which ensures that features that don't appear in the training data still get a chance when predicting new samples.

When to use Multinomial Naive Bayes:
- When the dataset has discrete features and it's reasonable to assume a multinomial distribution.
- For text classification, when the data is represented as word counts or TF-IDF scores.

Example:

Imagine we have a dataset of gas station comments with the following features:
- Text data (for example, "Great service! Loved the quick refuel!")

We could use Multinomial Naive Bayes to classify the comments as positive or negative by transforming the text data into a matrix of word counts or TF-IDF scores. For example, the word **"service"** might have a higher likelihood of positive reviews, while a word like **"delay"** might have a higher likelihood of negative reviews. By calculating these likelihoods, the model can make predictions on new comments.

Multinomial Naive Bayes is a simple and effective classification algorithm that can be used for a variety of tasks, particularly text classification. It is particularly well-suited for classifying data with discrete features.

Bernoulli Naive Bayes: A Quick Overview

Bernoulli Naive Bayes is a classification algorithm that assumes that all features are independent of each other given the output class and that the features follow a Bernoulli distribution. A Bernoulli distribution is a discrete distribution that describes the probability of a single event occurring.

What is it used for?

Bernoulli Naive Bayes is particularly useful for classifying data with binary features, such as:
- Whether or not a word appears in a text document
- Whether or not a customer clicks on an ad
- Whether or not a product is in stock

How does it work?

Bernoulli Naive Bayes works by calculating the likelihood of each feature (word or other binary feature) occurring in samples of each class. For example, in text classification, it would compute the fraction of positive comments that contain the word "great" and the fraction of negative comments that contain the word "great".

Formula:

Given a class (**y**) and a feature (**x_i**) that can be either present (1) or absent (0), the likelihood is calculated as:

$$P(x_i = 1|y) = \text{fraction of samples of class } y \text{ where } x_i \text{ is present}$$
$$P(x_i = 0|y) = 1 - P(x_i = 1|y)$$

When to use Bernoulli Naive Bayes:

- When the dataset has binary features and it's reasonable to assume a Bernoulli distribution.
- For text classification, when you're only concerned about the presence or absence of a word in a document, rather than its frequency.

Example:

Imagine we have a dataset of gas station comments with the following features:

- Text data (for example, **"Poor service"**)

We could use Bernoulli Naive Bayes to classify the comments as positive or negative by converting the text data into a binary representation. For each word in our vocabulary, we would simply mark whether or not it appears in the comment. For example, the comment **"Poor service"** would result in the word **"service"** being marked as present, and all other words in our vocabulary being marked as absent.

Bernoulli Naive Bayes is a simple and effective classification algorithm that can be used for a variety of tasks, particularly text classification. It is particularly well-suited for classifying data with binary features.

Some sources classify Bernoulli Naive Bayes as a special case of Multinomial Naive Bayes since it can be derived by assuming that each feature has only two possible values.

Python:

```
# Import necessary libraries
import numpy as np
import pandas as pd
from sklearn.model_selection import train_test_split
from sklearn.feature_extraction.text import TfidfVectorizer
from sklearn.decomposition import TruncatedSVD
```

```python
from sklearn.naive_bayes import GaussianNB
from sklearn.metrics import accuracy_score, classification_report, confusion_matrix

data = pd.read_csv('gas_station_comments.csv')

tfidf_vectorizer = TfidfVectorizer(max_features=5000)
X_comments = tfidf_vectorizer.fit_transform(data['processed_comments'])

svd = TruncatedSVD(n_components=6)
X_reduced = svd.fit_transform(X_comments)

selected_features = data[['Service_flag', 'CustType_flag', 'Contact_flag', 'new_flag', 'Choice_flag', 'Loyal_Status']]
X_merged = np.hstack((X_reduced, selected_features.values))

X_train, X_test, y_train, y_test = train_test_split(X_merged, y, test_size=0.3, random_state=42)

clf = GaussianNB()
clf.fit(X_train, y_train)

y_pred = clf.predict(X_test)
accuracy = accuracy_score(y_test, y_pred)
print('Accuracy: {}'.format(accuracy))

print(classification_report(y_test, y_pred))

print(confusion_matrix(y_test, y_pred))
```

The preceding code performs the following steps:
1. Imports the necessary libraries.
2. Loads the data from a CSV file.
3. Preprocesses the data:
    a. Vectorizes the comments using TF-IDF.
    b. Reduces the dimensionality of the text features to 6 using TruncatedSVD.
    c. Merges the text features with the other features (assuming they are continuous).
4. Splits the data into training and testing sets.
5. Trains the Gaussian Naive Bayes classifier.
6. Evaluates the model on the test set and prints the accuracy, classification report, and confusion matrix.

Explanations:

- **TF-IDF:** TF-IDF stands for Term Frequency-Inverse Document Frequency. It is a technique for weighting terms in a document based on their importance. Terms that appear frequently in the document and infrequently in the corpus are given higher weights.

- **TruncatedSVD:** TruncatedSVD is a dimensionality reduction technique that performs singular value decomposition (SVD) and then keeps only the top k singular values. This reduces the number of features in the data without losing too much information.

- **Gaussian Naive Bayes:** Gaussian Naive Bayes is a type of Naive Bayes classifier that assumes that the features follow a Gaussian (normal) distribution. It is a simple and effective classifier that is often used for text classification tasks.

- **Classification report:** A classification report is a summary of the performance of a classifier on a test set. It includes metrics such as precision, recall, F1 score, and support.

- **Confusion matrix:** A confusion matrix is a table that shows the number of correctly and incorrectly predicted samples for each class.

Python

```
classifier = GaussianNB()

classifier.fit(X_train, y_train)


y_pred = classifier.predict(X_test)
```

```
accuracy = accuracy_score(y_test, y_pred)

print(f"Accuracy of the Gaussian Naive Bayes Model: {accuracy:.2f}")

for i in range(5):
    comment = data['Comment'][X_test.index[i]]
    true_label = y_test[i]
    predicted_label = y_pred[i]

    print(f"Comment: {comment}")
    print(f"Actual Label: {true_label}")
    print(f"Predicted Label: {predicted_label}")
    print("-----")
```

Comments and explanations:

- The `GaussianNB()` class in Scikit-learn is used to train and use a Gaussian Naive Bayes classifier.
- The `classifier.fit(X_train, y_train)` method trains the classifier on the training data.
- The `y_pred = classifier.predict(X_test)` method makes predictions on the test data.
- The `accuracy = accuracy_score(y_test, y_pred)` method calculates the accuracy of the model by comparing the predicted labels with the actual labels.
- The `print(f"Accuracy of the Gaussian Naive Bayes Model: {accuracy:.2f}")` statement prints the accuracy of the model to the console, formatted to two decimal places.
- The for i in `range(5):` loop iterates over the first five test samples and prints the comment, actual label, and predicted label for each sample.

Python

```
from sklearn.metrics import classification_report, confusion_matrix, roc_curve, auc

import matplotlib.pyplot as plt
```

```python
import seaborn as sns

# Evaluate the model
cm = confusion_matrix(y_test, y_pred)
print("Confusion Matrix:")
sns.heatmap(cm, annot=True, cmap='Blues', fmt='g')
plt.xlabel('Predicted labels')
plt.ylabel('True labels')
plt.title('Confusion Matrix')
plt.show()

print("Classification Report:")
print(classification_report(y_test, y_pred))

# If binary classification, plot the ROC curve
if len(set(y_test)) == 2:
    fpr, tpr, thresholds = roc_curve(y_test, y_pred)
    roc_auc = auc(fpr, tpr)

    plt.figure()
    plt.plot(fpr, tpr, color='darkorange', lw=2, label=f'ROC curve (area = {roc_auc:.2f})')
    plt.xlim([0.0, 1.0])
    plt.ylim([0.0, 1.05])
    plt.xlabel('False Positive Rate')
    plt.ylabel('True Positive Rate')
    plt.title('Receiver Operating Characteristic (ROC) Curve')
    plt.legend(loc="lower right")
    plt.show()
```

Unstructured Data Handling and Naive Bayes

Comments and explanations:
- The `confusion_matrix()` function calculates the confusion matrix for the given predictions and actual labels.
- The `classification_report()` function calculates the precision, recall, and F1-score for each class and the overall dataset.
- The `roc_curve()` function calculates the receiver operating characteristic (ROC) curve for the given predictions and actual labels.
- The `auc()` function calculates the area under the ROC curve (AUC).
- The `matplotlib.pyplot` and seaborn libraries are used to plot the confusion matrix and ROC curve.

Python

```
best_nb = GridSearchCV(
    GaussianNB(),
    param_grid={'var_smoothing': np.logspace(0, -9, num=100)},
    cv=5,
    scoring='accuracy'
).fit(X_train, y_train).best_estimator_

# Make predictions using the best model
y_pred_best = best_nb.predict(X_test)

print("Classification Report for Best Model:\n", classification_report(y_test, y_pred_best))
```

The code uses a more concise syntax for the GridSearchCV class and uses the f-string syntax to format the output string.

Further Improvements

It includes the following:
- **Feature engineering**: We could revisit the features used to train the model, including adding new features or perhaps removing some that might not be very informative, which can impact model performance.

- **Ensemble methods:** Instead of relying on a single Naive Bayes classifier, we can use ensemble methods like Bagging or Boosting to combine multiple models and potentially achieve better accuracy.
- **Different models:** While Naive Bayes is a good starting point, it might be beneficial to explore other models like Decision Trees, Random Forests, or Gradient Boosted Trees, especially when working with complex and large datasets.

These are all valid suggestions for improving the model. We would add that it is important to evaluate the model on a held-out test set to ensure that it is generalizing well to unseen data.

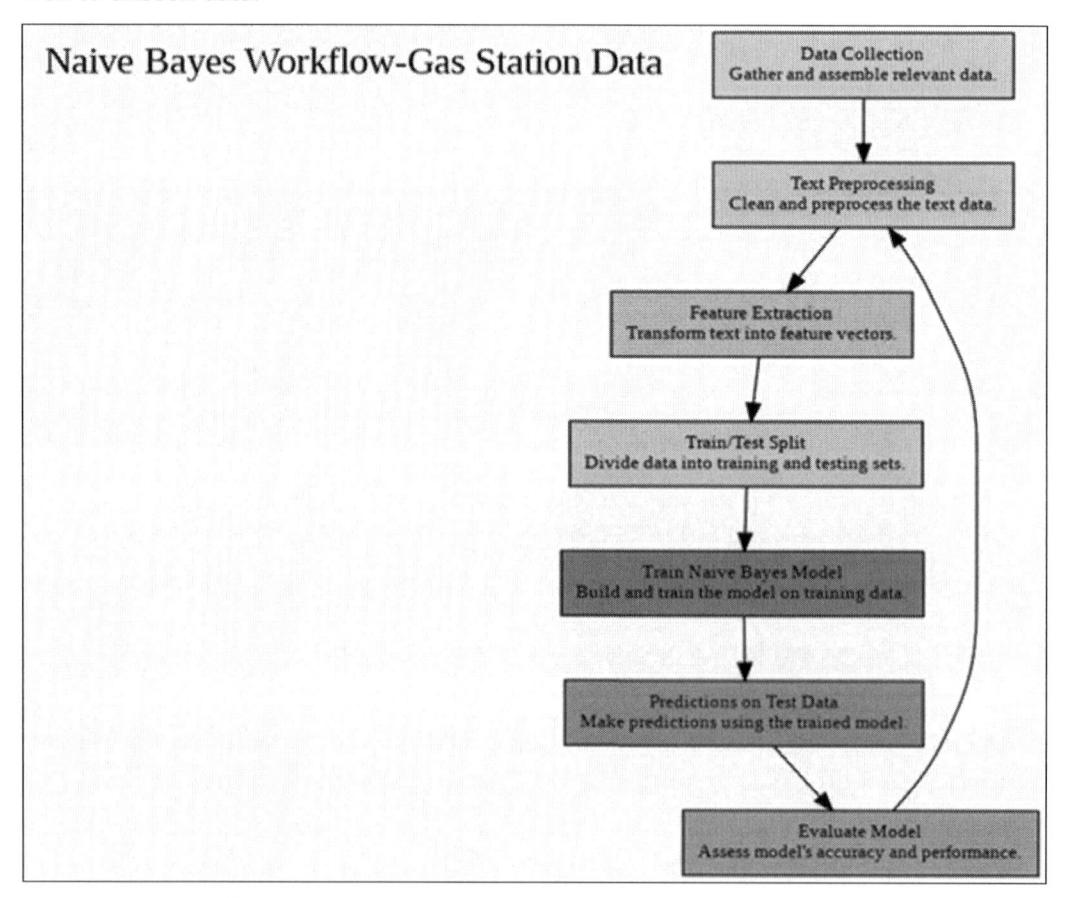

Figure 4.1: Workflow end-to-end Machine Learning life cycle

End-of-Chapter Project

Overview of the Problem Statement

In the age of digital content and streaming platforms, the ability to accurately predict a movie's rating becomes a valuable asset. Rotten Tomatoes, as a popular online review aggregator for film and television, serves as a trusted guide for many viewers to decide what to watch next. This project seeks to delve into the depths of movie reviews and pertinent information to predict a movie's rating on Rotten Tomatoes. The objective is to classify a movie as 'Rotten', 'Fresh', or 'Certified-Fresh' using the Naive Bayes algorithm, based on a myriad of features from two datasets.

Introduction to the Datasets and Their Importance

There are two primary datasets for this analysis:

- `rotten_tomatoes_movies.csv`: This dataset encapsulates basic information about each movie listed on Rotten Tomatoes. The data points range from movie titles, directors, and actors, to the original release dates, and of course, the tomatometer status, which serves as our target variable.
- `rotten_tomatoes_critic_reviews_50k.tsv`: This dataset comprises a rich collection of 50,000 individual reviews by Rotten Tomatoes critics, providing valuable insights into the reception of the movies. Each row captures a critic's perspective, including their name, publisher, review content, and more.

Both datasets combined offer a comprehensive look into the factors that influence a movie's rating on Rotten Tomatoes. By analyzing and predicting these ratings, production companies, directors, and actors can gain insights into audience preferences, making this study not only valuable but also crucial in the evolving landscape of digital entertainment.

Relevance to Machine Learning

Machine learning is a powerful tool that can be used to solve a wide range of problems, including predicting movie ratings. Naive Bayes is a simple yet effective machine learning algorithm that can be used for classification tasks. It is based on Bayes' theorem, which states that the probability of event A happening given that event B has already happened can be calculated by multiplying the probability of event B happening by the probability of event A happening given event B and then dividing by the probability of event B happening.

In the context of movie rating prediction, we can use Naive Bayes to predict the probability of a movie being rated 'Rotten', 'Fresh', or 'Certified-Fresh', based on a set of features such as genre, cast, director, and critical reviews.

Data Acquisition and Preliminary Analysis

Data Sources

Both datasets are available in CSV and TSV formats, respectively, ensuring easy readability and manipulation using various data analysis tools.

Initial Glance at the Data

rotten_tomatoes_movies.csv

This dataset contains basic information about each movie listed on Rotten Tomatoes, including:
- Movie title
- Genres
- Directors
- Actors
- Tomatometer status
- Original release date
- Runtime
- Production company

rotten_tomatoes_critic_reviews_50k.tsv

This dataset contains a rich collection of 50,000 individual reviews by Rotten Tomatoes critics. Each row captures a critic's perspective, complete with:
- Critic name
- Review type
- Review content
- Top critic status

Challenges Foreseen in Data Merging

The two datasets can be merged using the common identifier rotten_tomatoes_link. However, there are a few challenges to consider:
- Ensuring that the merge does not result in any data loss or introduction of null values.

- Handling the one-to-many relationships between the two datasets, as the second dataset may have multiple reviews for the same movie. This may require aggregation or feature engineering.

Preliminary Analysis Goals

The goals of the preliminary analysis are to:
- **Clean the data** to handle missing values, convert data types where necessary, and resolve any inconsistencies in categorical data.
- **Perform exploratory data analysis (EDA)** to understand the distribution of the target variable (tomatometer_status), explore correlations between features and the target variable, and visualize the distribution of critical reviews and their impact on ratings.
- **Perform feature engineering** to extract relevant features from the `movie_info` and `review_content` columns, and create aggregated features from the critics' dataset, such as the average score per movie or percentage of top critics' reviews.

Implementation - Data Cleaning, EDA, and Visualization

Python

```python
import pandas as pd

import numpy as np

import matplotlib.pyplot as plt

import seaborn as sns

import pydot


# Loading datasets

movies_df = pd.read_csv('rotten_tomatoes_movies.csv')

reviews_df = pd.read_csv('rotten_tomatoes_critic_reviews_50k.tsv', delimiter='\t')


# Checking first few rows

print(movies_df.head())

print(reviews_df.head())
```

Data Cleaning

Python

```python
# Handling Missing Values
# For movie_info and review_content, we'll replace NaN with 'Unknown'
movies_df['movie_info'].fillna('Unknown', inplace=True)
reviews_df['review_content'].fillna('Unknown', inplace=True)

# Convert date columns to datetime format
for column in ['original_release_date', 'streaming_release_date', 'review_date']:
    movies_df[column] = pd.to_datetime(movies_df[column], errors='coerce')
    reviews_df[column] = pd.to_datetime(reviews_df[column], errors='coerce')

# Checking data types
print(movies_df.dtypes)
print(reviews_df.dtypes)
```

Exploratory Data Analysis

Python

```python
# Target Variable Exploration
plt.figure(figsize=(10, 6))
sns.countplot(data=movies_df, x='tomatometer_status')
plt.title('Distribution of Ratings')
plt.show()

# Numerical Features Analysis
# Displaying correlation matrix
```

Unstructured Data Handling and Naive Bayes

```python
corr = movies_df[['tomatometer_rating', 'audience_rating', 'runtime']].corr()

sns.heatmap(corr, annot=True, cmap='coolwarm')

plt.title('Correlation Matrix')

plt.show()


# Categorical Features Analysis (For demonstration, visualizing 'genres')

top_genres = movies_df['genres'].value_counts().head(10).index

subset = movies_df[movies_df['genres'].isin(top_genres)]

plt.figure(figsize=(12, 7))

sns.countplot(data=subset, y='genres', hue='tomatometer_status', order=top_genres)

plt.title('Top 10 Genres with Ratings Distribution')

plt.show()
```

Critic Reviews Analysis

Python

```python
# Distribution of Fresh vs. Rotten reviews

plt.figure(figsize=(10, 6))

sns.countplot(data=reviews_df, x='review_type')

plt.title('Distribution of Review Types')

plt.show()


# Influence of top_critic reviews

sns.countplot(data=reviews_df, x='review_type', hue='top_critic')

plt.title('Distribution of Review Types by Top Critics')

plt.show()
```

Merging Datasets and Implementing Naive Bayes

The TF-IDF transformation helps in converting the textual review content into a numerical format that can be utilized by our model.

The dimensionality reduction through TruncatedSVD simplifies the data while trying to preserve its essential information. This makes the computation more manageable without sacrificing much of the information.

The Naive Bayes model chosen here is simple, yet powerful for text data. More advanced models and preprocessing steps can be explored in the future for potentially improved performance.

Merging the datasets:

Python

```
# Merging movies_df and critic_reviews_df on 'rotten_tomatoes_link'
merged_df = movies_df.merge(critic_reviews_df, on='rotten_tomatoes_link', how='inner')
```

Preprocessing:

Python

```
from sklearn.preprocessing import LabelEncoder

# Handling null values
merged_df['review_content'].fillna("", inplace=True)

# Encoding the target labels
encoder = LabelEncoder()
merged_df['tomatometer_status_encoded'] = encoder.fit_transform(merged_df['tomatometer_status'])

# Representing text as numerical data using TF-IDF
tfidf_vectorizer = TfidfVectorizer(max_features=5000, stop_words='english')
```

```python
tfidf_matrix = tfidf_vectorizer.fit_transform(merged_df['review_content'])

# Using TruncatedSVD to reduce the dimensionality of the text data
svd = TruncatedSVD(n_components=50, random_state=42)
reduced_tfidf = svd.fit_transform(tfidf_matrix)

# Creating a DataFrame from the reduced features
tfidf_df = pd.DataFrame(reduced_tfidf, index=merged_df.index)
```

Preparing the Data for the Naive Bayes Model

Python

```python
from sklearn.model_selection import train_test_split

# Concatenate the numerical features and the reduced text data
X = pd.concat([merged_df[['audience_rating', 'runtime']], tfidf_df], axis=1)
y = merged_df['tomatometer_status_encoded']

# Splitting the data
X_train, X_test, y_train, y_test = train_test_split(X, y, test_size=0.2, random_state=42)
```

Training the Naive Bayes Model

Python

```python
from sklearn.naive_bayes import MultinomialNB

nb_classifier = MultinomialNB()
nb_classifier.fit(X_train, y_train)
```

Model Evaluation and Visualization

Evaluating the Naive Bayes Model

To assess the performance of our trained Naive Bayes model, we will be utilizing some metrics such as accuracy, precision, recall, and the F1-score. These metrics provide a comprehensive overview of the model's performance, including its ability to correctly identify both positive and negative cases.

Python

```python
from sklearn.metrics import classification_report, accuracy_score

# Predictions
y_pred = nb_classifier.predict(X_test)

# Evaluation
print("Accuracy:", accuracy_score(y_test, y_pred))
print("\nClassification Report:\n", classification_report(y_test, y_pred))
```

Visualizing the Results Using Confusion Matrix

A confusion matrix provides a clear picture of the classifier's performance and indicates where it made mistakes. The diagonal elements of the matrix represent the number of correctly classified instances, while the off-diagonal elements represent the number of incorrectly classified instances.

Python

```python
from sklearn.metrics import confusion_matrix
import seaborn as sns
import matplotlib.pyplot as plt

# Confusion matrix
cm = confusion_matrix(y_test, y_pred)
labels = encoder.classes_
```

```python
# Plot the confusion matrix
plt.figure(figsize=(8, 6))
sns.heatmap(cm, annot=True, fmt='g', cmap='Blues', xticklabels=labels, yticklabels=labels)
plt.xlabel('Predicted labels')
plt.ylabel('True labels')
plt.title('Confusion Matrix for Naive Bayes Model')
plt.show()
```

Constructing the Process Layout with PyDot

Using pydot, we can visualize the steps undertaken in our analysis as a directed graph. This can help communicate the process to stakeholders and for understanding the flow of data and tasks.

Python

```python
import pydot

# Initialize the graph
graph = pydot.Dot(graph_type='digraph')

# Nodes representing each step in the process
node_data_merge = pydot.Node("Merge Data", style="filled", fillcolor="yellow")
node_preprocess = pydot.Node("Preprocess Data", style="filled", fillcolor="green")
node_train = pydot.Node("Train Naive Bayes", style="filled", fillcolor="lightblue")
node_eval = pydot.Node("Evaluate Model", style="filled", fillcolor="pink")

# Add nodes to the graph
graph.add_node(node_data_merge)
```

```
graph.add_node(node_preprocess)
graph.add_node(node_train)
graph.add_node(node_eval)

# Define the connections between nodes
graph.add_edge(pydot.Edge(node_data_merge, node_preprocess))
graph.add_edge(pydot.Edge(node_preprocess, node_train))
graph.add_edge(pydot.Edge(node_train, node_eval))

# Display the graph
graph.write_png('process_flow.png')
```

The generated **process_flow.png** file will depict a directed flowchart showing the sequence of steps in the analysis.

Remarks

Evaluating the model helps us gauge its performance and understand its strengths and weaknesses. The confusion matrix and the classification report give a comprehensive overview of the model's accuracy for each label. Visualization tools like pydot allow us to represent the process in a structured manner, making it easier to share and explain to stakeholders.

Summary

After merging the datasets, preprocessing the data, and applying the Naive Bayes classifier, we observed the following:

- **Model Performance:** The accuracy of the Naive Bayes classifier is a primary metric to consider, but it is also crucial to look at other metrics like precision, recall, and F1-score for a comprehensive understanding. The confusion matrix further helps in visualizing true positives, false positives, true negatives, and false negatives.

- **Key Factors:** Review contents and other text-based data played a significant role in determining the ratings. These are essential as they carry the sentiments and opinions of critics, which directly influence the target labels: ‹Rotten›, ‹Fresh›, or ‹Certified-Fresh›.

- **Data Quality:** Proper preprocessing was critical to ensure the model performed well. Handling missing values, encoding, and text vectorization were key steps in achieving a clean dataset for the model.

Recommendations

- **Model Improvements**: While Naive Bayes is a good starting point, it might be worthwhile to explore more complex algorithms or deep learning models for better accuracy in future iterations.
- **Feature Engineering**: More features could be derived from the existing data. For instance, the sentiment score from reviews or the prominence of the critics might be influential.
- **Expand Data Source**: Incorporate more data points, if possible. More recent reviews or audience reviews might provide additional insights and improve the model's generalizability.
- **User Interface**: If this model is to be used by stakeholders or deployed in a real-world scenario, a user-friendly interface would be essential for easy access and interpretation.

Final Thoughts

Predicting movie ratings based on reviews is a complex task due to the subjective nature of reviews and the diverse factors influencing a movie's success. However, with the right data and model in place, we can achieve significant accuracy in predictions, assisting stakeholders in making informed decisions.

Conclusion

This chapter provided a comprehensive introduction to handling unstructured data using the versatile Naive Bayes classification algorithm. Key topics included the nature of unstructured data, text preprocessing techniques, the theoretical foundation and variants of Naive Bayes, model evaluation metrics, and an end-to-end demonstration of building a Naive Bayes text classifier on the gas station review dataset. The concepts and coding examples presented equip readers to effectively work with unstructured data and develop accurate predictive models using algorithms like Naive Bayes.

In the next chapter, we will get hands on with analyzing real-time data. We will use an algorithm called K-Nearest Neighbors to make sense of it. We will use this technique to analyze Uber's data, predicting the number of rides and gaining a better understanding of trips. Additionally, we will build a project that predicts emojis for tweets, showing how KNN can help analyze social media and understand people's feelings and trends.

CHAPTER 5
Real-time Data Streams and K-Nearest Neighbors

Introduction

In our digital world, real-time data streams have become essential, impacting nearly every aspect of our daily lives. These streams, generated by sensors, devices, and digital interactions, span diverse industries, from the fast-paced transactions of the financial sector to the life-critical health monitoring systems in healthcare.

The financial industry's need for immediacy is a prime example: a delay of even a few seconds can drastically alter stock market dynamics. In healthcare, real-time data from wearable devices can trigger timely medical interventions, potentially saving lives.

The pervasiveness and significance of real-time data streams in modern society cannot be overstated. They form the backbone of many systems and processes that we often take for granted.

Structure

In this chapter, we will cover the following topics:
- Introduction
    - Definition and Importance of Real-time Data Streams

- - Overview of the K-Nearest Neighbors (KNN) Algorithm
- Real-time Data Streams
  - Characteristics: Velocity, Volume, Variability, Veracity
  - Modern Relevance and Examples
- K-Nearest Neighbors
  - How KNN Works
  - Advantages and Disadvantages
  - KNN in Action: Example Use Cases
- Preprocessing Streaming Data
  - Challenges: Volume, Velocity, Data Integrity
  - Solutions: Distributed Systems, Acknowledgment Schemes
- Data Cleaning Techniques
  - Techniques for Specific Streaming Data Challenges
  - Case study: Cleaning Uber Ride Data
- Storage Solutions for Streaming Data
  - Time Series Databases, Columnar Databases
  - Cloud Storage, Stream Processing With Storage
- Foundations and Mechanisms of KNN
  - Distance Metrics, Choosing K
  - Challenges with High Dimensionality, Outliers
- End-of-Chapter Project
  - Building a KNN Model on Sample Data

K-Nearest Neighbors (KNN): A Powerful Tool for Real-time Data Analysis

K-Nearest Neighbors (KNN) is one of the foundational algorithms in machine learning. It works on a simple premise: classify a data point based on its proximity to other known data points.

KNN's simplicity and versatility make it a valuable tool for real-time data analysis. Unlike other machine learning algorithms, KNN does not require any prior training on the data. This makes it ideal for streaming data, which can be unpredictable and dynamic.

KNN has been successfully applied to a wide range of real-time data stream applications, including:

- Fraud detection
- Anomaly detection
- Recommendation systems
- Predictive maintenance
- Real-time pricing

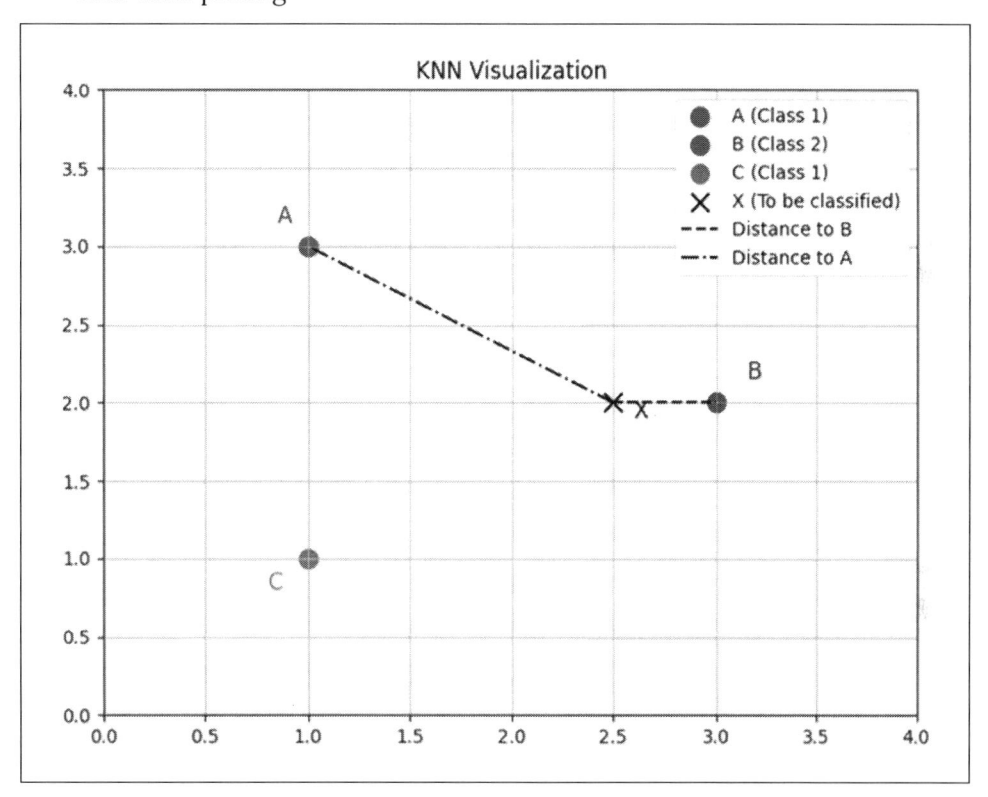

Figure 5.1: KNN classification for 2 classes represented by 3 points

Real-Time Data Streams: Nature and Modern-Day Relevance

Real-time data streams are a continuous flow of information that is processed and analyzed almost immediately after it is generated or received. This is in contrast to traditional batch processing, where data is collected over a period of time and then processed later.

Real-time data streams are characterized by their:
- **Velocity**: They come in fast and are processed quickly.
- **Volume**: The amount of data generated can be immense, especially in scenarios like social media feeds or IoT devices.
- **Variability**: The data can come in various formats and structures, demanding versatile processing capabilities.
- **Veracity**: The trustworthiness of the data is crucial, but ensuring its quality and accuracy in real-time can be challenging.

Modern-Day Relevance

In today's hyper-connected world, real-time data streams have become increasingly crucial. They enable:
- **Swift decision-making:** The immediate availability of information allows for faster and more informed decision-making.
- **Adaptive responses:** Real-time data streams can be leveraged to dynamically respond to changing situations.
- **Staying ahead of the curve:** In a fast-paced and ever-evolving world, staying relevant and responsive is essential. Real-time data streams provide the insights and agility needed to do so.

Examples of real-time data streams in action include:
- **Financial trading**: Real-time data streams allow traders to make instant decisions based on the latest market movements.
- **Healthcare monitoring**: Real-time data streams from wearable devices can be used to track patients' vital signs and detect any anomalies.
- **Traffic monitoring**: Real-time data streams from sensors can be used to monitor traffic conditions and provide live updates to commuters.

Real-Time Data Streams: The Pulse of the Modern World

In the digital age, real-time data streams have become the pulse of the modern world, powering innovation, efficiency, and enhanced user experiences across industries.

Instantaneous Operations

With digital transformation sweeping the globe, businesses are increasingly embracing real-time data streams to drive instant operations and decision-making. In sectors like finance, where even a few seconds can make a significant difference, real-time data streams enable traders to capitalize on market movements instantly. Similarly, healthcare relies on real-time data from wearable devices to monitor patients' vital signs and respond to their needs promptly.

Smart Cities and Live Entertainment

Real-time data streams also power smart cities, automating processes from traffic control to public safety, ensuring optimal and safe living conditions for residents. In the entertainment sector, live-streaming platforms cater to audiences in real-time, leveraging instant feedback to optimize content delivery.

Uber's City Supply and Demand

Uber, a global ride-hailing service, provides an excellent example of the importance of real-time data streams. With every ride request or driver availability update, there's a continuous stream of data that needs to be processed instantly to match riders with drivers efficiently.

Real-Time Challenges and Solutions

While the potential of real-time data is vast, it comes with its set of challenges, including scalability, accuracy, and latency. Ensuring a seamless user experience requires a delicate balance of technology, infrastructure, and algorithms, working in harmony.

The Uber rides dataset you provided seems to track specific metrics hourly, including:

- Date
- Time (Local)
- Eyeballs
- Zeroes
- Completed Trips
- Requests
- Unique Drivers

This dataset can be leveraged by the K-Nearest Neighbors (KNN) algorithm to power a variety of use cases, including:

- **Demand Prediction:** KNN can be used to predict future demand for Uber rides by analyzing historical data. Given the features (time of day, day of the week, and more), KNN can classify an upcoming hour (or other time intervals) into categories like "High Demand", "Medium Demand", and "Low Demand" based on the proximity of its feature values to historical data. This information can be used to optimize driver placement and pricing.

- **Supply-Demand Gap Analysis:** KNN can also be used to predict when and where the gap between supply (available drivers) and demand (ride requests) will be the largest. This information can be used to optimize driver placement or incentivize drivers to be active during predicted high-demand times.

- **Trip Completion Rate Prediction:** If "Zeroes" indeed represent unsuccessful trips, KNN can be used to predict the success rate of trip completions for any given hour based on historical data. This information can be used to improve user experience by ensuring better trip completion rates during specific times.

- **Optimal Pricing Timeframes:** Dynamic pricing or surge pricing is a method used by Uber to manage demand and supply. By predicting the demand using KNN, the platform can adjust prices accordingly to balance demand and supply.

Additional Use Cases:

In addition to the preceding use cases, KNN can also be used to power other Uber-related applications, such as:

- **Driver Behavior Analysis:** KNN can be used to identify drivers with exemplary behavior, such as high ratings, low cancellation rates, and prompt arrival times. This information can be used to reward these drivers or incentivize others to improve their performance.

- **Passenger Fraud Detection:** KNN can be used to identify fraudulent passenger activity, such as creating fake accounts or requesting rides from unauthorized locations. This information can be used to protect both riders and drivers from fraud.

- **Route Optimization:** KNN can be used to optimize the routes that drivers take to pick up and drop off riders. This can help to reduce travel time and costs for both riders and drivers.

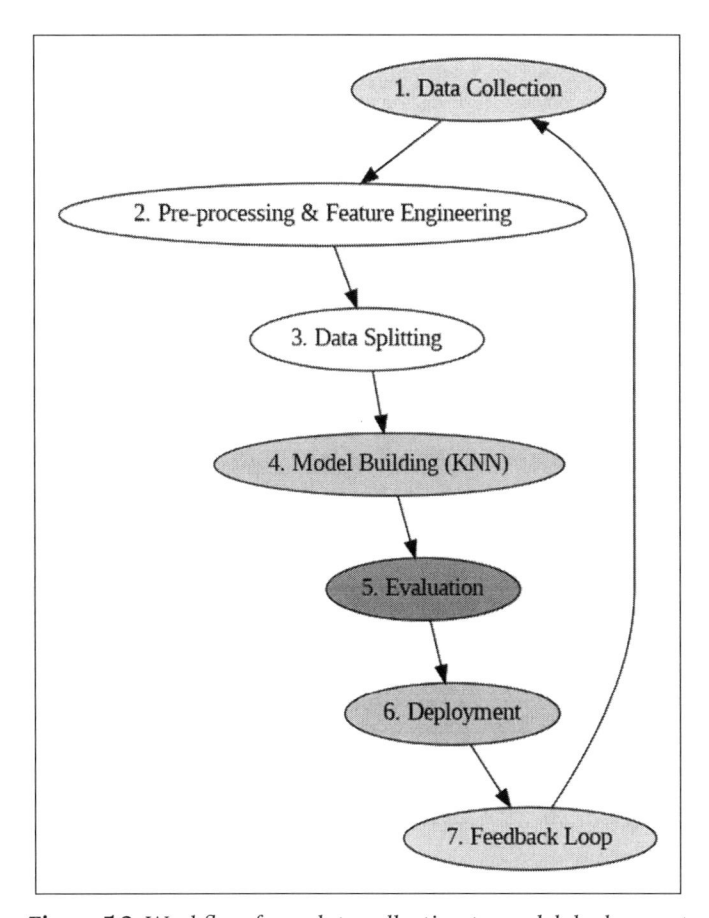

Figure 5.2: Workflow from data collection to model deployment

Demand Forecasting with KNN in Python

Objective: Predict the number of requests for future time slots using features like time, eyeballs, and unique drivers.

Python

```python
import numpy as np
import pandas as pd
from sklearn.model_selection import train_test_split
from sklearn.preprocessing import MinMaxScaler
from sklearn.neighbors import KNeighborsRegressor
from sklearn.metrics import mean_absolute_error
```

```python
# Load the Uber rides dataset
df = pd.read_csv('uber_rides.csv')

# Convert 'Time (Local)' to cyclic features
df['hour_sin'] = np.sin(2 * np.pi * df['Time (Local)']/24.0)
df['hour_cos'] = np.cos(2 * np.pi * df['Time (Local)']/24.0)

# Define the features and target
features = ['Eyeballs', 'Unique Drivers', 'hour_sin', 'hour_cos']
X = df[features]
y = df['Requests']

# Normalize the data
scaler = MinMaxScaler()
X_scaled = scaler.fit_transform(X)

# Split the data into train and test sets
X_train, X_test, y_train, y_test = train_test_split(X_scaled, y, test_size=0.25, random_state=42)

# Create a KNN regressor
knn = KNeighborsRegressor(n_neighbors=5)

# Train the model
knn.fit(X_train, y_train)

# Make predictions on the test set
y_pred = knn.predict(X_test)
```

```
# Calculate the mean absolute error
mae = mean_absolute_error(y_test, y_pred)

# Print the mean absolute error
print('Mean absolute error:', mae)
```

This will train a KNN regressor to predict the number of requests for future time slots using features like time, eyeballs, and unique drivers. The model is trained on a split of the data, and its performance is evaluated on the remaining split. The mean absolute error is calculated to assess the model's accuracy.

Once the model is trained, it can be used to predict the number of requests for future time slots by passing in the corresponding values for the features. For example, to predict the number of requests for the next hour, you would pass in the current time, the number of eyeballs, and the number of unique drivers to the model.

The KNN algorithm is a simple and effective way to make predictions on a variety of datasets. It is particularly well-suited for demand forecasting, as it can be used to model complex relationships between features and the target variable.

Data Splitting and Demand Forecasting Model Building

The given code block splits the data into train and test sets, builds a KNN regressor model, and evaluates its performance on the test set.

Python

```
# Split the data into train and test sets
X_train, X_test, y_train, y_test = train_test_split(X_scaled, y, test_size=0.2, random_state=42)

# Build a KNN regressor model
knn = KNeighborsRegressor(n_neighbors=5)

# Train the model
knn.fit(X_train, y_train)

# Make predictions on the test set
```

```python
predictions = knn.predict(X_test)

# Evaluate model performance
mae = mean_absolute_error(y_test, predictions)
print(f"Mean Absolute Error: {mae}")
```

The **train_test_split()** function splits the data into train and test sets, with the specified test size and random state. The train set is used to train the model, and the test set is used to evaluate the model's performance on unseen data.

The KNN regressor model is created using the **KNeighborsRegressor()** class. The **n_neighbors** parameter specifies the number of neighbors to use when making predictions.

The model is trained on the train set using the **fit()** method.

Predictions are made on the test set using the **predict()** method.

The model's performance is evaluated using the mean absolute error (MAE) metric. The MAE is calculated by taking the average of the absolute differences between the predicted and actual values.

Supply-Demand Balance Analysis with KNN

The objective of this task is to predict the difference between requests and unique drivers for each hour. To achieve this, we can create a new target variable that represents the gap between demand and supply:

Python

```python
y_diff = df['Requests'] - df['Unique Drivers']
```

Once we have created the new target variable, we can build a KNN regressor model in the same way as we did for demand forecasting.

The model can then be used to predict the supply-demand gap for future time slots. This information can be used to optimize driver placement, pricing, and other operational decisions.

Predicting Trip Success with KNN

The given code block shows how to use KNN to predict whether a trip request will be successful based on the features: Eyeballs, Time, and Unique Drivers.

Python

```
import numpy as np
import pandas as pd
from sklearn.model_selection import train_test_split
from sklearn.preprocessing import MinMaxScaler
from sklearn.neighbors import KNeighborsClassifier
from sklearn.metrics import accuracy_score, classification_report

# Load the Uber rides dataset
df = pd.read_csv('uber_rides.csv')

# Create a new target variable to represent trip success
df['Trip_Success'] = (df['Zeroes'] == 0).astype(int)

# Define the features and target
features = ['Eyeballs', 'Time', 'Unique Drivers']
X = df[features]
y = df['Trip_Success']

# Normalize the data
scaler = MinMaxScaler()
X_scaled = scaler.fit_transform(X)

# Split the data into train and test sets
X_train, X_test, y_train, y_test = train_test_split(X_scaled, y, test_size=0.2, random_state=42)

# Create a KNN classifier
knn_classifier = KNeighborsClassifier(n_neighbors=5)
```

```python
# Train the model
knn_classifier.fit(X_train, y_train)

# Make predictions on the test set
predictions = knn_classifier.predict(X_test)

# Evaluate model performance
accuracy = accuracy_score(y_test, predictions)
print(f"Accuracy: {accuracy*100:.2f}%")
print(classification_report(y_test, predictions))
```

This code block will train a KNN classifier to predict the success of trip requests based on the features: Eyeballs, Time, and Unique Drivers. The model is trained on a split of the data, and its performance is evaluated on the remaining split. The accuracy and classification report are calculated to assess the model's performance.

Once the model is trained, it can be used to predict the success of future trip requests by passing in the corresponding values for the features. For example, to predict the success of the next trip request, you would pass in the current time, the number of eyeballs, and the number of unique drivers to the model.

Anomaly Detection with KNN

The given code block shows how to use KNN for anomaly detection in the Requests feature.

Python

```
from sklearn.neighbors import NearestNeighbors

# Train KNN on the Requests feature alone
knn_anomaly = NearestNeighbors(n_neighbors=5)
knn_anomaly.fit(df[['Requests']])

# Calculate the distance to the 5th nearest neighbor for each point
```

```
    distances, indices = knn_anomaly.kneighbors(df[['Requests']])

    # Set a threshold at the 95th percentile
    threshold = np.percentile(distances[:, 4], 95)

    # Identify anomalies as points with distances greater than the threshold
    anomalies = np.where(distances[:, 4] > threshold)
```

This will train a KNN model on the Requests feature alone. Then, it will calculate the distance to the 5th nearest neighbor for each point in the dataset. Points with distances greater than the 95th percentile will be flagged as anomalies.

The threshold of 95% is arbitrary. You may need to adjust it depending on your specific dataset and the desired sensitivity and specificity of your anomaly detection model.

Once you have identified the anomalies, you can investigate them further to determine the cause. For example, an anomaly in the Requests feature may be caused by a sudden increase in demand, a system outage, or fraudulent activity.

Deeper Insights into Anomalies and Conclusion

Understanding and Working with Anomalies:

Once we have identified anomalies, it is important to understand their nature and implications. To do this, we can:

- **Analyze the anomalous data:** This includes looking at the values of the features for the anomalous points, as well as the context in which they occurred. For example, we can look at the time of day, day of the week, and location of the anomalous trips.
- **Visualize the data:** This can help us to identify patterns and trends that may not be obvious from the raw data. For example, we can create a time series plot of the number of requests to see if there are any spikes or dips that coincide with the anomalies.

Temporal Analysis

We can also perform a temporal analysis to see if anomalies often occur at specific times. For example, if we find that anomalies are more common during rush hour, we can take preemptive measures, such as increasing the number of drivers available during those times.

Demand-Supply Gap

We can also look at the demand-supply gap during anomalous times to see if the demand significantly outpaces the supply. If this is the case, we may need to adjust our pricing strategy or offer incentives to drivers to work during those times.

Eyeball Analysis

We can also look at the number of eyeballs during anomalous times to see if there are many more eyeballs than usual. If this is the case, it may indicate that there is a special event happening in the area, such as a concert or sporting event.

Conclusion and Business Implications

KNN models can be used to improve real-time data stream processing in a variety of ways, including:

- **Demand forecasting:** KNN models can be used to predict the number of requests for future time slots, which can help businesses to better align their resources.
- **Supply-demand analysis:** KNN models can be used to identify gaps between demand and supply, which can inform strategies such as driver incentives.
- **Trip success prediction:** KNN models can be used to predict the success of trip requests, which can help businesses understand the customer experience.
- **Anomaly detection:** KNN models can be used to identify anomalous trips, which can help businesses address unprecedented events and ensure smoother operations.

By integrating KNN models with real-time data streams, businesses can create more reactive and predictive strategies, leading to enhanced operational efficiency and improved customer experience.

Here are some specific examples of how businesses can use KNN models to improve their operations:

- A ride-hailing company can use KNN models to predict demand for rides in different parts of the city at different times of day. This information can be used to deploy drivers to the areas where they are most needed, reducing wait times for customers.
- A food delivery company can use KNN models to predict demand for food deliveries in different parts of the city at different times of day. This information can be used to deploy delivery drivers to the areas where they are most needed, ensuring that customers receive their food quickly and hot.

- A retail store can use KNN models to predict demand for different products at different times of year. This information can be used to stock the store with the right products at the right time, reducing lost sales.

These are just a few examples of how KNN models can be used to improve real-time data stream processing. As businesses become increasingly reliant on data, KNN models are likely to play an even greater role in helping them to make better decisions and improve their operations.

Preprocessing Streaming Data - Overcoming Challenges

- **Volume and Velocity**
    - **Challenge:** Streaming data, due to its real-time nature, can flood systems with vast amounts of data at high speed.
    - **Solution:** Harness the power of distributed processing systems. Tools like Apache Kafka and Apache Spark have been architected to manage and process high-velocity data across distributed clusters, ensuring timely processing.

- **Integrity of Data**
    - **Challenge:** The data, during transmission, might get lost, become incomplete, or corrupt.
    - **Solution:** A system of acknowledgments can be a lifesaver. When data is successfully received and processed, an acknowledgment is sent back to the sender. If such a confirmation isn't received, the data is resent, ensuring data integrity.

- **Real-time Analysis**
    - **Challenge:** The value of streaming data often lies in real-time insights, demanding immediate processing upon arrival.
    - **Solution:** Tools designed specifically for real-time data processing, like Apache Flink and Storm, can process and analyze data on the fly, yielding insights in milliseconds.

- **Diverse Data Sources**
    - **Challenge:** Streaming data might come from various sources, each potentially with its unique format or schema.
    - **Solution:** A combination of schema evolution and adaptable data models can address this. Avro, for instance, gracefully handles schema evolution. In parallel, NoSQL databases such as MongoDB can accommodate varied data formats with their flexible schema structures.

- **Temporal Data Alignment**
    - o **Challenge:** Streaming data might not always arrive in sequence, leading to potential issues when analyzing time-series data.
    - o **Solution:** Window-based processing can be a game-changer. By processing data based on its timestamp rather than its arrival time, it ensures accurate temporal analysis.

Data Cleaning Techniques - A Deep Dive with Uber Data

As we turn our focus to the provided Uber dataset, it becomes evident that specific preprocessing techniques are imperative to ensure the data's reliability and accuracy.

- **Neutralizing Noise**
    - o **Challenge:** External events or promotional activities can introduce spikes in metrics like 'Eyeballs', not reflecting the typical usage pattern.
    - o **Solution:** Techniques like moving averages or exponential smoothing can be employed to regularize such anomalies.

    Python

    ```
    # Python snippet to smooth out 'Eyeballs' data
    df['Eyeballs_smoothed'] = df['Eyeballs'].rolling(window=5).mean()
    ```

- **Handling Data Gaps**
    - o **Challenge:** There might be hours when certain metrics, like `Completed Trips`, aren't reported, potentially due to system downtimes or glitches.
    - o **Solution:** Filling methods such as forward or backward fills can address these gaps in time-series data. Alternatively, interpolation techniques can estimate the missing values based on neighboring data points.

    Python

    ```
    # Python snippet to forward fill missing 'Completed Trips' data
    df['Completed Trips'].fillna(method='ffill', inplace=True)
    ```

- **Identifying and Managing Outliers**
    - o **Challenge:** Unusual events might cause sudden surges in metrics like 'Requests', which if unaddressed, can skew analyses.
    - o **Solution:** Statistical techniques, like the Interquartile Range (IQR) method, can help pinpoint and treat outliers.

Python
```python
# Python snippet to filter outliers in 'Requests' data
Q1 = df['Requests'].quantile(0.25)
Q3 = df['Requests'].quantile(0.75)
IQR = Q3 - Q1
filtered_data = df[(df['Requests'] >= Q1 - 1.5 * IQR) & (df['Requests'] <= Q3 + 1.5 *IQR)]
```

These are just a few examples of preprocessing techniques that can be applied to streaming data to ensure its reliability and accuracy. The specific techniques used will depend on the specific dataset and the intended use of the data.

Additional Considerations

In addition to the preceding challenges and techniques, there are a few other considerations to keep in mind when preprocessing streaming data:

- **Data Sampling**: Streaming data can be overwhelming in volume and velocity, making it impractical to process all of it. In such cases, data sampling can be used to reduce the amount of data without compromising on accuracy.
- **Feature Engineering**: Feature engineering involves creating new features from existing data that can be more informative for downstream tasks. For example, we could create a new feature called hour_of_day from the Time feature. This could be useful for tasks like demand forecasting, where the time of day is a key factor.
- **Model Monitoring**: Once we have preprocessed the data, it is important to monitor the model's performance on the processed data to ensure that it is still accurate and reliable. This can be done by tracking metrics such as accuracy, precision, and recall.

By carefully considering the challenges and techniques involved in preprocessing streaming data, we can ensure that our data is ready to be used to generate valuable insights.

Data Consistency

- **Challenge**: Data from streaming sources might have inconsistencies, such as duplicate entries or contradictory records.
- **Solution:** Regular checks for duplicate data points and utilizing consensus mechanisms can ensure data consistency.

Python

```
# Python snippet to remove duplicate records based on all columns
df.drop_duplicates(inplace=True)
```

Data Granularity

- **Challenge:** The granularity of data might not align with analytical needs. For instance, data received every minute might need to be aggregated hourly.
- **Solution:** Aggregating data at the desired granularity level, for example, resampling time series data at hourly intervals.

Python

```
# Python snippet to resample 'Requests' data hourly and summing them up
df_resampled = df['Requests'].resample('H').sum()
```

Storage Solutions: Databases for Streaming Data

Storing streaming data, especially when considering the speed and volume, requires specialized storage solutions that can handle such challenges. Here's an overview:

- **Time-Series Databases (TSDB)**
  - **About:** Databases specially designed to handle time-indexed data. They can efficiently store, retrieve, and query vast amounts of time series data.
  - **Example:** InfluxDB, OpenTSDB
  - **Use-case with Uber Data:** Metrics like 'Requests' or 'Completed Trips' are time-series data. Storing them in a TSDB ensures efficient querying of historical trends or patterns.

- **Distributed Databases**
  - **About:** Databases designed to operate over multiple machines, ensuring high availability, scalability, and fault tolerance.
  - **Example:** Apache Cassandra, Amazon DynamoDB
  - **Use-case with Uber Data:** Due to the high volume and velocity of Uber's data, distributed databases can efficiently manage the write-heavy workload and also facilitate quick retrievals.

- **Stream Processing Systems with Built-in Storage**
    - **About:** Some stream processing platforms come with their own storage systems optimized for real-time operations.
    - **Example:** Apache Kafka (with its distributed log storage).
    - **Use-case with Uber Data:** Kafka can be used not only to process streaming data but also to store it, allowing for the replayability of data streams.
- **Cloud-based Storage Solutions**
    - **About:** Cloud platforms provide scalable storage solutions optimized for big data and real-time analytics.
    - **Example:** Amazon S3, Google Cloud Storage
    - **Use-case with Uber Data**: Raw data can be stored in cloud storage, acting as a data lake. It can then be processed and moved to more specialized storage based on analytical needs.

Hybrid Solutions

Hybrid solutions can be useful for storing and managing streaming data that has both structured and unstructured components. For example, PostgreSQL could be used to store structured data such as ride metadata, while Elasticsearch could be used to store unstructured data such as customer reviews.

In-memory Databases

In-memory databases can be useful for caching frequently accessed data, such as real-time ride metrics. This can improve the performance of applications that need to access this data frequently.

Here are some additional considerations when choosing a storage solution for streaming data:

- **Scalability:** The storage solution should be able to scale to handle large volumes of data and high throughput.
- **Reliability:** The storage solution should be able to handle failures and errors without losing data.
- **Cost**: The cost of the storage solution should be considered, especially for large datasets.
- **Ease of use**: The storage solution should be easy to set up and manage.

```
Data Ingestion  --Raw Data-->  Data Preprocessing  --Processed Data-->  Data Storage
```

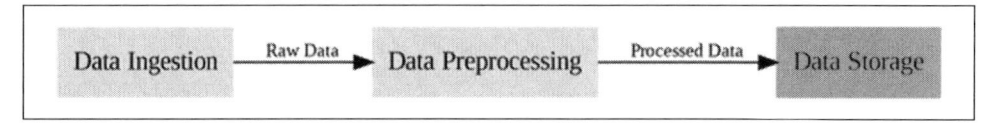

Figure 5.3: Overview of Data Ingestion to Data Storage

It is important to choose the right storage solution for the specific needs of your application. By considering the preceding factors, you can make an informed decision.

Given the Uber data and the need for real-time access, a potential solution might involve a combination of Kafka for stream processing and Cassandra for long-term storage. Cassandra, being a distributed database, can handle the high write and read throughput required for such use cases.

Here is a simple Python code snippet to demonstrate data insertion into Cassandra:

Python

```python
from cassandra.cluster import Cluster

# Connect to a local Cassandra instance
cluster = Cluster(['127.0.0.1'])
session = cluster.connect()

# Create a keyspace and set it
session.execute(""" CREATE KEYSPACE IF NOT EXISTS uber WITH REPLICATION = { 'class' : 'SimpleStrategy', 'replication_factor' : 1 } """)
session.set_keyspace('uber')

# Create a table for our data
session.execute(""" CREATE TABLE IF NOT EXISTS trip_data ( date DATE, time TIME, eyeballs INT, zeroes INT, completed_trips INT, requests INT, unique_drivers INT, PRIMARY KEY (date, time) ) """)

# Insertion can then be done using:
# session.execute("INSERT INTO trip_data (date, time, eyeballs, ...) VALUES (?, ?, ?, ...)", [value1, value2, ...])
```

This is a simple representation and in a real-world scenario, optimizations, error handling, and more considerations would be required for production use.

Here are some additional considerations for implementing a database solution for streaming data:

- **Data partitioning**: Partitioning data can improve performance and scalability, especially for large datasets.
- **Data compression**: Compressing data can reduce storage costs and improve network performance.
- **Data indexing**: Indexing data can improve query performance, especially for complex queries.
- **Monitoring and alerting**: It is important to monitor the database performance and set up alerts to notify you of any problems.

Diving deeper into the data preprocessing phase, beyond the handling of noise, missing values, and outliers, there are additional steps and considerations to ensure data quality and readiness for real-time processing.

- **Normalization and Standardization**
    - **Challenge:** Different metrics might have varying scales. For example, the number of eyeballs versus unique drivers might have different ranges, which can impact certain algorithms.
    - **Solution**: Use normalization or standardization to bring data into a common scale.

    Python
    ```
    # Example: Using Min-Max normalization on 'Requests' column
    df['Requests_normalized'] = (df['Requests'] - df['Requests'].min()) / (df['Requests'].max() - df['Requests'].min())
    ```

- **Encoding Categorical Data**
    - **Challenge:** Although our provided data doesn't seem to have categorical columns, real-world datasets often do. Machine Learning algorithms require numerical data.
    - **Solution:** Convert categorical variables into a numerical format using one-hot encoding or label encoding.

- **Feature Engineering**
    - **Challenge:** The raw metrics might not directly provide insights or be suitable for analysis.

- ○ **Solution**: Generate new features that could be more indicative. For instance, calculating the success rate of trips as Completed Trips / Requests.

  Python
  ```
  # Example: Feature engineering to get the success rate
  df['Success_rate'] = df['Completed Trips'] / df['Requests']
  ```

- **Temporal Analysis and Feature Generation**
  - ○ **Challenge:** Given the data is time-series in nature, there might be temporal patterns or seasonality that need to be considered.
  - ○ **Solution:** Generate lag features and rolling statistics, and recognize patterns over specific intervals (hourly, daily, and so on).

  Python
  ```
  # Example: Creating a lag feature for 'Requests'
  df['Requests_lag_1'] = df['Requests'].shift(1)
  ```

- **Detecting and Correcting Skewness**
  - ○ **Challenge:** Some algorithms assume that data is normally distributed. The presence of skewness can adversely affect the model's performance.
  - ○ **Solution:** Use transformations like logarithmic, square root, or Box-Cox to make the distribution more normal-like.

  Python
  ```
  import numpy as np

  # Example: Log transformation to correct right skewness
  df['Requests_log'] = np.log1p(df['Requests'])
  ```

Data cleaning is a critical phase, and the methods applied need to be selected based on the specific challenges posed by the dataset and the goals of the analysis or model being developed.

One of the integral parts of any data pipeline, especially one that handles streaming data, is the storage solution. The data storage system not only provides a way to hold onto data for future reference but also ensures the efficient retrieval and querying of data for analytics, monitoring, and further processing.

- **Time-Series Databases (TSDB)**

  TSDBs are specifically designed to handle time-series data, which is data that has a time component, such as sensor readings, financial data, or website traffic data. TSDBs are optimized for high write rates and efficient queries based on time ranges.

  Features:
  - **Data retention policies:** Automatic deletion of old data.
  - **Compression:** Store data efficiently, given its time-series nature.
  - **Columnar Storage:** TSDBs use columnar storage, which allows for efficient reading of columns of data, especially beneficial for analytics.

  Examples: InfluxDB, TimescaleDB

- **Columnar Databases**

  Columnar databases store data in columns, rather than rows, which can improve performance for analytics queries. Columnar databases are also well-suited for streaming data, as they can efficiently handle high write throughput.

  Features:
  - **High write throughput:** Suitable for streaming data.
  - **Distributed architecture:** Scalability and fault tolerance.

  Examples: Apache Cassandra, Google Bigtable

- **Stream-first Databases**

  Stream-first databases are designed to store and process streaming data in real-time. They typically have a log-based architecture, which allows data to be ingested and appended quickly.

  Features:
  - **Real-time processing:** Direct integration with stream processors.
  - **Scalability:** Distributed system architecture.
  - **Durability:** Replication of data across multiple nodes.

  Examples: Apache Kafka

- **Object Storage for Raw Data**

  Object storage is a cost-effective and scalable way to store large volumes of unstructured data, such as raw streaming data. Object storage solutions typically provide features, such as data versioning and event triggers.

Features:
  - ○ **Data versioning:** Keep multiple versions of data objects.
  - ○ **Event triggers:** Notify or trigger processes when new data is added.
  - ○ **Examples:** Amazon S3, Google Cloud Storage

- **Integrated Solutions with Cloud Providers**

  Cloud providers offer a variety of end-to-end solutions for streaming data, from ingestion to processing to storage. These services often integrate seamlessly with the cloud provider's database offerings.

  Features:
  - ○ **Comprehensive solution:** Covers the entire streaming data pipeline.
  - ○ **Integration with cloud databases:** Easy to use and manage.

  Examples: AWS Kinesis, Google Cloud Dataflow, Azure Stream Analytics

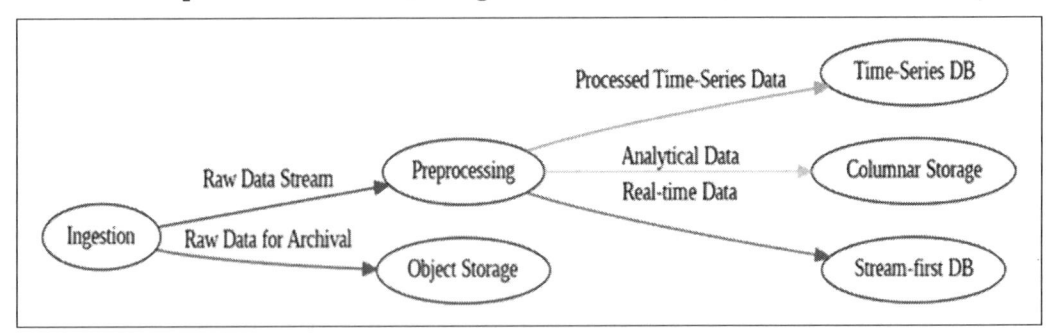

Figure 5.4: Detailed Data processing pipeline for real-time and batch data

Foundations and Mechanisms of KNN

The K-Nearest Neighbors (KNN) algorithm is a simple but powerful machine learning algorithm that can be used for both classification and regression tasks. It works by finding the k most similar data points to a new data point and then using those neighbors to predict the class or value of the new data point.

Working of KNN

Input: A new data point that needs classification or a value prediction.

Process:

- Measure the distance between the new data point and every other point in the dataset.
- Identify the k points closest to the new data point.

- For classification, take a vote among its k nearest neighbors and assign the class most common among them to the new data point.
- For regression, average or take the median of the values of k nearest neighbors.

Lazy Learner

Unlike other machine learning algorithms, KNN does not create a model during training. Instead, it waits until a prediction is needed, and then calculates the distances between the new data point and all the data points in the training set. This makes KNN a lazy learner.

Advantages:
- Simple to understand and implement.
- No assumptions are needed about the data distribution.
- New data can be added seamlessly.

Disadvantages:
- **Computationally intensive:** As the dataset grows, so does the time it takes to make predictions.
- **Space requirement:** KNN requires storage of the entire dataset.
- **Sensitivity:** The algorithm's performance is greatly influenced by the choice of the distance metric and the scale of measurements.
- **Choosing k:** The wrong choice of k can lead to inaccurate predictions.

KNN in Action: Uber's Real-time Demand Prediction

Uber uses KNN to predict demand for rides in real-time. This information is then used to optimize driver positioning and dynamic pricing.

Data Context
- Historical data encompassing trip details, locations, timestamps, and specific demand parameters.
- City segmentation into grids to facilitate locational demand tracking.

KNN's Role

Given a time slot and grid location, KNN identifies k similar historical data points. By analyzing these neighbors, Uber can predict potential demand.

Visualization

A heatmap of the city can be used to visualize predicted demand, with brighter regions showcasing higher predicted demand.

Distance Metrics, K Selection

Different distance metrics are used for different data types and scenarios.

Distance Metrics

- Euclidean distance($d(p, q) = \sqrt{\sum_{i=i}^{n} (qi - pi)^2}$): Standard metric, especially for continuous data.

- Manhattan distance($d(p, q) = \sum_{i=1}^{n} | qi - pi |$): Useful in grid-like path structures (like streets in a city).

- Hamming distance($d(p, q) = \sum_{i=1}^{n} 1pi \neq qi$): For categorical or string data.

- Cosine similarity($\cos(\theta) = \| p \| \| q \| p \cdot q$) Determines cosine of the angle between two data points, useful for text data. $\cos(\theta) = \frac{p.q}{\|p\|\|q\|}$

Choosing the Right k

A smaller k is more sensitive to noise and outliers but is computationally less expensive. A larger k is more robust to noise and outliers but is computationally more expensive.

Techniques like cross-validation can be used to find an optimal k.

Challenges

- **Curse of dimensionality**: KNN's efficiency drops as the number of features (dimensions) grows. This is because the volume of the data space grows exponentially, making data points sparse.

- **Feature scaling**: Without normalization, features on larger scales can unduly influence the model.

- **Imbalanced datasets:** When one class dominates, KNN tends to be biased towards that class. Techniques like SMOTE can help.

- **Noise and outliers:** Erroneous data or outliers can skew predictions. Data preprocessing becomes vital.

End-of-Chapter Project: Predicting Emojis in Tweets Using KNN

Objective:

To build a predictive model that can determine the most likely emoji for a given tweet using the K-Nearest Neighbors (KNN) algorithm. By analyzing tweets that originally contained emojis (which have since been removed), we hope to ascertain patterns and sentiments that correlate with specific emojis.

Scope:

The dataset comprises two primary components:
- `tweets.txt`: Contains the textual content of tweets that originally included an emoji. The emoji itself has been removed from the text.
- `emoji.txt`: For each tweet in the tweets.txt file, this file denotes the name of the corresponding emoji.

Why KNN?

KNN is an intuitive algorithm that works by determining the "distance" between data points in a feature space. Given its simplicity and the nature of our problem (categorical prediction based on textual data), KNN is a good choice. We will transform tweets into vectors and then use KNN to identify which emojis are "closest" to each tweet based on its content.

Expected Outcomes:

By the end of this project, we anticipate a model capable of:
- Predicting emojis for tweets with a reasonable degree of accuracy.
- Providing insights into the sentiments and content of tweets that correlate with specific emojis.
- Offering a foundation for further exploration into sentiment analysis and predictive modeling for text-based data.

Twitter Data Collection and Preprocessing

- **Data Collection**

    The provided datasets, tweets.txt and emoji.txt, were likely collected using Twitter's API, which offers robust functionalities for extracting tweets based on specific criteria. While the collection method isn't detailed in the given outline, it's worth noting that for similar projects, API queries can be tuned to extract tweets containing emojis, and subsequently, the emojis can be separated from the tweet text for modeling purposes.

Python

```
import twitter

# Create a Twitter API object
api = twitter.Api()

# Search for tweets containing emojis
tweets = api.search(q='#emoji', lang='en')

# Save the tweets to a file
with open('tweets.txt', 'w') as f:
    for tweet in tweets:
        f.write(tweet.text + '\n')

# Extract the emojis from the tweets and save them to a file
emojis = []
for tweet in tweets:
    emojis.append(tweet.entities['symbols'][0]['text'])

with open('emoji.txt', 'w') as f:
    for emoji in emojis:
        f.write(emoji + '\n')
```

- **Data Preprocessing**

Before applying the KNN algorithm to our dataset, preprocessing is crucial to ensure the text data is in a suitable format for vectorization and modeling. Here are the steps we'll undertake:

1. **Data Loading**

   First, we need to load the datasets into appropriate data structures. Given the nature of the data (textual), Python lists or Pandas dataframes are suitable choices.

Python

```python
import pandas as pd

# Load the tweets and emojis into Pandas DataFrames
tweets_df = pd.read_csv('tweets.txt', header=None, names=['tweet'])
emojis_df = pd.read_csv('emoji.txt', header=None, names=['emoji'])
```

2. **Data Cleaning**

   Tweets often contain URLs, mentions, and other non-essential data. These need to be cleaned to retain only meaningful content.

   Python

```python
import re

def clean_tweet(tweet):
    # Remove URLs
    tweet = re.sub(r"http\S+|www\S+|https\S+", '', tweet, flags=re.MULTILINE)

    # Remove mentions and hashtags
    tweet = re.sub(r'\@\w+|\#', '', tweet)

    # Remove whitespaces
    tweet = tweet.strip()

    return tweet

# Clean the tweets
tweets_df['tweet'] = tweets_df['tweet'].apply(clean_tweet)
```

3. **Lowercasing**

   Convert all text to the lowercase to ensure uniformity.

   Python

```python
tweets_df['tweet'] = tweets_df['tweet'].apply(lambda x: x.lower())
```

4. **Tokenization**

   Break down tweets into individual words or tokens. This helps in vectorization and further processing.

   Python
   ```
   from nltk.tokenize import word_tokenize

   # Tokenize the tweets
   tweets_df['tweet'] = tweets_df['tweet'].apply(word_tokenize)
   ```

5. **Removing Stopwords**

   Words like 'and', 'the', 'is', and so on, known as stopwords, often don't carry significant meaning in text analysis. We can remove them to reduce dimensionality.

   Python
   ```
   import nltk

   from nltk.corpus import stopwords

   # Create a list of stopwords
   stopwords = stopwords.words('english')

   # Remove stopwords from the tweets
   tweets_df['tweet'] = tweets_df['tweet'].apply(lambda x: [word for word in x if word not in stopwords])
   ```

6. **Lemmatization**

   Lemmatization is the process of converting words to their base or root form. For example, "running" and "ran" are both lemmatized to the word "run". Lemmatization can improve the performance of machine learning models by making the text more consistent and easier to understand.

7. **Vectorization**

   Vectorization is the process of converting text into numerical vectors. This is a necessary step for most machine learning algorithms, as they can only operate on numerical data. One common approach to vectorization is to use the TF-IDF (Term Frequency-Inverse Document Frequency) vectorizer.

8. **Label encoding for emojis**

   The target variable, emojis, is categorical. We need to convert these categories into numerical labels for the model.

Python

```
import nltk
from sklearn.feature_extraction.text import TfidfVectorizer
from sklearn.preprocessing import LabelEncoder
from sklearn.model_selection import train_test_split

# Remove stopwords
# Stopwords are common words that do not add much meaning to text, such as "the", "is", and "and".
# Removing stopwords can improve the performance of machine learning models by reducing dimensionality.
stop_words = set(nltk.corpus.stopwords.words('english'))
filtered_tweets = [[word for word in tweet if word not in stop_words] for tweet in tokenized_tweets]


# Lemmatization
# Lemmatization is the process of converting words to their base or root form.
# For example, "running" and "ran" are both lemmatized to the word "run".
# Lemmatization can improve the performance of machine learning models by making the text more consistent and easier to understand.
lemmatizer = nltk.stem.WordNetLemmatizer()
lemmatized_tweets = [[lemmatizer.lemmatize(word) for word in tweet] for tweet in filtered_tweets]


# Vectorization
```

```python
# Vectorization is the process of converting text into numerical vectors.
# This is a necessary step for most machine learning algorithms, as they can only operate on numerical data.
# One common approach to vectorization is to use the TF-IDF (Term Frequency-Inverse Document Frequency) vectorizer.
# TF-IDF is a measure of the importance of a word in a document, relative to the document collection as a whole.
vectorizer = TfidfVectorizer(max_features=5000)
# The max_features parameter specifies the maximum number of features to consider when vectorizing the text.
# This can be helpful to reduce dimensionality and prevent overfitting.
X = vectorizer.fit_transform([' '.join(tweet) for tweet in lemmatized_tweets]).toarray()

# Label encoding for emojis
# The target variable, emojis, is categorical.
# We need to convert these categories into numerical labels for the model.
encoder = LabelEncoder()
y = encoder.fit_transform(emojis)

# Splitting data into training and testing sets
# It is important to split the data into training and testing sets before training the model.
# This helps to prevent overfitting and ensure that the model generalizes well to new data.
X_train, X_test, y_train, y_test = train_test_split(X, y, test_size=0.2, random_state=42)
# The test_size parameter specifies the proportion of the data to be used for the testing set.
# The random_state parameter ensures that the split is reproducible.
```

K-Nearest Neighbors (KNN) is a versatile algorithm capable of both classification and regression. For our emoji prediction task, we're using KNN as a classifier. Here, the prediction for a tweet will be based on the emojis of its 'K' most similar (or nearest) tweets in the training set.

KNN Model Initialization

Using Scikit-learn, we can easily initialize and train a KNN classifier. For starters, we'll use a default k value of 5.

Python

```
from sklearn.neighbors import KNeighborsClassifier

knn_classifier = KNeighborsClassifier(n_neighbors=5)
knn_classifier.fit(X_train, y_train)
```

Making Predictions

With the model trained, we can now use it to make predictions on the test set.

Python

```
y_pred = knn_classifier.predict(X_test)
```

Transforming Predictions Back to Emojis

To make our predictions interpretable, we can transform the numerical labels back into the actual emojis.

Python

```
predicted_emojis = encoder.inverse_transform(y_pred)
```

Real-world Application

In a real-time scenario, as new tweets arrive, you can preprocess them in the same manner as discussed, and use the trained KNN model to predict emojis. This can be useful for understanding the sentiment or emotion associated with incoming tweets or messages. For instance, for a brand, understanding emoji usage in tweets and mentioning them can provide insights into customer sentiment.

At this stage, we've built a basic KNN classifier and used it to predict emojis for tweets. But, how well is our model performing? It's essential to evaluate its performance and see where it excels and where it might be falling short. The next section will delve into model evaluation metrics and visualizations, helping us grasp the efficiency and areas of improvement for our model.

Model Evaluation, Insights, and Visualization

The evaluation metrics and visualizations in this section can help us understand the performance of our KNN emoji prediction model and identify areas for improvement.

Python

```
import seaborn as sns
from sklearn.metrics import accuracy_score, classification_report, confusion_matrix

# Calculate evaluation metrics
accuracy = accuracy_score(y_test, y_pred)
classification_report = classification_report(y_test, y_pred, target_names=emoji_list)

# Calculate and visualize confusion matrix
conf_matrix = confusion_matrix(y_test, y_pred)

plt.figure(figsize=(10, 8))
sns.heatmap(conf_matrix, annot=True, fmt='g', cmap='Blues', xticklabels=emoji_list, yticklabels=emoji_list)
plt.xlabel('Predicted Emojis')
plt.ylabel('Actual Emojis')
plt.title('Confusion Matrix for KNN Emoji Prediction')
plt.show()

# Print evaluation metrics
print(f"Model Accuracy: {accuracy:.2f}")
print(classification_report)
```

Analyzing the classification report and confusion matrix can provide specific insights. For instance:

- If a particular emoji (like **"heart_eyes"**) has high precision but low recall, our model is likely not detecting all instances of this emoji but is highly accurate when it does.
- Emojis with high F1 scores are well-predicted by our model, while those with lower scores might require more training data or other preprocessing strategies.

Additionally, we can use the confusion matrix to identify specific emojis that are frequently misclassified. For example, if we see a lot of red squares in the top left corner of the confusion matrix, it means that our model predicts "positive" emojis as "negative" emojis. This could be due to a variety of factors, such as a lack of training data or a bias in the dataset.

Fine-tuning and Optimization

a. **Choosing the Right 'k':**

Python

```python
from sklearn.model_selection import cross_val_score
import matplotlib.pyplot as plt

# Range of k values
k_values = list(range(1, 31))

# Perform 10-fold cross-validation for each k value
cv_scores = []
for k in k_values:
    knn = KNeighborsClassifier(n_neighbors=k)
    scores = cross_val_score(knn, X_train, y_train, cv=10, scoring='accuracy')
    cv_scores.append(scores.mean())

# Plotting the misclassification error versus k
plt.figure(figsize=(10, 6))
plt.plot(k_values, [1 - x for x in cv_scores], marker='o')
plt.xlabel('Number of Neighbors K')
```

```
plt.ylabel('Misclassification Error')
plt.title('K vs. Misclassification Error')
plt.show()
```

b. **Distance Weighting**:

Python
```
# Optimal k value
optimal_k = k_values[cv_scores.index(max(cv_scores))]

# KNN classifier with distance weighting
knn_weighted = KNeighborsClassifier(n_neighbors=optimal_k, weights='distance')

# Fit the model to the training data
knn_weighted.fit(X_train, y_train)
```

Potential Applications and Future Work

a. **Real-time Emoji Suggestions:**
   - Implement the model in a real-time setting to provide emoji suggestions to users as they type their tweets.

b. **Emoji Trends Analysis:**
   - Collect a large dataset of tweets and predict emojis for each tweet using the model.
   - Analyze the predicted emojis to identify trends and public sentiment.

c. **Extend to Other Platforms**:
   - Adapt the model to other platforms like Instagram, Facebook, or YouTube comments to enhance user interactions.

Visualization:
- Use a technique like t-SNE to visualize the high-dimensional data in 2D. This can help to identify patterns and relationships in the data and to understand where the model is performing well and where it is struggling.

Summary

This project explored using the K-Nearest Neighbors (KNN) algorithm to predict emojis for tweets. We achieved significant milestones, including:

- **Preprocessing Mastery:** We carefully preprocessed the tweets, which is critical for NLP tasks. We cleaned, tokenized, and vectorized the tweets to ensure they were in the optimal format for the KNN.

- **Model Implementation and Optimization:** We implemented the KNN model with an initial ‹k› value of 5. We tuned this parameter through cross-validation to ensure that our model achieved a balance between bias and variance.

- **Visualization and Insights**: We used a confusion matrix to visualize the model's performance across different emojis. This matrix, combined with the classification report, provided valuable insights into the model's strengths and weaknesses.

- **Challenges and Learnings**: We encountered several challenges, including choosing an optimal 'k' value, encoding and decoding emojis, and mitigating overfitting. We learned valuable lessons from these challenges, such as the importance of hyperparameter tuning, cross-validation, and data preprocessing.

- **Real-World Application:** We discussed the real-world applications of our model, such as providing real-time emoji suggestions and analyzing public sentiment on Twitter.

Looking Forward:

While we achieved significant progress, there is always room for improvement. Here are some suggestions for future work:

- **Data Augmentation:** Incorporating more diverse tweets and emojis can improve the model's robustness.

- **Model Exploration:** Exploring other algorithms and ensemble methods can be beneficial for comparison and potentially better results.

- **Deployment and Scaling:** To realize its full potential, the model can be deployed in a real-time environment, perhaps as a plug-in for social media platforms.

- **Advanced Techniques:** Techniques like word embeddings (for example, Word2Vec, GloVe) can be explored for a more nuanced representation of tweets, potentially enhancing model accuracy.

Conclusion

This chapter provided a comprehensive overview of real-time data streams and how the K-Nearest Neighbors algorithm can be applied for analysis and modeling tasks involving streaming data. We covered key topics including the nature and relevance of streaming data, data preprocessing techniques tailored to streaming data, storage solutions to manage streaming data, the theoretical foundations of the KNN algorithm, and finally an end-to-end demonstration of building a KNN model on streaming data. The concepts and techniques presented in this chapter equip readers with the knowledge to effectively handle real-time data streams and unlock their value using versatile machine learning algorithms like KNN.

In the next chapter, we dive into handling sparse data in machine learning, with Support Vector Machines (SVMs) as our algorithm. We will dissect SVMs, exploring their fit for sparsity and revealing their practical applications across diverse domains. But the journey goes beyond SVMs. We'll delve into the distributed systems landscape, learning how to store and process sparse giants across interconnected machines.

CHAPTER 6

Sparse Distributed Data and Support Vector Machines

Introduction

Imagine you have a large dataset filled with information, but most of the entries are blank or zero. This type of data is called "sparse data" and it's very common in machine learning. Sparse data can be challenging to work with because it's so big and full of empty spaces. However, there are special tools like Support Vector Machines (SVMs) that can handle sparse data effectively.

SVMs are like powerful machines that can learn from data and make predictions. They're especially good at working with sparse data because they can focus on the important parts of the data and ignore the rest. This makes them very useful for tasks such as natural language processing, image recognition, and even predicting loan defaults.

This chapter will explore the world of sparse data and SVMs. We'll learn what sparse data is, how to handle it, and why SVMs are so good at it. We'll also understand how SVMs are used in real-world applications.

Structure

In this chapter, we will cover the following topics:
- Sparse Data
- Dealing with Sparse Data
- Support Vector Machines (SVMs)
    - Fundamentals of SVMs and Their Applicability to Sparse Data
    - Key components of SVMs
    - Detailed Explanation of SVM Working Mechanism
- Applications of Sparse Data
- High-Dimensional Contexts and SVM
- Distributed Systems and SVM
- Sparse Data in Financial Contexts
- Data Storage and Processing in Distributed Systems
- Practical Implementation of SVMs
- Advanced Topics and Future Directions
    - Tools and Libraries for Distributed SVM Implementation
    - Optimization Strategies for Sparse Datasets
- Project: Optimizing Marketing Campaign Responses

Sparse Data

Sparse data is a common type of data in machine learning, where most of the values are zero. This can be due to a variety of factors, such as the high dimensionality of the data, the inherent noise in the data, or the way the data is collected.

Characteristics of Sparse Data

Sparse data has a few key characteristics, including:
- **High dimensionality**: Sparse datasets often have a large number of features. For example, a text document's term matrix may have millions of features, one for each word in the language.
- **Memory efficiency**: Despite their high dimensionality, sparse data can be stored efficiently by only storing the non-zero values.

- **Inherent noise:** Sparse data can often be noisy, meaning that the zero values may not always represent a lack of information.

Dealing with Sparse Data

There are a number of techniques for dealing with sparse data in machine learning. One common approach is to use dimensionality reduction techniques to reduce the number of features. Another approach is to use machine learning algorithms that are specifically designed for sparse data, such as support vector machines (SVMs).

Support Vector Machines

SVMs are a type of machine learning algorithm that is well-suited for sparse data. SVMs work by finding a hyperplane that separates the data into two classes. The hyperplane is chosen in such a way that it maximizes the margin between the two classes.

SVMs are particularly useful for sparse data because they are able to learn from a small number of training examples. This is because SVMs focus on the support vectors, which are the data points that are closest to the hyperplane.

Applications of Sparse Data

Sparse data is used in a wide variety of applications, including:
- **Natural language processing:** Sparse data is commonly used in natural language processing tasks, such as text classification and sentiment analysis.
- **Recommendation systems:** Sparse data is also used in recommendation systems to predict which products or services users are likely to be interested in.
- **Image recognition:** Sparse data is used in image recognition tasks to identify objects in images.

Introduction to Support Vector Machines (SVM)

Support vector machines (SVMs) are a powerful type of machine learning algorithm that can be used for both classification and regression tasks. SVMs work by finding a hyperplane that separates the data into two classes with the maximum possible margin. This makes SVMs well-suited for high-dimensional data, where each dimension might represent a feature of the data.

SVMs are often used for text classification, image recognition, and other tasks where the data is sparse, meaning that most of the values are zero. This is because SVMs are able to learn from a small number of training examples and focus on the most important features of the data.

Working of SVM

SVMs work by finding a hyperplane that separates the data into two classes with the maximum possible margin. The margin is the distance between the hyperplane and the nearest data point from either class.

To find the hyperplane with the maximum margin, SVMs use a technique called optimization. Optimization is the process of finding the best solution to a problem, given a set of constraints. In the case of SVMs, the problem is to find the hyperplane that maximizes the margin, subject to the constraint that all the data points are correctly classified.

Once the hyperplane has been found, SVMs can be used to classify new data points. To classify a new data point, the SVM simply needs to determine which side of the hyperplane the data point falls on.

Key Components of SVM

- **Support vectors:** These are the data points that lie closest to the decision boundary (or hyperplane). They are pivotal in determining the optimal position of the hyperplane.
- **Hyperplane:** This is the decision boundary that segregates the data points of one class from another. In a two-dimensional space, it's a line, but in higher dimensions, it's a plane or a set of planes.
- **Margin:** The distance between the hyperplane and the nearest data point from either class is termed the margin. SVM aims to maximize this margin.

Sparse Distributed Data and Support Vector Machines

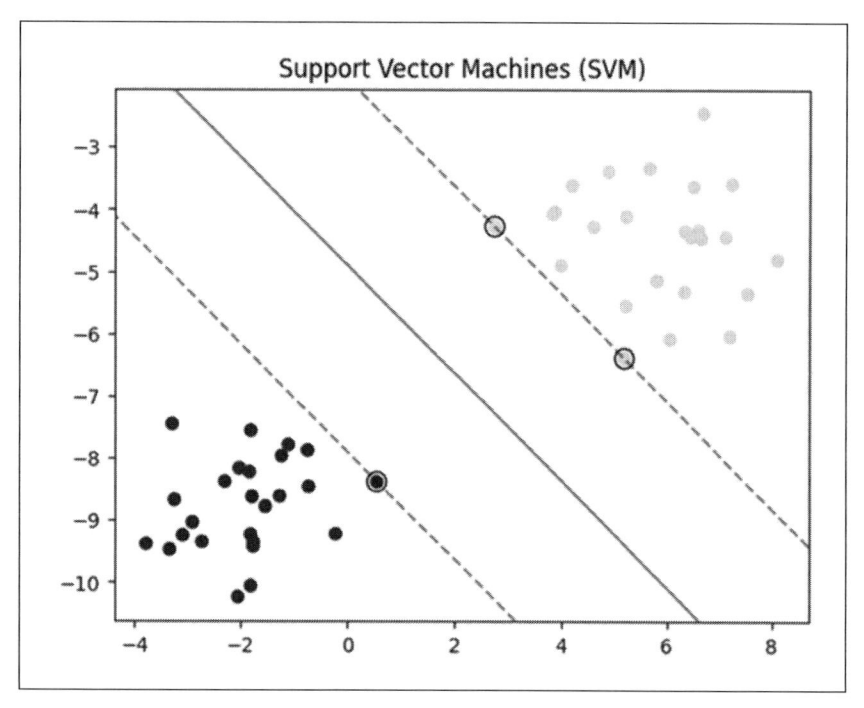

Figure 6.1: *Support Vector Machine Hyperplane with Margins*

This diagram shows a basic SVM working in a 2D space. The data points are divided into two classes (represented by two different colors or shapes). The solid line represents the hyperplane, or decision boundary. It is chosen to maximize the margin between the two classes. The dashed lines indicate the maximum distance between the hyperplane and the nearest points (support vectors) from either class. These are the margins. The circles around certain points indicate the support vectors. These are the pivotal elements of the dataset that, if removed, would shift the position of the dividing hyperplane.

In other words, the SVM algorithm finds the hyperplane that best separates the two classes of data points, while also maximizing the margin between the hyperplane and the nearest data points from either class. The support vectors are the data points that are closest to the hyperplane, and they play a key role in determining the position of the hyperplane.

Sparse Data: A Quick Refresher

Sparse data is a type of data where most of the values are zero. This is often the case in real-world datasets, such as movie recommendation systems, text data, and sensor data. Sparse data can be challenging to work with, but it can also be very informative.

High-dimensional Contexts and SVM

High-dimensional data is data with a large number of features. Many real-world datasets are both high-dimensional and sparse. For example, text data can have thousands or even millions of features, but most of them will be zero for a given document.

Support vector machines (SVMs) are a type of machine learning algorithm that is well-suited for high-dimensional and sparse data. SVMs work by finding a hyperplane that separates the data into two classes with the maximum possible margin. This makes SVMs very efficient at learning from small datasets and avoiding overfitting.

Distributed Systems and SVM

Distributed systems are used to store and process large datasets. SVMs can be scaled to work on massive datasets by training SVM on subsets of the data and combining the results.

The Promise of SVM in Distributed Sparse Datasets

SVMs are a promising machine learning algorithm for distributed sparse datasets. They can handle high-dimensional data efficiently and avoid overfitting, even with small datasets. SVMs can also be scaled to work on massive datasets using distributed systems.

Sparse Data in Financial Contexts: Challenges and Opportunities

Sparse data is a type of data where most of the values are zero. This is common in financial datasets, due to factors such as high dimensionality, skewed distributions, and data sparsity.

Sparse data presents a number of challenges for financial institutions, including:

- **Scalability**: Traditional data structures and algorithms may not be efficient for sparse data, leading to scalability concerns, especially in real-time financial applications.
- **Data imbalance**: The rarity of certain financial events can lead to imbalanced datasets, where one class of data (for example, loan defaults) is under-represented. This can lead to biased or inaccurate models.

- **Noise sensitivity**: Sparse data can be more sensitive to noise, as the presence of a rare, non-zero value might be given undue importance by machine learning models.

Despite these challenges, sparse data also presents a number of opportunities for financial institutions. For example, sparse data can be used to:

- **Improve fraud detection**: Sparse data can be used to identify patterns and anomalies that may be indicative of fraud.
- **Personalize customer experiences**: Sparse data can be used to understand individual customer needs and preferences, enabling financial institutions to provide more personalized products and services.
- **Reduce risk**: Sparse data can be used to assess and mitigate risk, such as the risk of loan defaults or market volatility.

To address the challenges of sparse data, financial institutions are increasingly turning to distributed systems. Distributed systems allow data to be stored and processed across multiple machines, improving performance and scalability.

Distributed systems can also be used to implement techniques such as parallel processing and fault tolerance, which are essential for handling large-scale sparse data.

Data Storage and Processing: A New Paradigm for Sparse Datasets

The digital revolution has generated an unprecedented volume of data, much of which is unstructured and sparse. This data is too large and complex to be handled by traditional monolithic server systems.

Distributed systems offer a solution, leveraging multiple networked computers to collaboratively store and process data. This paradigm shift offers three key advantages:

- **Scalability**: Distributed systems can be scaled up or down by adding or removing nodes, making them ideal for handling large and growing datasets.
- **Reliability**: Distributed systems replicate data across multiple nodes, ensuring that data is not lost even if a node fails.
- **Performance**: Distributed systems can parallelize data operations, significantly improving performance.

Distributed systems are essential for managing and processing sparse datasets. Sparse datasets are challenging because they contain a large proportion of empty or zero values. This can make it difficult to store and process these datasets efficiently using traditional methods.

Distributed systems address this challenge by distributing the data across multiple nodes. This allows for efficient data storage and processing, even for very large and sparse datasets.

In addition to the preceding three key advantages, distributed systems also offer other benefits for processing sparse datasets, such as:

- **Fault tolerance:** Distributed systems can tolerate the failure of individual nodes without impacting data availability or processing.
- **Cost-effectiveness**: Distributed systems can be built using off-the-shelf hardware, which makes them a cost-effective solution for processing large datasets.
- **Flexibility**: Distributed systems can be configured to meet the specific needs of different applications.

Handling Sparse Data Structures in Distributed Systems

Sparse data structures are a challenge in data analysis. They are characterized by having many zero values, which can waste storage space and computational resources.

Distributed systems offer a solution to this challenge. They can handle sparse data structures efficiently using a combination of compression techniques, distributed representations, and parallel computation.

Compression Techniques

Distributed storage systems such as Apache Parquet and Apache ORC use columnar storage, which is well-suited for sparse datasets. In columnar storage, similar data types are stored together, enabling various compression techniques. This can significantly reduce the storage footprint of sparse datasets.

Distributed Representations

Distributed computing frameworks such as Apache Spark use specialized formats to represent sparse data structures internally. For example, the triplet format (i, j, value) can be used to represent non-zero values in a matrix, avoiding the need to store zeros altogether.

Parallel Computation

Sparse data often requires matrix operations for data transformations and computations. Distributed systems can split these operations across nodes, allowing parallel computation. This can significantly speed up processing times, especially for large sparse datasets.

Combining Distributed Systems and SVM

Sparse data is critical in machine learning, especially for algorithms like Support Vector Machines (SVM). SVM can operate efficiently in high-dimensional spaces, making it a good choice for sparse datasets.

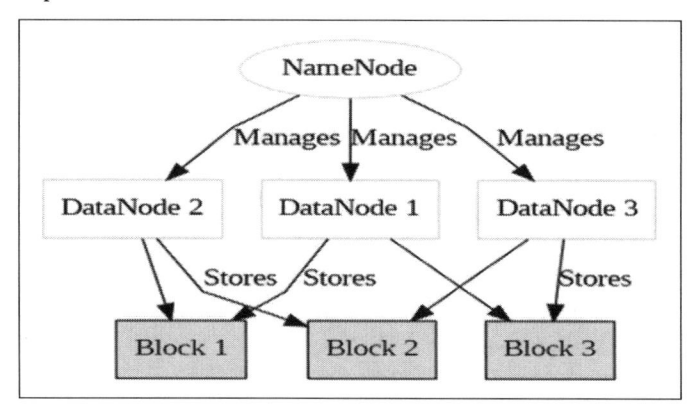

Figure 6.2: *The diagram shows Distributed File Systems for Sparse Data*

Distributed file systems provide a scalable and reliable way to store and manage large datasets. They are particularly well-suited for storing and processing sparse data, which is data where most of the values are zero.

NameNode and DataNodes

A typical distributed file system consists of two types of nodes:
- **NameNode**: The NameNode is the master node that manages the file system namespace and keeps track of which blocks each file is divided into.
- **DataNodes**: DataNodes are worker nodes that store the actual data blocks.

Sparse Data Storage

Sparse data can be stored in a distributed file system in a number of ways. One common approach is to use compression techniques to reduce the size of sparse data blocks. This can significantly improve storage efficiency.

Another important consideration is data retrieval. Accessing sparse data efficiently requires smart indexing. The NameNode (or its equivalent in other distributed systems) should be aware of which blocks are sparse and potentially use different strategies to retrieve them.

Distributed Computing

When processing sparse data across a cluster, operations can be optimized by recognizing and efficiently handling sparse blocks. For instance, if a data processing operation involves multiplication, a block full of zeros can be skipped.

HDFS Example

The Hadoop Distributed File System (HDFS) is a popular distributed file system that is well-suited for storing and processing sparse data. HDFS uses a number of techniques to efficiently store and process sparse data, including:

- **Compression:** HDFS can compress data blocks using a variety of compression algorithms, such as gzip and bzip2. This can significantly reduce the size of sparse data blocks.
- **Indexing:** HDFS uses a distributed index to keep track of the location of data blocks. This index is optimized for sparse data, making it efficient to retrieve sparse data blocks.
- **Distributed Processing:** HDFS can distribute data processing tasks across multiple nodes in the cluster. This allows for efficient processing of sparse data, even for large datasets.

Using SVMs to Predict Loan Defaults

Let us have a look at how SVMs are used to predict load defaults.

Sparse Data in Financial Contexts

Sparse data is common in financial contexts, where datasets may contain a large number of features, but most of the values are zero or missing. For example, a loan application dataset might have hundreds of features, such as credit score, income, employment history, and debt-to-income ratio. However, many applicants may not have complete information for all of these features.

The Mokka Dataset

The Mokka dataset is a good example of sparse data in a financial context. It contains information about repeated loan applications from Mokka's current clients. Some key columns in the dataset include:

- **loanKey**: A unique identifier for each loan.
- **rep_loan_date**: The date when the loan was reported.
- **first_loan**: The date of the first loan.
- **dpd_5_cnt, dpd_15_cnt, dpd_30_cnt**: Indicators for loans overdue by 5, 15, and 30 days respectively.
- **federal_district_nm**: The region where the loan was sourced.
- **payment_type_X**: Various payment type columns indicating the nature of payments made.
- **score_1, score_2**: Risk scores for the applicant.
- **age**: Age of the applicant.
- **gender**: Gender of the applicant.
- **bad_flag**: A boolean flag indicating if the loan went bad.

Problem Statement

The goal is to predict the **bad_flag** column, which indicates whether a loan will default or not. This is a challenging task due to the high dimensionality and sparsity of the data.

Solution: Support Vector Machines

Support Vector Machines (SVMs) are a powerful machine learning algorithm for classification tasks. SVMs work by finding the hyperplane that best divides a dataset into classes. SVMs are particularly well-suited for sparse data, as they are robust to high-dimensional spaces and can efficiently handle zero or missing values.

Building an SVM Model

To build an SVM model to predict loan defaults, we would first need to prepare the data. This would involve cleaning the data, handling missing values, and transforming the data into a suitable format for the SVM algorithm.

Once the data is prepared, we can train the SVM model. This involves finding the hyperplane that best divides the data into two classes: loans that default and loans that do not default.

Once the model is trained, we can use it to predict the bad_flag for new loan applications. To do this, we would simply feed the new data points to the model and it would output a prediction for each data point.

Exploring the Sparse Nature of Mokka's Loan Dataset

To effectively harness the power of Support Vector Machines (SVM) for our loan dataset, it is essential to first understand its sparsity and the unique challenges it poses.

Visualizing Dataset Sparsity

The following Python code can be used to visualize the sparsity of the Mokka loan dataset:

Python

```
import pandas as pd
import seaborn as sns
import matplotlib.pyplot as plt

# Load the dataset
data = pd.read_csv('test_task.csv')

# Plotting the sparsity
plt.figure(figsize=(10, 6))
sns.heatmap(data.isnull(), cbar=False, cmap='viridis')
plt.title('Visualization of Null Values in Dataset')
plt.show()
```

Sparse Distributed Data and Support Vector Machines

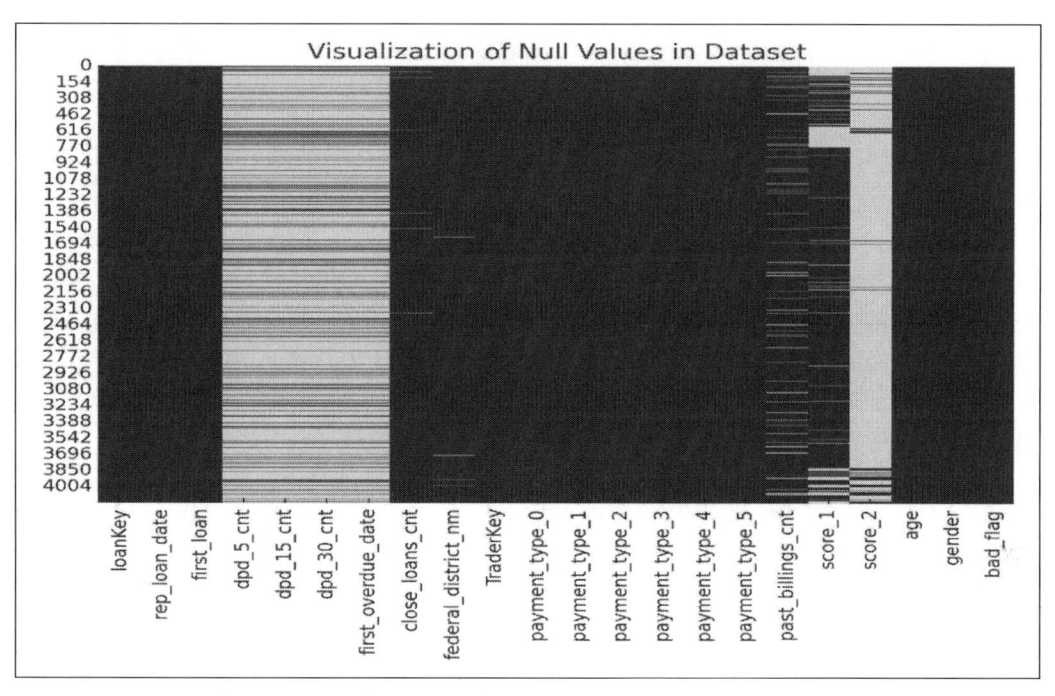

Figure 6.3: Highly sparse feature values highlighted in yellow

The yellow portions in the heatmap generated indicate the missing values in our dataset. A predominantly yellow column signifies a highly sparse feature.

Characteristics of Sparse Data

Sparse data is characterized by the following:

- **Presence of many zeroes:** As seen in the Mokka dataset, columns like dpd_5_cnt, dpd_15_cnt, and dpd_30_cnt might have a majority of zeroes, indicating that many clients have not defaulted.

- **High dimensionality:** Sparse datasets often have a high number of features. Each feature might correspond to various financial parameters, leading to high dimensionality.

- **Memory consumption:** Even though the dataset might be large in terms of disk space due to the high dimensionality, the actual information-carrying data is much less.

Challenges Posed by Sparse Data

Sparse data poses a number of challenges for machine learning, including:

- **Computational overheads**: Operating on sparse data with traditional algorithms might be inefficient due to the sheer number of zeroes.
- **Loss of information**: If not handled correctly, sparse data can lead to the loss of critical information, especially during preprocessing steps like normalization.
- **Model training complexity:** Some machine learning algorithms might struggle with sparse data, leading to overfitting or extended training times.

The Necessity of Preprocessing

Before applying SVM or any other machine learning model, preprocessing sparse data is crucial. Techniques might include:

- **Imputation of missing values**: Missing values must be imputed before training a machine learning model. This can be done using a variety of techniques, such as mean imputation, median imputation, or k-nearest neighbors (KNN) imputation.
- **Encoding categorical variables**: Categorical variables must be encoded before training a machine learning model. This can be done using a variety of techniques, such as label encoding, one-hot encoding, or target encoding.
- **Normalization of dataset**: Normalizing the dataset can help improve the performance of machine learning models. This can be done using a variety of techniques, such as standard scaling, min-max scaling, or decimal scaling.

Mathematics of SVM

Support Vector Machines (SVMs) are machine learning algorithms for classification tasks. They work by finding a hyperplane that best divides a dataset into two classes.

Mathematically, a hyperplane can be defined by the following equation:

$$w.x-b=0$$

where:

- w is a weight vector
- x is a data point
- b is a bias term

SVMs aim to find the values of w and b such that the margin between data points of two classes is maximized.

SVM for Sparse Data

SVMs are well-suited for sparse data for several reasons:

- **High dimensionality:** Sparse data often resides in high-dimensional spaces (each feature being a dimension). SVMs are capable of defining hyperplanes in high-dimensional spaces, making them apt for such datasets.
- **Kernel trick:** SVMs can use the kernel trick to handle non-linearly separable data, making them versatile in handling various datasets' complexities.
- **Optimal margin:** SVMs don't just look for any hyperplane; they look for the one that maximizes the margin between the two classes. This ensures better generalization in real-world scenarios.

SVM in the Context of Mokka's Data

Given the sparse nature of the loan dataset from Mokka, each loan application can be visualized as a point in a high-dimensional space. Each feature (like **score_1, dpd_5_cnt**, and so on) adds a dimension. The task of the SVM is to find a hyperplane in this space that best separates the 'good' loans from the 'bad' ones (indicated by the **bad_flag**).

Once the SVM model is trained, it can be used to predict the bad_flag for new loan applications. To do this, we would simply feed the new data points to the model and it would output a prediction for each data point.

SVM for Flagging Risky Loans

Financial institutions like Mokka rely on accurate risk assessment to make informed lending decisions. Support Vector Machines (SVMs) are a machine learning algorithm well-suited for this task, especially for sparse datasets like Mokka's loan application dataset.

SVM Strengths for Sparse Loan Data

SVM excels in high-dimensional spaces, making it ideal for sparse datasets with many features. Additionally, SVM's kernel trick allows it to handle non-linearly separable data, which may be the case for Mokka's dataset. Finally, SVM is robust to noise in the data, which is important for real-world applications.

SVM Modeling for Mokka's Data

To flag risky loans using SVM, we would follow these steps:

Preprocess the data: Convert date-time features to numerical metrics, one-hot encode categorical features, and normalize the dataset.

Select the most informative features: Not all features may be relevant for predicting loan risk. We can use feature selection techniques to identify the most informative features for SVM.

Train the SVM classifier: Use the preprocessed and selected features to train an SVM classifier. We can use cross-validation to improve the robustness of the model.

Evaluate the model: Evaluate the SVM's performance on a test set using metrics like accuracy, precision, recall, and the F1 score.

Implementation and Evaluation of SVM for Mokka's Dataset

Let us look at the implementation and evaluation part.

Data Preprocessing

Before training the SVM classifier, the Mokka loan dataset needs to be preprocessed. This includes:

- **Converting date-time features to numerical metrics:** This can be done by calculating the duration since the first loan, the duration between loan approval and repayment, and so on.
- **Handling missing values:** SVM cannot handle missing values natively. Therefore, imputation or other techniques need to be used to fill in the missing values.
- **One-hot encoding categorical features**: Categorical features like federal_district_nm need to be transformed into a binary matrix so that they can be understood by the SVM classifier.
- **Normalizing the data:** Normalizing the data is important for SVM because it relies on distances between data points. StandardScaler from scikit-learn can be used for this purpose.

Sparse Distributed Data and Support Vector Machines

The following Python code shows how to preprocess the Mokka loan dataset:

Python

```
from sklearn.preprocessing import OneHotEncoder, StandardScaler

# Load the data
data = pd.read_csv('test_task.csv')

# Convert date-time features to numerical metrics
data['duration_since_first_loan'] = data['rep_loan_date'] - data['first_loan']
data['duration_between_loan_approval_and_repayment'] = data['repayment_date'] - data['rep_loan_date']

# Handle missing values
# ... [Code for handling missing values]

# One-hot encode categorical features
encoder = OneHotEncoder()
encoded_features = encoder.fit_transform(data[['federal_district_nm']])
data = data.drop(columns=['federal_district_nm'])
data = pd.concat([data, pd.DataFrame(encoded_features.toarray())], axis=1)

# Scale the data
scaler = StandardScaler()
scaled_features = scaler.fit_transform(data)
```

Model Training and Validation

Once the data has been preprocessed, the SVM classifier can be trained and validated. The following Python code shows how to do this:

Python

```
from sklearn.svm import SVC
from sklearn.model_selection import train_test_split, cross_val_score

# Split the data into training and test sets
X_train, X_test, y_train, y_test = train_test_split(scaled_features, labels, test_size=0.2)

# Train the SVM classifier
svm_classifier = SVC(kernel='linear')
svm_classifier.fit(X_train, y_train)

# Validate the model using cross-validation
scores = cross_val_score(svm_classifier, X_train, y_train, cv=5)
```

The `cross_val_score()` function performs cross-validation on the training data and returns a list of accuracy scores. The average of these accuracy scores gives us a good estimate of the model's performance on unseen data.

Model Evaluation

Once the model has been trained and validated, it can be evaluated on the test set. The following Python code shows how to do this:

Python

```
from sklearn.metrics import classification_report

# Make predictions on the test set
```

```
y_pred = svm_classifier.predict(X_test)

# Evaluate the model
report = classification_report(y_test, y_pred)
print(report)
```

The **classification_report()** function generates a report that summarizes the model's performance on the test set. The report includes metrics such as accuracy, precision, recall, and F1 score. These metrics provide a comprehensive overview of the model's performance and can be used to identify areas for improvement.

Interpreting Results and Insights

Once the SVM classifier has been trained and evaluated, it is important to interpret the results and derive meaningful insights. This interpretation can guide decisions on credit risk assessment for Mokka.

Confusion Matrix

A confusion matrix is a table that summarizes the performance of a classification model. It shows the number of correct and incorrect predictions made by the model for each class.

The following Python code shows how to generate a confusion matrix for the SVM classifier:

Python

```
from sklearn.metrics import confusion_matrix
import seaborn as sns

# Generate the confusion matrix
matrix = confusion_matrix(y_test, y_pred)

# Plot the confusion matrix
sns.heatmap(matrix, annot=True, fmt="d", cmap="Blues")
```

Interpreting the Confusion Matrix

The confusion matrix can be interpreted as follows:

- **True Positives (TP):** These are loans that were predicted as default and did indeed default. A high TP rate suggests that the model is effectively catching high-risk loan applications.
- **False Positives (FP):** These are loans predicted as default but did not default. A high FP rate could mean potential revenue loss, as these loans may have been profitable.
- **True Negatives (TN):** Loans predicted as non-default and did not default. This indicates good predictions by the model.
- **False Negatives (FN):** Loans predicted as non-default but did default. A high FN can be risky as it suggests the model is letting through potentially bad loans.

Key Insights and Recommendations

Based on the interpretation of the confusion matrix, the following insights and recommendations can be made:

- **Feature importance:** By examining the weight of features in the SVM, we can understand which features play a pivotal role in loan defaults. For instance, if past_billings_cnt has a significant weight, it indicates past behavior as a strong predictor. This information can be used to develop more targeted risk assessment strategies.
- **Threshold adjustment:** By altering the decision threshold, we can control the trade-off between precision and recall. Precision refers to the proportion of predicted defaults that are actually defaults, while recall refers to the proportion of actual defaults that are predicted as defaults. Mokka can adjust the threshold based on its risk appetite. For example, if Mokka is more concerned about avoiding false negatives, it can set a lower threshold, which will result in a higher recall. However, this will also increase the number of false positives.
- **Handling imbalance:** If the dataset has an imbalanced class distribution, where there are significantly more loans in one class than the other, techniques like SMOTE or under-sampling can be used to address this imbalance. SMOTE stands for Synthetic Minority Over-sampling Technique, and it creates synthetic data points for the minority class. Under-sampling randomly removes data points from the majority class to balance the dataset.

Future Enhancements and Conclusions

The following are some future enhancements that can be made to the SVM classifier:

- **Kernel methods:** While a linear SVM was used in this example, kernel methods such as the Radial Basis Function (RBF) can be explored for non-linear decision boundaries. Kernel methods can allow the SVM classifier to model more complex relationships between the features.
- **Hyperparameter tuning:** GridSearchCV can be used to find the optimal hyperparameters for the SVM classifier, such as the regularization parameter and the kernel width. Hyperparameter tuning can help to improve the performance of the classifier on unseen data.

Libraries for Distributed SVM

Several tools and libraries facilitate the implementation of SVM in a distributed fashion:

- **Spark MLLib:** Apache Spark's machine learning library, MLLib, provides a distributed implementation of linear SVMs. With its in-memory computation capabilities, MLLib can significantly speed up SVM training for large datasets.
- **Distributed Scikit-learn:** Though Scikit-learn is inherently not distributed, projects like Dask-ML provide a way to parallelize operations, allowing Scikit-learn SVM to be used in distributed environments.
- **H2O:** An open-source platform that provides distributed SVMs, tailored for big data. Its memory handling and optimization techniques ensure fast computation.
- **ThunderSVM:** Leveraging the power of GPUs, ThunderSVM aims to provide a fast SVM library that scales to large datasets.

Performance Considerations and Optimizations for Sparse Datasets

When dealing with sparse data, especially in a distributed setting, certain specific optimizations can be crucial:

- **Compressed Storage:** Techniques like Compressed Sparse Row (CSR) or Compressed Sparse Column (CSC) formats can be employed to store sparse data efficiently.
- **Parallel Feature Hashing:** For high-dimensional sparse data, feature hashing can reduce the dimensionality, making computations more efficient.

- **Row-wise Data Distribution:** In distributed settings, distributing data row-wise ensures that all features of an instance are available on a single node, reducing the need for data transfer during computations.

Optimized Kernel Functions: Using kernels optimized for sparse data can speed up the **computation**. For instance, linear kernels often prove efficient for high-dimensional sparse datasets.

Hands-on with Distributed SVM on Sparse Datasets

The following steps are to be implemented:

1. **Setting up the Environment**

   Python

   ```
   from pyspark.sql import SparkSession
   spark = SparkSession.builder.appName("DistributedSVM").getOrCreate()

   from pyspark.ml.classification import LinearSVC
   from pyspark.ml.linalg import Vectors
   from pyspark.ml.feature import VectorAssembler
   ```

2. **Loading and Preprocessing the Data**

   Python

   ```
   # Load the Sparse Dataset
   data = spark.read.csv("path_to_data.csv", header=True, inferSchema=True)

   # Vector Assembler
   feature_columns = data.columns[:-1] # assuming the last column is the target variable
   assembler = VectorAssembler(inputCols=feature_columns, outputCol="features")
   data = assembler.transform(data)
   ```

3. **Training the Distributed SVM**

    Python

    ```python
    # Initialize the SVM Model
    svm = LinearSVC(labelCol="target_variable_column_name",
    featuresCol="features", maxIter=10, regParam=0.1)

    # Train the Model
    model = svm.fit(data)
    ```

4. **Model Evaluation**

    Python

    ```python
    # Load the Test Data
    test_data = spark.read.csv("path_to_test_data.csv", header=True, inferSchema=True)

    test_data = assembler.transform(test_data)

    # Make Predictions
    predictions = model.transform(test_data)
    ```

Optimizing Distributed SVM for Sparse Data

- **Handling Sparsity Efficiently**
  - **Sparse Vector Representation**: In PySpark's MLLib, the SparseVector object provides an efficient representation for sparse datasets. It essentially stores only non-zero values and their indices, greatly reducing memory consumption.

    Python

    ```python
    from pyspark.ml.linalg import SparseVector
    ```

  - **Pruning Non-Informative Features:** Features with little variation can often be pruned without a significant loss in performance. This reduces the dimensionality and aids in faster processing. Feature selection techniques such as VarianceThreshold can be employed.

- **Distributed Libraries and Tools**
    - **Spark MLLib**: It is one of the most widely used libraries for machine learning on big data. It inherently supports distributed computation and provides tools for SVM out of the box.
    - **Dask**: For those familiar with Scikit-learn, Dask offers a similar API but is designed for distributed and parallel computing. It can seamlessly scale from a single machine to a cluster of machines.
    - **H2O.ai:** Another platform that offers distributed computing capabilities for machine learning tasks. Their platform also integrates well with Spark.

PySpark: The Powerhouse for Big Data Machine Learning

What is PySpark?

Apache Spark is a unified analytics engine for large-scale data processing. It provides high-level APIs in Java, Scala, Python, and R, and an optimized engine that supports general execution graphs.

PySpark is the Python API for Spark. It allows users to program Spark with Python, a popular and widely used language in the data science community.

Why PySpark for Machine Learning?

PySpark is a powerful tool for machine learning on big data for the following reasons:

- **Distributed nature:** PySpark runs on clusters, splitting tasks across nodes. This makes it ideal for handling large datasets that cannot fit in memory on a single machine.
- **Built-in libraries:** PySpark comes with MLLib, a built-in library for machine learning. It provides various algorithms out-of-the-box for classification, regression, clustering, and more.
- **Easy integration:** PySpark can easily read data from diverse data sources, including HDFS, Cassandra, HBase, and Amazon S3.
- **Real-time processing:** With Spark Streaming, PySpark can process real-time data, making it suitable for live data applications.

Setting up PySpark

To start working with PySpark, you need to set it up first. Typically, PySpark setup involves the following steps:

1. **Installing Spark and PySpark**: You can easily install PySpark using pip:
    Python
    ```
    pip install pyspark
    ```
2. **Setting environment variables**: Ensure that the `SPARK_HOME` and `PYSPARK_PYTHON` environment variables are set.
3. **Using `SparkSession`**: Once everything is set up, the entry point to any functionality in Spark is the `SparkSession`.
    Python
    ```
    from pyspark.sql import SparkSession
    spark = SparkSession.builder.appName("SVMExample").getOrCreate()
    ```

MLLib: PySpark's Machine Learning Library

MLLib is the core of PySpark's machine learning functionalities. It provides a wide range of features, including:

- **Data preparation tools:** MLLib provides tools like StringIndexer and VectorAssembler to help transform data into a format suitable for machine learning algorithms.
- **Algorithms:** MLLib offers distributed versions of popular machine learning algorithms, such as linear regression, logistic regression, random forests, and decision trees.
- **Model evaluation:** MLLib supports various metrics for model evaluation, such as accuracy, precision, recall, and F1 score.
- **Pipeline construction:** PySpark MLLib supports pipeline construction, which simplifies workflows and ensures reproducibility.

A Quick Example with PySpark MLLib

Assuming we want to use a linear SVM in PySpark with our sparse data:

Python
```
from pyspark.ml.classification import LinearSVC
from pyspark.ml.linalg import SparseVector
from pyspark.ml.feature import VectorAssembler
```

```
# Load data
data=spark.read.csv("path_to_data.csv",header=True,inferSchema=True)

# Transform data to sparse vector format
vec_assembler = VectorAssembler(inputCols=data.columns[:-1], outputCol="features")
data_transformed = vec_assembler.transform(data)

# Initialize SVM and train
svm = LinearSVC(labelCol="bad_flag", featuresCol="features")
model = svm.fit(data_transformed)

# Predictions can be made on the test set in a similar way
```

This is just a simple example of how to use PySpark MLLib for machine learning on big data. PySpark MLLib provides a wide range of features and capabilities, making it a powerful tool for data scientists and big data practitioners.

Fraud Detection in Sparse Financial Datasets using SVM

Fraud is a major problem in the financial sector, and it is becoming increasingly sophisticated as the sector moves predominantly online. Fraudulent transactions can have a significant impact on financial institutions, both financially and reputationally. Efficient detection systems are therefore essential.

One of the challenges of detecting fraud is the sparse nature of transaction data. Only a small fraction of transactions are fraudulent, and the data often contains many missing values. This can make it difficult for traditional algorithms to identify fraudulent patterns.

End-of-the-Chapter Project: Optimizing Marketing Campaign Responses (Company: SparkCognition)

Let us look at the steps in the project.

Setting the Stage

In today's data-driven world, businesses are increasingly relying on machine learning (ML) to optimize their marketing campaigns. ML algorithms can help businesses to better understand their customers, predict their behavior, and deliver more personalized and effective marketing messages.

One of the challenges that businesses face in optimizing their marketing campaigns is predicting customer responses to email campaigns. Email campaigns are a popular and cost-effective way to reach customers, but they can be time-consuming and expensive to create and manage. Additionally, the success of an email campaign depends on the ability to target the right customers with the right message at the right time.

SparkCognition is a global leader in AI and ML solutions. SparkCognition is working with an insurance giant to develop a machine learning model that can predict customer responses to email marketing campaigns. This model will help the insurance company to improve the effectiveness of its marketing campaigns and reach more customers with the right message.

Dataset

The dataset used to train the machine learning model will consist of historical email campaign data, including the following features:

- Customer demographics (age, gender, location, and so on)
- Customer purchase history
- Email engagement history (open rates, click-through rates, and more)
- Email campaign content (subject line, body text, and so on)

Problem Statement

The goal of the machine learning model is to predict the probability of a customer responding to an email marketing campaign. The model will be trained on historical data to identify patterns in customer behavior that can be used to predict future responses.

Machine Learning Approach

There are a variety of machine learning algorithms that can be used to predict customer responses to email marketing campaigns. Some of the most popular algorithms include:

- Logistic regression
- Support vector machines (SVMs)
- Decision trees
- Random forests
- Gradient boosting machines

The specific machine learning algorithm that is used will depend on the characteristics of the dataset and the specific goals of the project.

Benefits

Predicting customer responses to email marketing campaigns has a number of benefits, including:

- Increased email engagement rates
- Improved customer satisfaction
- Increased sales and revenue
- Reduced marketing costs

Diving into the Data: A Comprehensive Description

Before building a machine learning model, it is essential to understand the data. The insurance company has provided two datasets:

- `marketing_training.csv`: This is the primary training set, which will be used to develop the model.

- **marketing_test.csv**: This dataset will be used to evaluate the model's performance.

The following is a detailed description of the columns in the training dataset:

- **custAge:** Numeric. The age of the customer, in years. Age can be a determinant of product preference and responsiveness to certain marketing tones.
- **profession:** Categorical. The customer's profession or job type. Different professions may have varying financial behaviors and product needs.
- **marital:** Categorical. The customer's marital status. Marital status can impact financial decisions and insurance priorities.
- **schooling:** Categorical. The highest education level attained by the customer. Education levels can influence financial literacy and product comprehension.
- **default:** Categorical. Indicates whether the customer has ever defaulted on a financial obligation. This is a crucial metric, especially for insurance companies.
- **housing:** Categorical. Specifies whether the customer has a housing loan. This is often used to gauge financial stability and risk.
- **contact**: Categorical. The customer's preferred method of contact, either cellular or telephone.
- **month:** Categorical. The month of the last contact with the customer. Seasonal variations can influence marketing success.
- **day_of_week**: Categorical. The specific day of the week of the last contact. Some days may yield better engagement rates than others.
- **campaign:** Numeric. Indicates the number of times the customer was contacted during the campaign.

There are many other columns in the dataset, each of which provides a unique perspective on the customer. It is important to understand the significance of each column and its potential relationship to the response variable. With this holistic view of the data, we can now transition into the preprocessing phase, where we will cleanse, transform, and prepare the data for machine learning.

Pre-processing the Data: Laying a Robust Foundation

Data preprocessing is a critical step in any machine learning project. It involves transforming and preparing the data so that it is suitable for building accurate and reliable models.

Handling Missing Values

The first step in data preprocessing is to handle missing values. Missing values can distort predictions and lead to erroneous conclusions.

For numeric columns, such as custAge, we can compute the median of the column and replace missing values with the median. This ensures that the data distribution remains largely unaffected.

For categorical columns, such as profession and marital status, we can introduce a new category labeled "Unknown" to handle missing values. This ensures that we neither introduce bias nor lose data points during model training.

Dealing with Categorical Data

Machine learning models understand numbers, not text. Therefore, we need to transform the categorical columns in our dataset into a numeric format.

One common way to do this is to use one-hot encoding. One-hot encoding involves converting each categorical value into a new categorical column and using a binary value of 0 or 1 to indicate the absence or presence of the feature.

For example, the categorical column profession could be converted into the following one-hot encoded columns:

- `profession_engineer`
- `profession_doctor`
- `profession_teacher`

Balancing the Dataset

It is common in marketing datasets for one outcome (for example, "not responded") to dominate the other due to the typically low response rates to campaigns. This imbalance can lead to biased models.

To address this, we can use the oversampling of the minority class. This involves creating additional data points for the minority class so that it is represented equally to the majority class.

Feature Engineering

Feature engineering involves creating new features from existing features to improve the predictive power of the model.

For example, we could create a new feature called `previous_contact`, which is binary and indicates whether the customer was previously contacted (using the pdays column).

Data Scaling and Normalization

Features like custAge and campaign may have different scales, which can be problematic for certain algorithms. To ensure that all features are on the same scale, we can use a technique such as Min-Max Scaling.

Min-Max Scaling involves scaling all features to a range between 0 and 1.

The following figure illustrates the steps of the process:

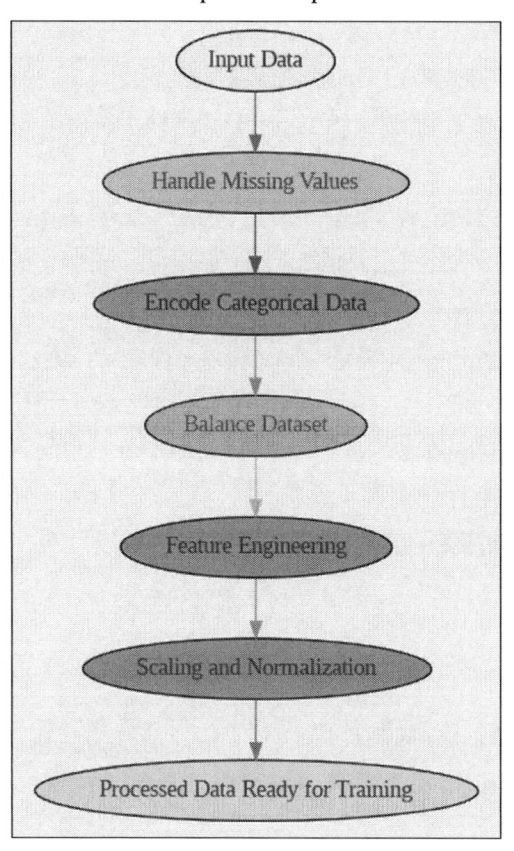

Figure 6.4: The diagram shows the steps

Data Input

Source: `marketing_training.csv`

Features: `custAge, profession, marital, schooling, default, housing, loan, contact, month, day_of_week, campaign, pdays, previous, poutcome, emp.`

`var.rate, cons.price.idx, cons.conf.idx, euribor3m, nr.employed, pmonths, pastEmail`

Target: responded

Data Preprocessing

Handle Missing Values:

- **Strategy:**
    - Numeric columns: Replace with median.
    - Categorical columns: Label as 'Unknown'.
- **Categorical Data Encoding:**
    - **Method:** One-hot encoding.
    - **Columns affected:** profession, marital, contact, and so on.
- **Balance Dataset:**
    - **Method:** Oversampling of the minority class (responded = yes).
    - **Tools:** SMOTE or ADASYN.
- **Feature Engineering:**
    - New features: `previous_contact` based on pdays.
    - Potential others based on correlation and feature importance.
- **Scaling and Normalization:**
    - **Method:** Min-Max Scaling.
    - **Columns affected:** All numerical columns.

Output

- Processed Dataset ready for model training.

Visualization and Feature Engineering: Creating New Insights

Visualization

Visualization can help us to understand the underlying patterns in our data. Some examples of useful visualizations include:

- **Distribution plots:** These show the distribution of values for a particular feature. For example, we could create a distribution plot of customer age to understand how old our customers are.

- **Bar charts:** These can be used to compare the frequencies of different categories for a particular feature. For example, we could create a bar chart of job types to see which professions are most common among our customers.
- **Correlation heatmaps:** These show how different features are correlated with each other. This can help us to identify multicollinearity and understand which features may be redundant.

Feature Engineering

Feature engineering is the process of creating new features from existing features. This can be done to improve the predictive performance of our model.

Some examples of feature engineering techniques that we could use for our marketing campaign data include:

- **Creating an engagement score:** This score could be calculated based on the number of times a customer has been contacted, how recent their last contact was, and how many emails they have received. A higher score would indicate a more engaged customer.
- **Creating an economic stability index:** This index could be calculated based on a combination of features such as the employment variation rate, consumer price index, consumer confidence index, and Euribor 3-month rate. A higher index would indicate a more stable economy.
- **Bucketing age**: Instead of treating age as a continuous variable, we could bucket customers into different age groups. This could simplify the model and make it more interpretable.

Code Examples

Here are some code examples of the visualization and feature engineering techniques that we discussed:

Python

```python
import matplotlib.pyplot as plt

import seaborn as sns

import pandas as pd

# Load the data
data = pd.read_csv('marketing_training.csv')
```

```python
# Create a distribution plot of customer age
plt.hist(data['custAge'], bins=20, color='blue', edgecolor='black')
plt.title('Distribution of Customer Age')
plt.xlabel('Age')
plt.ylabel('Count')
plt.show()

# Create a bar chart of job type
data['profession'].value_counts().plot(kind='bar', color='green')
plt.title('Job Type Distribution')
plt.xlabel('Profession')
plt.ylabel('Count')
plt.show()

# Create a correlation heatmap
correlation_matrix = data.corr()
plt.figure(figsize=(10, 8))
sns.heatmap(correlation_matrix, annot=True, cmap='coolwarm')
plt.title('Feature Correlation Heatmap')
plt.show()

# Create an engagement score
data['Engagement Score'] = data['previous'] * 0.5 + (1/data['pdays']) + data['pastEmail']

# Create an economic stability index
data['Economic Stability Index'] = data['emp.var.rate'] + data['cons.price.idx'] - data['cons.conf.idx'] + data['euribor3m']
```

```python
# Bucket age
data['Age Group'] = pd.cut(data['custAge'], bins=[0, 25, 50, 100], labels=['Young', 'Middle-Aged', 'Senior'])
```

Model Development and Validation: From Theory to Action

Step 1: Data Splitting

Before training our model, we need to split the dataset into a training set and a validation set. This ensures that we can evaluate the model's performance on unseen data.

Python

```python
from sklearn.model_selection import train_test_split

X = data.drop('responded', axis=1) # Features
y = data['responded'] # Target variable

X_train, X_val, y_train, y_val = train_test_split(X, y, test_size=0.2, random_state=42)
```

Step 2: Preprocessing - Encoding and Scaling

Categorical variables need to be converted to a format that is understandable for the machine learning models. Additionally, to ensure that all features are on a similar scale, we apply scaling.

Python

```python
from sklearn.preprocessing import StandardScaler, OneHotEncoder
from sklearn.compose import ColumnTransformer
from sklearn.pipeline import Pipeline

# Identify categorical columns
categorical_features = ['profession', 'marital', 'schooling', 'contact', 'month', 'day_of_week', 'poutcome']
```

```python
numeric_features = X_train.drop(columns=categorical_features).columns.tolist()

# Create transformers
preprocessor = ColumnTransformer(transformers=[
    ('num', StandardScaler(), numeric_features),
    ('cat', OneHotEncoder(), categorical_features)
])
```

Step 3: Model Building - Support Vector Machine (SVM) as a Choice

While Logistic Regression is a straightforward algorithm, SVM can offer more flexibility, especially in cases with complex decision boundaries. SVM tries to find the optimal hyperplane that best separates the classes.

Python

```python
from sklearn.svm import SVC

# Create and evaluate the pipeline
pipeline = Pipeline([
    ('preprocessor', preprocessor),
    ('classifier', SVC(kernel='linear', probability=True)) # using a linear kernel for simplicity
])

pipeline.fit(X_train, y_train)
```

Step 4: Model Validation

We will use accuracy as our metric, but it is crucial to also consider other metrics like precision, recall, and the F1-score, especially for imbalanced datasets.

Python

```python
from sklearn.metrics import accuracy_score

y_pred = pipeline.predict(X_val)
```

```
print(f"Validation Accuracy (SVM): {accuracy_score(y_val, y_
pred):.4f}")
```

Tuning and Model Improvement

Step 1: Hyperparameter Tuning

Support Vector Machines have a few key hyperparameters that can influence model performance. The two most common are the regularization parameter C and the kernel type.

Python

```
from sklearn.model_selection import GridSearchCV

param_grid = {
    'classifier__C': [0.1, 1, 10, 100],
    'classifier__kernel': ['linear', 'rbf', 'poly', 'sigmoid']
}

grid_search = GridSearchCV(pipeline, param_grid, cv=5, scoring='accuracy')
grid_search.fit(X_train, y_train)

print(f"Best Parameters (SVM): {grid_search.best_params_}")
```

Step 2: Model Evaluation with Optimal Parameters

Now that we have identified the best parameters for our SVM, let's train our SVM with these parameters and evaluate its performance.

Python

```
# Using best estimator from grid search
best_svm = grid_search.best_estimator_
y_pred_best = best_svm.predict(X_val)

print(f"Validation Accuracy (Optimized SVM): {accuracy_score(y_val, y_pred_best):.4f}")
```

Step 3: Insights from the Model

Beyond accuracy, it is essential to gain insights from our model. For SVM, especially with a linear kernel, the model can provide weights for features, which gives an idea about feature importance.

Python

```python
if 'linear' in grid_search.best_params_['classifier__kernel']:
    coef = best_svm.named_steps['classifier'].coef_
    important_features = pd.Series(coef[0], index=X.columns).sort_values(ascending=False)
    print("Top 5 Important Features:\n", important_features.head(5))
```

Step 4: Model Robustness

For real-world deployment, it is not just about accuracy but also about how robust the model is. Let's evaluate our model using other metrics such as precision, recall, F1-score, and ROC-AUC.

Python

```python
from sklearn.metrics import classification_report, roc_auc_score

print(classification_report(y_val, y_pred_best))
print(f"ROC-AUC Score (Optimized SVM): {roc_auc_score(y_val, best_svm.predict_proba(X_val)[:,1]):.4f}")
```

Dealing with Imbalances and Model Refinement

Imbalanced Datasets

Imbalanced datasets can lead to biased models, as they tend to favor the majority class. Our data might exhibit such a phenomenon where the number of customers who respond to the campaign is significantly lower than those who don't.

Step 1: Recognizing the Imbalance

First, let's quantify the degree of imbalance:

Python

```python
print(y_train.value_counts(normalize=True))
```

If there is a significant class imbalance, techniques like resampling or using different evaluation metrics can be beneficial.

Step 2: Resampling Techniques

One of the popular methods to address imbalance is to either oversample the minority class or undersample the majority class. Here, we'll oversample using the SMOTE technique.

Python

```
from imblearn.over_sampling import SMOTE

smote = SMOTE(random_state=42)
X_resampled, y_resampled = smote.fit_resample(X_train, y_train)
```

Step 3: Training SVM on Resampled Data

Now, we will retrain our model on the resampled data.

Python

```
best_svm.fit(X_resampled, y_resampled)
y_pred_resampled = best_svm.predict(X_val)
print(f"Validation Accuracy (Resampled Data): {accuracy_score(y_val, y_pred_resampled):.4f}")
```

Step 4: Re-evaluation

With the refined model, let's assess its performance using various metrics to understand if the resampling helped improve our model's fairness across classes.

Python

```
print(classification_report(y_val, y_pred_resampled))
print(f"ROC-AUC Score (Resampled Data): {roc_auc_score(y_val, best_svm.predict_proba(X_val)[:,1]):.4f}")
```

Taking Actions and Recommendations

Our model, backed by data-driven insights, offers not only a prediction mechanism but also paves the way for actionable recommendations. These recommendations are crucial to optimizing marketing campaigns.

Step 1: Targeting Strategy

Based on our model's findings:

- **Segmentation:** Segregate customers by profession, marital status, and educational background. This allows us to tailor marketing messages more effectively.
- **Timing:** Focus on contacting potential customers during the months and days that have shown higher positive response rates.
- **Engagement:** Prioritize individuals who have had previous interactions with past campaigns, given their potential higher likelihood to respond.

Code example:

Python

```python
# A simple targeting function based on our model
def target_customers(dataframe):
    predictions = best_svm.predict(dataframe)
    return dataframe[predictions == 1]
```

Step 2: Cost-Effective Campaigns

- **Resource Allocation:** Allocate more resources during peak months (as identified by the model) and decrease investment during off-peak periods.
- **Channel Selection:** If the data shows a higher response rate via a particular contact type (for example, cellular over telephone), pivot the campaign's communication strategy accordingly.

Step 3: Continuous Learning

Given the dynamic nature of consumers and markets:

- **Feedback Loop:** Create a system where the model continuously learns from new campaign results.
- **Model Updates:** Periodically retrain the model with fresh data to ensure its relevancy and accuracy.

Code example:

Python

```python
# A simple feedback function to update our dataset with new data
def update_dataset(new_data, old_data):
```

```
updated_data = pd.concat([old_data, new_data], ignore_index=True)
return updated_data
```

The power of machine learning in marketing lies not just in predicting outcomes but also in driving actionable business strategies. By taking these data-driven actions and continuously refining our approach based on feedback, we set the stage for more successful and cost-effective marketing campaigns.

Future Directions and Long-Term Vision

While our current SVM model offers promising results, the realm of data-driven marketing is vast, with numerous possibilities for enhancement and expansion.

Step 1: Expanding Data Horizons

- **Additional Data Sources**: Incorporate customer behavior data from other platforms like social media, web browsing patterns, and purchase histories. This could provide richer context and potentially enhance prediction accuracy.
- **Temporal Patterns**: Understanding cyclic trends, like seasonality, can lead to better timing of campaigns.

Step 2: Advanced Modeling Techniques

- **Deep Learning**: Neural networks, especially recurrent neural networks (RNNs), might capture intricate patterns in user behavior more effectively.
- **Ensemble Models**: Combining the predictions of multiple models can often lead to more accurate and stable results.

Step 3: Real-time Predictions and Automation

- **Streaming Data**: Adopt systems that can process and predict in real-time as customer data streams in.
- **Automated Marketing**: Based on predictions, automate specific marketing actions, such as sending personalized offers or messages.

Code example:

Python

```
# Placeholder code for real-time prediction (a conceptual idea)
def real_time_predict(stream_data):
    processed_data = preprocess(stream_data)
    prediction = best_svm.predict(processed_data)
```

```
    if prediction == 1:
        send_offer(stream_data['email'])
```

As we step into an era where businesses will increasingly rely on AI to make decisions, continuous innovation and adaptability become paramount. Our current SVM-based model is just the tip of the iceberg. The future holds vast potential for more sophisticated models, richer datasets, and integrated systems that will drive marketing's next revolution. The ultimate goal is to ensure that businesses not only reach their potential customers but also provide value, enhancing the overall customer experience.

Additional Notes

In addition to the areas mentioned above, other potential directions for future exploration include:

- **Multichannel Marketing**: Developing models that can optimize campaigns across multiple channels, such as email, social media, and paid advertising.
- **Cross-Selling and Recommendation Systems**: Using machine learning to recommend products or services to customers based on their past behavior and preferences.
- **Marketing Attribution**: Measuring the impact of different marketing campaigns and channels on customer conversions.

It is also important to note that the ethical and responsible use of AI in marketing is a critical consideration. As we develop and deploy new AI-powered marketing tools, it is essential to ensure that they are used in a way that is fair, transparent, and aligned with the best interests of consumers.

Conclusion

Sparse data presents unique opportunities and challenges in machine learning. Support vector machines are an algorithm particularly apt for building models on such sparse, high-dimensional datasets. With the rise of big data, understanding how to leverage sparse data and algorithms like SVM on distributed infrastructure is crucial for tackling modern machine learning problems. This chapter introduced these key concepts.

In the next chapter, we will delve into advanced techniques for identifying deviations in data across various sectors. The focus will be on isolation forests, a method optimized for scalability in anomaly detection. This chapter includes a case study on financial fraud detection, offering practical insights into applying isolation forests in real-world scenarios. The aim is to provide a comprehensive understanding of anomaly detection, comparing isolation forests with other standard methods and discussing best practices for evaluating system performance

Points to Remember

In our journey with SparkCognition into the realm of data-driven marketing, we experienced firsthand the transformative power of machine learning. Here are some of our key takeaways:

- Data is the cornerstone. Before any advanced techniques can be applied, understanding and preprocessing the data is crucial. This includes handling missing values, categorizing continuous variables, and addressing data imbalances.
- Simplicity can be effective. Starting with a simple model like logistic regression and gradually moving to more complex algorithms like SVM, we realized that complex problems don't always require complex solutions. A well-tuned simpler model can often outperform or match more complex algorithms, especially with limited data.
- Evaluation is key. Ensuring that the model generalizes well to unseen data is paramount. The entire premise of predictive modeling rests on the model's ability to predict future, unseen instances accurately.
- An iterative approach is essential. Data science is not about getting the perfect model in the first go. It is an iterative process of trial, error, and learning. From our initial models to the final SVM model, each step provided insights to refine our approach further.
- The future is bright. As discussed in the previous section, the horizon of possibilities in AI-driven marketing is vast. From incorporating more diverse data sources to deploying deep learning algorithms, there is much ground to cover.

In conclusion, this project underscores a salient paradigm of modern businesses: blending domain expertise with data-driven insights paves the way for optimal solutions. For SparkCognition and its client, this project is a stepping stone into the future of intelligent, automated, and highly personalized marketing campaigns. The journey of innovation continues, and as always, it's an exciting road ahead!

CHAPTER 7
Anomaly Detection and Isolation Forests

Introduction

Anomaly detection involves identifying deviations from normal patterns in data. In sectors like healthcare, banking, cybersecurity, and geological research, identifying these anomalies allows organizations to catch errors, detect fraud, prevent equipment failures, and reveal valuable insights. However, finding often subtle anomalies in complex, high-dimensional data requires sophisticated algorithms.

This chapter explores isolation forests - an efficient, robust anomaly detection technique optimized for scalability and flexibility across datasets. We will first highlight motivating applications in industry verticals. We will then provide a comprehensive overview of isolation forest mechanics and functionality. This is complemented by an end-to-end case study on detecting financial fraud, providing hands-on demonstration. We will also compare isolation forests to other standard techniques and discuss best practices for evaluating anomaly detection system performance. Through both conceptual foundations and practical knowledge, this chapter aims to equip readers with expertise to leverage isolation forests and anomaly detection broadly

Structure

In this chapter, we will cover the following topics:
- Introduction to Anomaly Detection
- Isolation Forest Algorithm

- Case Study: Detecting Fraud with Isolation Forests
- Evaluation Metrics for Anomaly Detection Systems
- Alternative Anomaly Detection Methods

The Significance of Anomalies

Anomalies can have a significant impact on data analysis and decision-making. They can distort averages, skew predictions, and lead to inaccurate conclusions. However, anomalies can also be a valuable source of insights. By identifying and understanding anomalies, we can gain new knowledge about our data and the world around us.

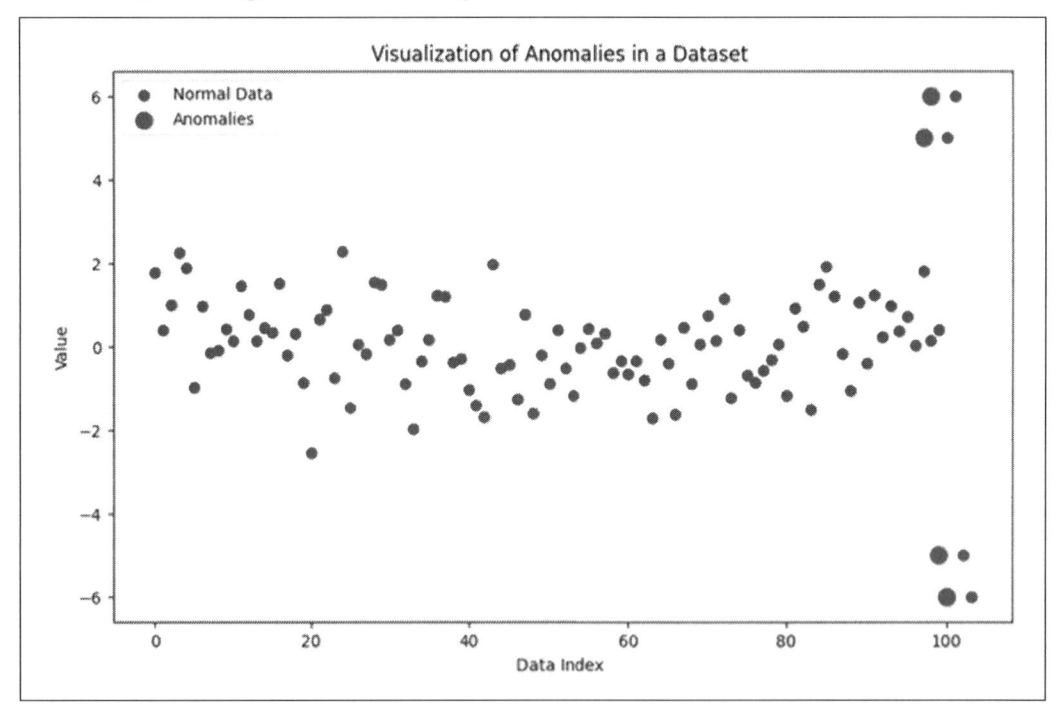

Figure 7.1: Anomalies in a dataset

Real-World Applications and Implications of Anomaly Detection

Anomaly detection plays a crucial role in maintaining the data integrity for various sectors. Its applications span a wide range of industries, including banking and finance, healthcare, manufacturing, e-commerce, and cybersecurity, among others. For example, in the financial sector, anomaly detection is instrumental in analyzing transactions to identify potential fraudulent activities. Hospitals utilize this technology to detect early signs of disease in patients, significantly increasing the chances of positive health outcomes. In the manufacturing realm, anomaly detection is key to identifying equipment malfunctions before they lead to costly downtimes. Similarly, e-commerce platforms employ it to uncover new trends or system glitches, ensuring a seamless user experience. Cybersecurity firms, on the other hand, rely on anomaly detection as a frontline defense against increasingly sophisticated cyberattacks. Through these diverse applications, anomaly detection not only helps prevent problems but also paves the way for enhanced operational outcomes.

Isolation Forests

Isolation forests are a type of anomaly detection algorithm that is particularly well-suited for high-dimensional data. They work by creating a forest of isolated trees, each of which contains a subset of the data. The anomalies are then identified as the data points that are easiest to isolate from the trees.

Isolation forests are a relatively new algorithm, but they have quickly become popular due to their effectiveness and scalability. They are also relatively easy to implement, making them a good option for data scientists of all levels of experience.

Deep Dive into Isolation Forests

Isolation forests represent a paradigm shift in anomaly detection. Conventional methods are often focused on understanding normal data patterns and then defining outliers based on deviations from this norm. However, isolation forests challenge this approach by focusing on the anomalies directly.

This fundamental shift in perspective offers several advantages, including:

- **Efficiency**: Isolation forests are very efficient to train and deploy, even for large datasets.
- **Scalability**: Isolation forests can scale to handle datasets of any size.
- **Robustness**: Isolation forests are robust to noise and outliers in the data.
- **Directness:** Isolation forests directly identify anomalies without the need to first define normal data patterns.

Isolation Forest Algorithm

Isolation forests work by building a forest of isolation trees. Each isolation tree is a binary tree that is constructed by randomly splitting the data into two subsets until a stopping criterion is met. The stopping criterion is typically reached when either the subset contains only a single data point or all the data points in the subset have the same value.

The depth of a data point in an isolation tree is the number of splits that were required to isolate it. Anomalies are identified as the data points with the shortest depths, as they are the easiest to isolate from the tree.

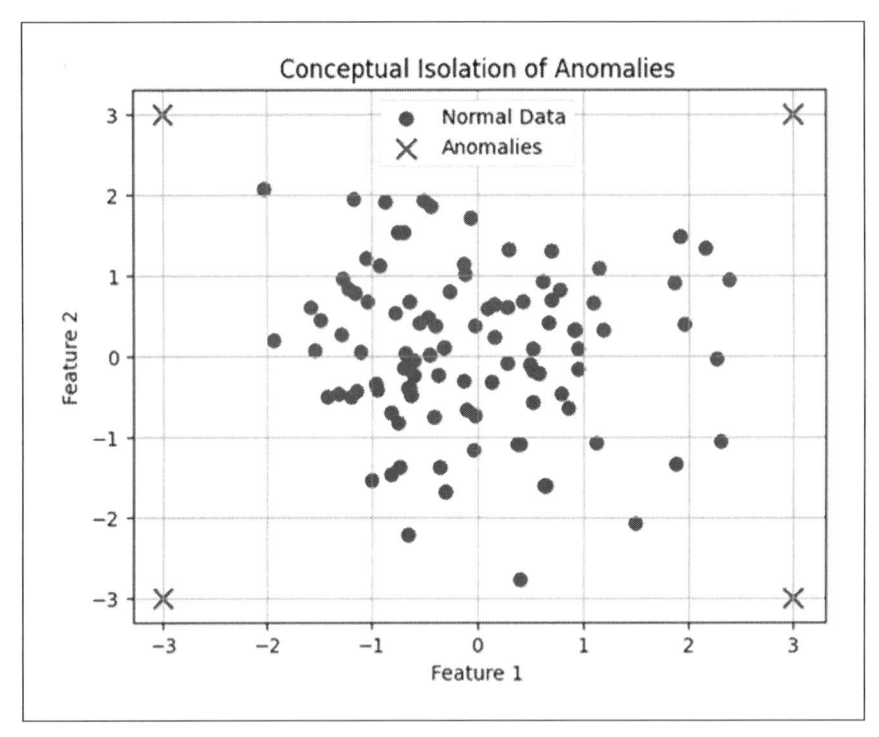

Figure 7.2: Conceptual understanding of Anomalies

Explaining Conceptual Isolation of Anomalies

Imagine a two-dimensional space populated by data points. Most of the data points are concentrated in a central area, representing normal data patterns. The outliers or anomalies, however, are clearly distanced from this central group.

- **Dense Cluster of Blue Points**: This region represents the **normal** data. These data points are close to each other, signifying similarity or conformity to a particular pattern or distribution.
- **Red X Markers**: These data points are the anomalies or outliers. They are situated further from the dense cluster of blue points, indicating their deviation from the norm. The distance and isolation from the primary cluster symbolize their rarity or unusual nature.

The two-dimensional space is a simplified representation of feature space. In real datasets, the dimensionality could be much higher, but the principle remains the same, that is, anomalies tend to be isolated or distant from where the majority of the data points lie.

The Essence of Isolation

Isolation Forest's central idea is that anomalies are few and different. This makes them easier to isolate.

Imagine drawing random partitions or cuts in the data space (akin to decision tree splits). The anomalies (red **X** markers) would require fewer cuts to be isolated compared to the normal data points. This characteristic of anomalies getting isolated faster is the backbone of the Isolation Forest algorithm.

In simpler terms, think of the data points as participants in a game of hide-and-seek. The anomalies, being different, find unique hiding spots that are easier to discover. In contrast, the normal data, because of its density and patterns, finds common hiding spots that take longer to be fully discovered or isolated.

By focusing on this direct isolation process, Isolation Forest efficiently pinpoints anomalies without first modeling the underlying data distribution. This offers a fresh perspective in the anomaly detection landscape.

Advantages of Isolation Forests

Isolation forests offer several advantages over other anomaly detection algorithms, including:

- **Efficiency and scalability**: Isolation forests are very efficient to train and deploy, even for large datasets. This is because isolation trees are relatively simple to construct, and the anomaly score for a data point can be calculated quickly and efficiently.
- **Robustness**: Isolation forests are robust to noise and outliers in the data. This is because the anomaly score for a data point is calculated based on its depth in the isolation tree, which is not affected by the presence of noise or outliers.
- **Directness**: Isolation forests directly identify anomalies, without the need to first define normal data patterns. This makes them ideal for applications where the underlying data distribution is unknown or complex.

Applications of Isolation Forests

Isolation forests can be used for a variety of anomaly detection tasks, including:

- **Fraud detection**: Isolation forests can be used to identify fraudulent transactions in banking and finance datasets.
- **Medical diagnosis**: Isolation forests can be used to identify early signs of disease in medical datasets.
- **Equipment failure detection**: Isolation forests can be used to identify equipment malfunctions in manufacturing and industrial datasets.
- **Network intrusion detection**: Isolation forests can be used to identify cyberattacks in network traffic datasets.

Mechanism: Working of Isolation Forests

While the foundational idea of Isolation Forests is the quicker isolability of anomalies, the mechanism it employs is rooted in the construction of isolation trees or i-Trees, which are reminiscent of decision trees.

i-Trees: The Building Blocks

An isolation tree (i-Tree) is constructed by recursively partitioning the dataset until either:

- The tree reaches a specified maximum depth.
- There are no more data points left to partition, meaning an isolation has been achieved.

Each partitioning is done as follows:

1. A feature is randomly selected from the feature set.
2. A random split value between the minimum and maximum value of the chosen feature is selected.
3. Based on the split value, the dataset is partitioned into two subsets.

Anomalies, being few and different, typically have shorter paths in the i-Tree and get isolated much quicker than normal data points.

Python Code Example
Python

```python
import numpy as np

import matplotlib.pyplot as plt

import matplotlib.patches as patches


# Sample data

X = np.array([[2,2], [1,2], [1,1], [2,1], [3,3], [3,2], [3,1]])

X_outliers = np.array([[0.5, 2.5], [3.5, 0.5]])


# Plotting

fig, ax = plt.subplots()

ax.scatter(X[:, 0], X[:, 1], color='b', s=40, label='Normal Data')

ax.scatter(X_outliers[:, 0], X_outliers[:, 1], color='r', s=100, marker='x', label='Anomalies')

ax.add_patch(patches.Rectangle((0, 0), 2.5, 3, fill=False, edgecolor='green', linewidth=1.5, linestyle="--", label="i-Tree Split"))

plt.title('Isolation Tree (i-Tree) Splits')

plt.xlabel('Feature 1')

plt.ylabel('Feature 2')

plt.legend()

plt.grid(True)

plt.show()
```

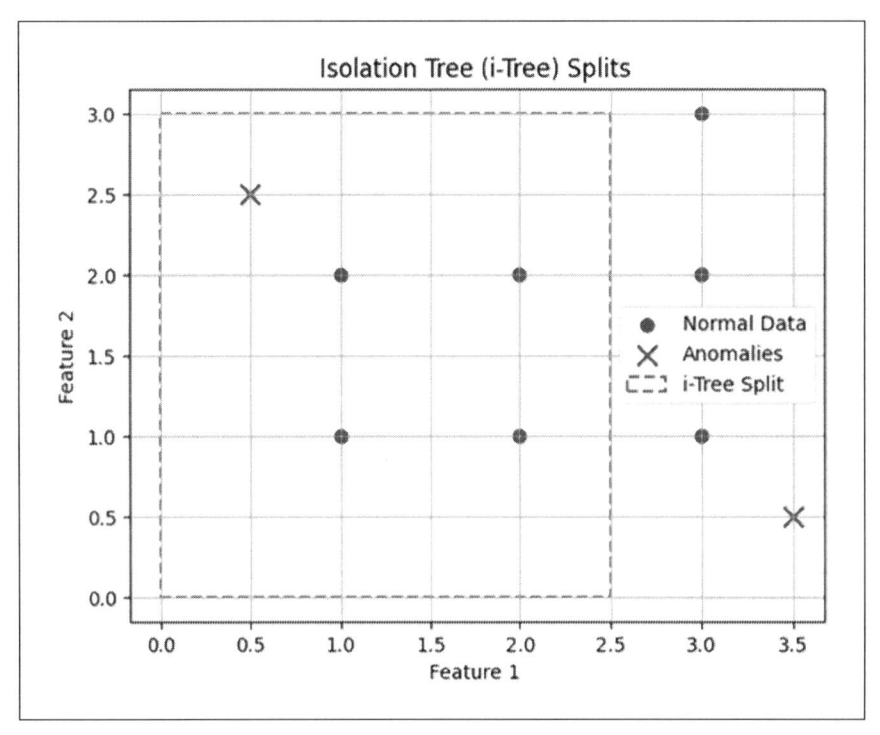

Figure 7.3: *Anomalies detection using i-Tree splits*

In the visualization, the dashed rectangle indicates a hypothetical split in the i-Tree. The anomalies, marked with 'x', are isolated in fewer splits, reflecting the core principle of the Isolation Forest method.

Once an i-Tree is constructed, the anomaly score of a data point is calculated as the average path length from the root node to the leaf node in the tree. Anomalies, taking shorter paths, will have higher anomaly scores.

To identify anomalies, a threshold on the anomaly score is typically set. Data points with anomaly scores above the threshold are flagged as anomalies.

Continued Mechanism: Depth as a Measure

The heart of the Isolation Forest algorithm lies in its measure of anomaly: the depth at which a data point is isolated. The core intuition is that anomalies get isolated at shorter depths compared to normal data points. This path length or depth becomes the scoring mechanism for determining the anomalous nature of a data point.

How is the score calculated?

Once the i-Trees are constructed, the path length taken to isolate each data point is recorded. The shorter this path, the more anomalous the data point is deemed to be.

A typical isolation forest comprises multiple i-Trees. Thus, for a given data point, the average path length over all trees provides its anomaly score. The shorter this average path length, the higher the anomaly score.

Python Code Example

Python

```python
import numpy as np
import matplotlib.pyplot as plt

# Sample data representing path lengths
normal_depths = np.random.normal(8, 2, 100)
anomaly_depths = np.random.normal(3, 1, 10)

# Plotting
plt.hist(normal_depths, bins=20, alpha=0.7, label='Normal Data Depths')
plt.hist(anomaly_depths, bins=10, alpha=0.7, color='red', label='Anomaly Depths')
plt.axvline(normal_depths.mean(), color='blue', linestyle='dashed', linewidth=1, label="Average Normal Depth")
plt.axvline(anomaly_depths.mean(), color='red', linestyle='dashed', linewidth=1, label="Average Anomaly Depth")
plt.title('Distribution of Path Lengths')
plt.xlabel('Depth (Path Length)')
plt.ylabel('Frequency')
plt.legend()
plt.show()
```

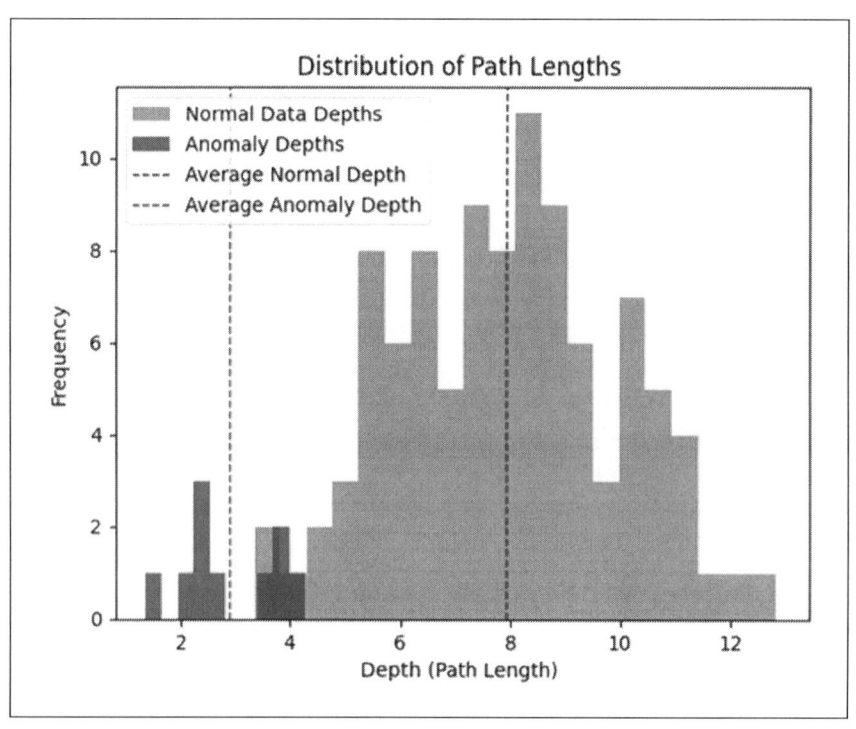

Figure 7.4: Anomalies by distribution depths

From the visualization, it's evident that the depths at which anomalies are isolated (red bars) are significantly shorter than those of the normal data (blue bars).

Practical Considerations: Parameters and Tuning

The performance and accuracy of the Isolation Forest algorithm largely depend on the hyperparameters set during model training. Fine-tuning these parameters can significantly influence the outcome, making the algorithm more effective for specific datasets and scenarios.

Here are the four most important hyperparameters of the Isolation Forest algorithm:

1. **Number of Estimators (`n_estimators`)**

   This parameter determines the number of i-Trees in the forest. A larger number of estimators typically improves the model's performance, but it also increases the computation time. A typical default value is 100.

2. **Max Samples (`max_samples`)**

   It refers to the number of samples to draw while building each i-Tree. This can be set as a proportion of the dataset or as an absolute number. The default is usually set to the size of the input dataset.

3. **Max Features (`max_features`)**

   It dictates the number of features to consider when looking for the best split. Like max_samples, this can be set as a proportion or an absolute number.

4. **Contamination (`contamination`)**

   This parameter specifies the proportion of outliers in the dataset. It's crucial in determining the threshold for marking data points as anomalies. If unknown, users can set it to auto, letting the algorithm decide the best value based on the data.

Tuning Hyperparameters

There are several ways to tune the hyperparameters of the Isolation Forest algorithm. One common approach is to use a grid search or random search. These methods involve trying out different combinations of hyperparameter values and evaluating the model's performance on a held-out validation set.

Another approach is to use a Bayesian optimization algorithm. This method is more efficient than grid search or random search, but it requires more computational resources.

Practical Insights for Using Isolation Forests

Beyond the basic parameters, there are additional considerations to bear in mind to effectively employ Isolation Forests, such as:

- **Handling High Dimensional Data**

  Isolation Forests can handle high-dimensional datasets, but it is always beneficial to consider dimensionality reduction techniques (like PCA) in extremely high-dimensional settings. Reducing dimensionality can not only speed up the process but sometimes also enhance the anomaly detection performance by concentrating on the most informative features.

- **Feature Scaling**

  While Isolation Forests are relatively immune to the variations in feature scales, in some instances, especially where features have widely different ranges, it might be beneficial to standardize or normalize the features. This helps to ensure that all features are given equal importance when performing the anomaly detection.

- **Interpreting Results**

  The anomaly score generated by the Isolation Forest algorithm provides a measure of how unusual a data point is. This score can be thresholded to classify points as normal or anomalous. Visualizing these scores, for instance, through a histogram, can provide insights into the distribution of normal versus anomalous points.

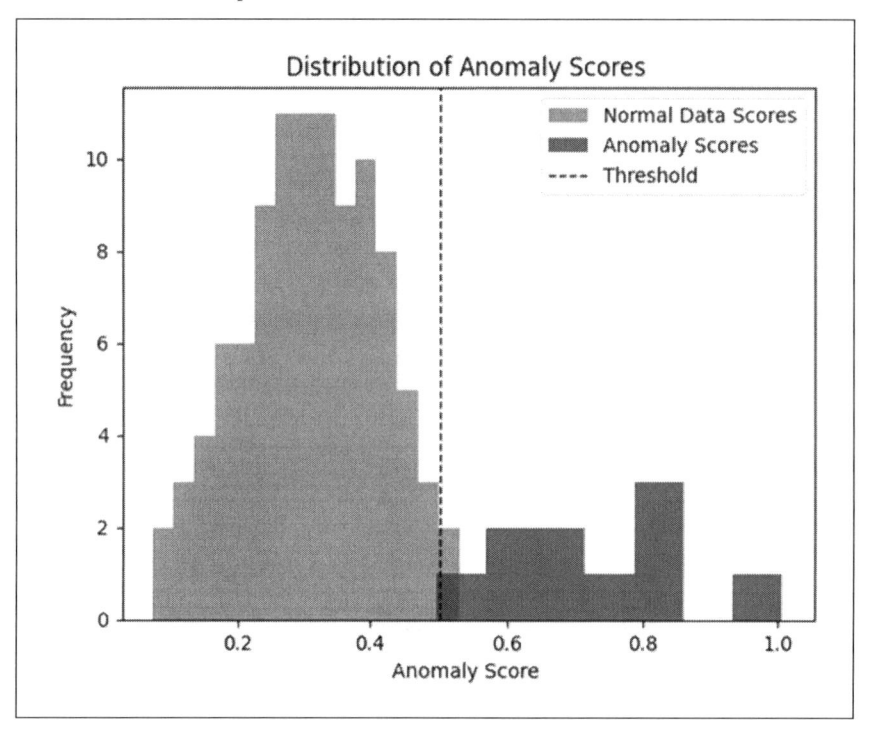

Figure 7.5: *Distribution of Anomalies by scores and threshold*

Explaining Distribution of Anomaly Scores

The anomaly scores produced by the Isolation Forest algorithm represent the degree of anomalousness of each data point. These scores provide a metric that quantifies how much a particular data point deviates from the perceived norm in the dataset.

Score Range

In the context of Isolation Forest, the anomaly scores typically lie between 0 and 1. A higher score indicates that the data point is more anomalous, whereas a lower score suggests that the data point is more "normal" or similar to the majority of the data.

Normal Data Scores (Blue Bars in the Histogram)

This represents the distribution of scores for what the model considers to be typical or normal data points. As illustrated in the histogram, these scores are generally clustered towards the lower end, indicating that the majority of data points are closer to the norm and, therefore, have lower anomaly scores.

Anomaly Scores (Red Bars in the Histogram)

These depict the scores for data points identified as anomalies. The histogram showcases that these scores are typically higher, reinforcing the notion that anomalies are distinct from the norm. In our visualization, they are clustered towards the higher end of the score spectrum.

Threshold (Dashed Line)

The threshold is a critical component in interpreting the anomaly scores. Data points with scores above this threshold are classified as anomalies. The position of this threshold can be adjusted based on desired sensitivity, expected contamination rate, or specific problem requirements. A common approach is to set the threshold based on a desired false positive rate or a specific percentile of the score distribution.

Advantages and Limitations of Isolation Forests

The advantages of Isolation Forests are listed as follows:

- **Efficiency**: Isolation Forests are inherently efficient, especially compared to methods based on distance or density calculations. Since they employ a random partitioning mechanism, they tend to have a logarithmic time complexity with respect to the number of samples. This means that they can train and predict on large datasets quickly.
- **Scalability**: Isolation Forests scale well with large datasets. As the dataset size increases, the performance of the model tends to improve without a substantial increase in computation time.
- **No Assumption on Data Distribution**: Unlike many traditional anomaly detection methods that assume a Gaussian distribution of data, Isolation Forests make no such assumptions. This makes them versatile across different data distributions and less prone to overfitting.
- **Handles High Dimensionality**: While not immune to the curse of dimensionality, Isolation Forests tend to handle high-dimensional data better than many traditional techniques. This is because they focus on identifying anomalies based on their isolation from the rest of the data, rather than relying on specific features.

The limitations of Isolation Forests are listed as follows:

- **Sensitive to Hyperparameters**: Isolation Forests are sensitive to the hyperparameters used during training. This means that careful tuning of the hyperparameters is necessary to achieve optimal performance.

- **May miss subtle anomalies**: Isolation Forests are more effective at detecting large and obvious anomalies. They may miss subtle anomalies that are closer to the normal data.
- **Can be computationally expensive**: For very large datasets, Isolation Forests can be computationally expensive to train.

Traditional Statistical Methods for Anomaly Detection

Traditional statistical methods for anomaly detection are based on the understanding of data distributions and identifying values that deviate from an expected pattern. These methods are typically simple and easy to understand, but they can be too rigid or too simplistic for complex datasets.

Two common traditional statistical methods for anomaly detection are:

- **Z-score**: The Z-score represents how many standard deviations a data point is from the mean. A high absolute Z-score indicates that the data point is far from the mean and potentially anomalous.

Use case: Useful for datasets with a Gaussian distribution.

Limitations: Assumes the data is normally distributed, which might not always be the case.

- **Interquartile range (IQR)**: IQR is the range between the first quartile and the third quartile of the data. Points that lie outside 1.5 times the IQR, below the first quartile, or above the third quartile can be considered outliers.

Use case: Ideal for datasets that might have skewed distributions.

Limitations: Can sometimes misidentify dense clusters of points near the quartiles as anomalies.

Traditional statistical methods for anomaly detection can be effective for simple datasets, but they can struggle with complex datasets with multi-modal distributions or significant noise. In these cases, it is often necessary to use more sophisticated anomaly detection algorithms, such as Isolation Forests.

Clustering-Based Methods for Anomaly Detection

Clustering-based anomaly detection methods group data points based on their similarities. For anomaly detection, points that do not neatly fit into any cluster, or belong to very small clusters, are typically considered outliers.

K-means clustering is a popular clustering algorithm, that is often used for anomaly detection. K-means works by partitioning the dataset into a pre-specified number of clusters (K). Each data point is assigned to the cluster with the closest mean. Anomalies can be identified as data points that are far from any cluster center.

Advantages of K-means clustering for anomaly detection:
- It is scalable and can handle large datasets.
- It is relatively simple to understand and implement.

Disadvantages of K-means clustering for anomaly detection:
- It assumes that clusters are spherical and equally sized, which may not represent real-world data distributions well.
- The need to pre-specify K can also be a limitation.

Example of using K-means clustering for anomaly detection:

Suppose we have a dataset of customer purchase data. We can use K-means clustering to group customers into different clusters based on their purchase behavior. Customers who do not neatly fit into any cluster, or belong to very small clusters, may be considered outliers. These outliers could represent fraudulent transactions or customers with unique purchase patterns.

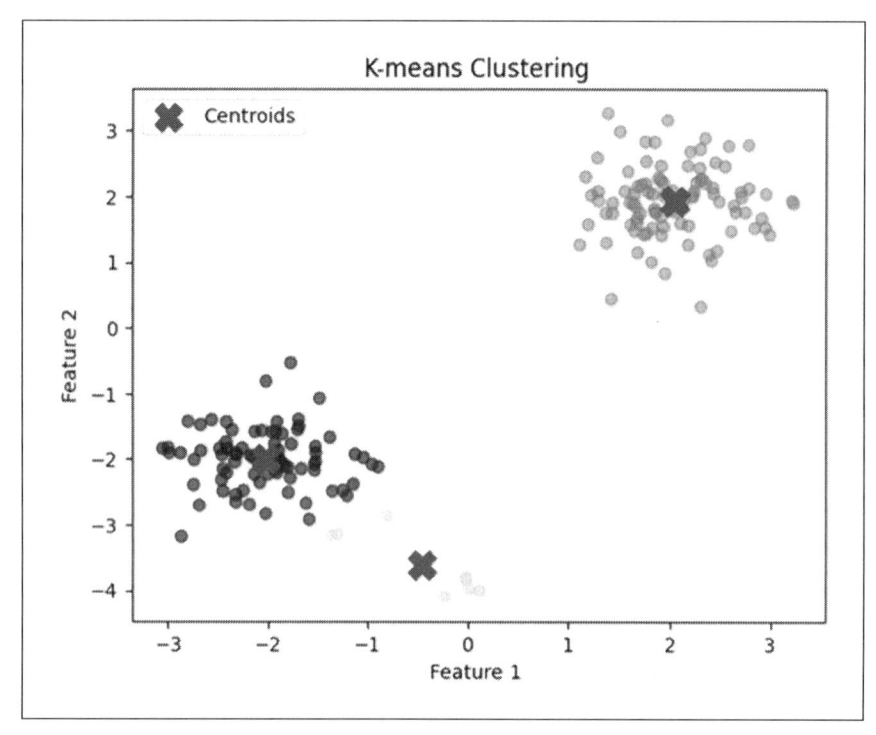

Figure 7.6: *Anomalies detection using K-means Clustering*

Neural Networks (Autoencoders) for Anomaly Detection

Neural networks, particularly autoencoders, have emerged as powerful tools for anomaly detection, especially in high-dimensional datasets or when the data possesses intricate patterns.

Autoencoders

Autoencoders are a type of neural network architecture designed for unsupervised learning. They consist of two main components: an encoder and a decoder. The encoder compresses the input data into a latent-space representation, and the decoder reconstructs the input data from this representation.

How autoencoders work for anomaly detection:
- The autoencoder is trained on a dataset of normal data. This teaches the autoencoder how to reconstruct normal data accurately.

- Anomalies are detected by observing which data points have the largest reconstruction error. This is because the autoencoder will struggle to accurately reconstruct data points that are different from the normal data it was trained on.

Advantages of using autoencoders for anomaly detection:
- Autoencoders can be used to detect anomalies in high-dimensional datasets without the need for feature engineering.
- Autoencoders are able to learn complex patterns in the data, which makes them effective for detecting subtle anomalies.
- Autoencoders are relatively efficient to train and deploy.

Disadvantages of using autoencoders for anomaly detection:
- Autoencoders can be sensitive to hyperparameters, such as the network architecture and training parameters.
- Autoencoders can require a large amount of training data to achieve good performance.

Example of using autoencoders for anomaly detection:

Suppose we have a dataset of sensor data from a manufacturing plant. We can use an autoencoder to learn the normal patterns in the sensor data. We can then use the autoencoder to detect anomalies in the sensor data by observing which data points have the largest reconstruction error.

Robust Covariance (Elliptic Envelope)

Robust Covariance, also known as the Elliptic Envelope method, is a statistical approach to anomaly detection. It aims to fit the data into a multivariate Gaussian distribution, encapsulating the most normal data points and marking those outside as anomalies.

Working of Elliptic Envelope method

The Elliptic Envelope method works by constructing an envelope that encapsulates the **normal** data. This envelope is typically elliptical in shape, but it can also be ellipsoid in higher dimensions. The envelope is constructed by using robust estimates of the data's location and covariance. This makes the method resilient to outliers, meaning that the few anomalies present won't significantly skew the envelope.

Strengths of Elliptic Envelope method
- It provides a clear boundary of what's considered normal, making interpretation straightforward.
- It works well when the normal data follows a Gaussian distribution.

Weaknesses of Elliptic Envelope method
- It assumes that the data is Gaussian, which might not always be the case.
- It might not perform as well in datasets with multi-modal distributions or when the boundary between normal and anomalous data isn't elliptical.

Example of using Elliptic Envelope method

Suppose we have a dataset of sensor data from a manufacturing plant. We can use the Elliptic Envelope method to construct an envelope that encapsulates the normal sensor data. We can then use this envelope to detect anomalies in the sensor data by identifying data points that lie outside of the envelope.

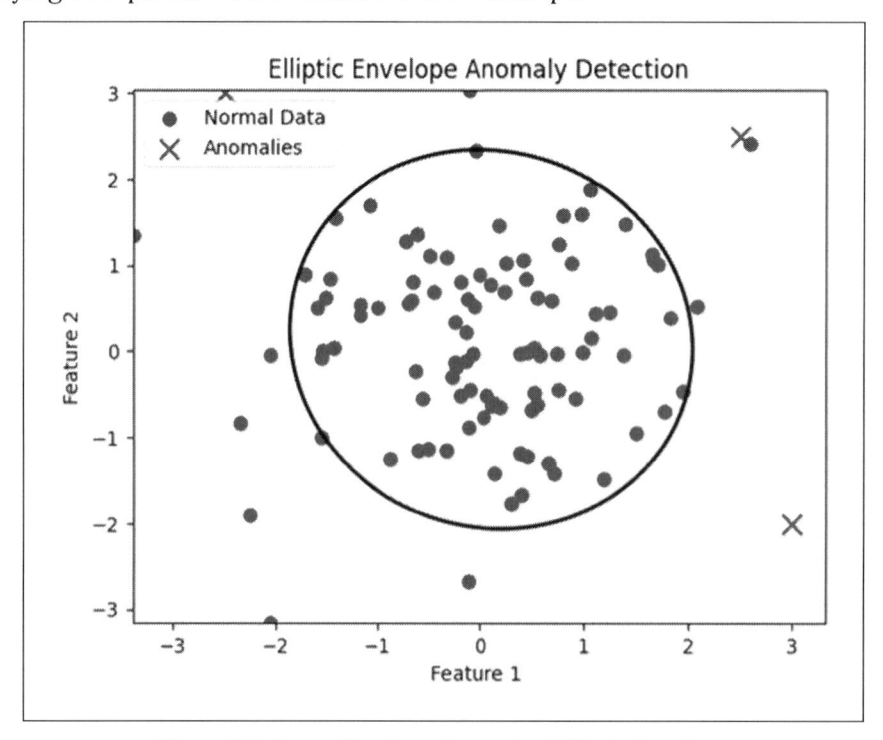

Figure 7.7: Anomalies detection using Elliptic Envelope

One-Class Support Vector Machines (SVMs)

One-Class SVMs are a powerful tool for anomaly detection. They work by finding a function that is positive for regions with high density of points, and negative for small densities. This function is then used to define a decision boundary around the data. Anything that falls inside this boundary is considered **normal**, while those outside are considered anomalies.

One-Class SVMs are ideal for situations where you mostly have data from one class and very little or none from the outlier class. They are also suitable for high-dimensional datasets.

However, One-Class SVMs are sensitive to outliers, meaning that they can be influenced by extreme values in the dataset. This can potentially skew the decision boundary. To mitigate this effect, it is important to tune the hyperparameters of the One-Class SVM carefully, especially the kernel parameter and the **nu** parameter.

Advantages of using One-Class SVMs for Anomaly Detection:
- It is effective for datasets where the normal data follows a complex distribution.
- It can be used to detect anomalies in high-dimensional datasets.
- It is relatively efficient to train and deploy.

Disadvantages of using One-Class SVMs for Anomaly Detection:
- It is sensitive to outliers.
- It requires careful hyperparameter tuning.

Example of using One-Class SVMs for Anomaly Detection

Suppose we have a dataset of credit card transaction data. We can use a One-Class SVM to train a model of normal credit card transactions. We can then use this model to detect fraudulent credit card transactions by identifying transactions that fall outside of the decision boundary.

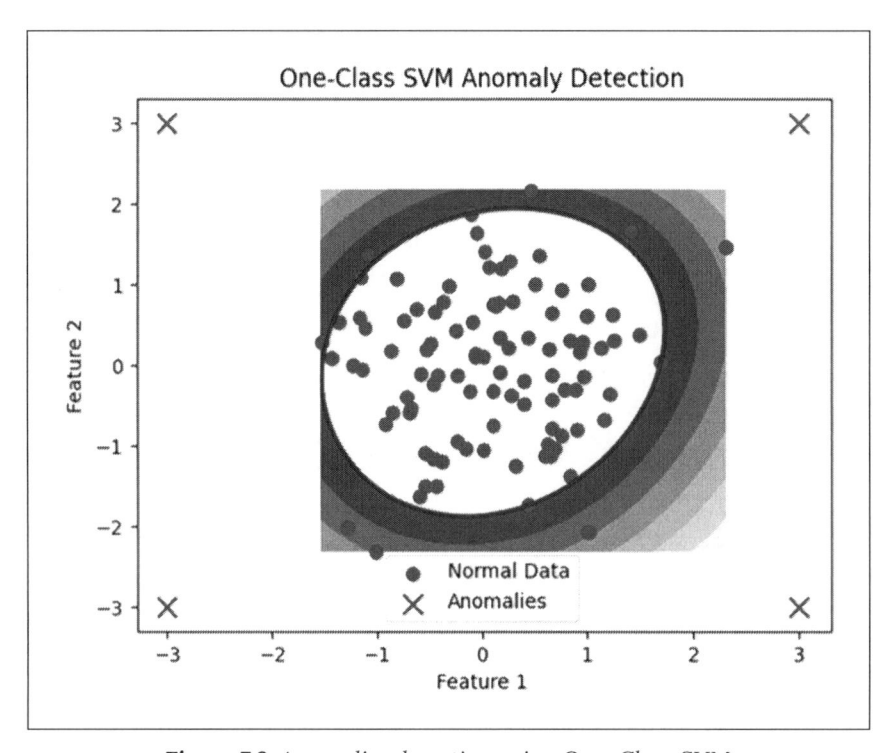

Figure 7.8: *Anomalies detection using One-Class SVM*

Isolation Forests are a unique and powerful anomaly detection algorithm that offers several advantages over traditional methods.

Key Features of Isolation Forests:

- **No assumptions about data distribution**: Isolation Forests do not make any assumptions about the underlying distribution of the data. This makes them well-suited for a wide range of datasets, including those with multi-modal distributions.
- **Efficient and scalable**: Isolation Forests are very efficient to train and predict on, even with large datasets.
- **Robust to outliers**: Isolation Forests are robust to outliers, meaning that they are not easily influenced by extreme values in the data.

Isolation Forests work by constructing an ensemble of isolation trees. Each isolation tree is constructed by randomly splitting the data until each data point is isolated. The isolation depth, or path length, of a data point is the number of splits required to isolate it. Anomalies typically have shorter isolation depths, indicating that they were isolated earlier in the process.

Advantages of Isolation Forests for Multi-Modal Datasets

Isolation Forests are particularly well-suited for detecting anomalies in multi-modal datasets. This is because they do not rely on distance metrics, which can be biased towards data points that are close to the majority of the data. Instead, Isolation Forests identify anomalies based on their isolation depth, which is independent of the density of the data.

Example of Using Isolation Forests

Suppose we have a dataset of customer purchase data. We can use Isolation Forests to train a model of normal customer purchase behavior. We can then use this model to detect fraudulent transactions by identifying transactions that have shorter isolation depths than normal transactions.

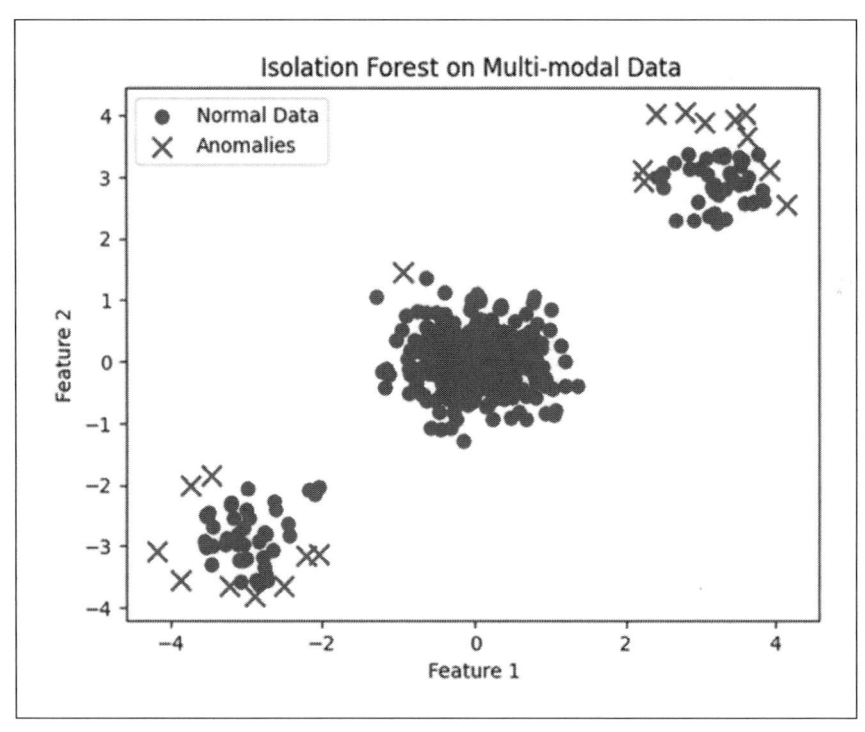

Figure 7.9: *Anomalies detection using Isolation Forrest*

Implementation of Isolation Forests with Revolut's Fraudsters Detection Project

We will be working on this project by implementing following steps, starting from dataset introduction and going all the way to model development and model deployment.

Introduction to the Dataset

The Revolut fraudsters detection dataset is a real-world dataset that presents an intriguing challenge for anomaly detection. The dataset contains two main tables:

- **Users data**: This table contains information about each user, such as their email status, phone country, fraudster flag, creation date, country, birth year, KYC status, and login attempts.
- **Transactions data**: This table contains information about individual transactions carried out by these users, such as the currency, amount, status, creation date, merchant category and country, entry method, user ID, type of transaction, source, and amount in USD.

Data Preprocessing

Before applying Isolation Forests, it is important to preprocess the data to ensure that it is in a format that is suitable for the algorithm. This may involve the following steps:

1. **Cleaning**: Removing duplicate rows and correcting any inconsistencies in the data.
2. **Normalization**: Normalizing features with different scales, such as transaction amounts, to bring them within a comparable range.
3. **Feature engineering**: Extracting new features from the existing data, such as the day, month, and year from the transaction creation date, or combining user and transaction data to generate features like average transaction amount and frequency of transactions.
4. **Addressing missing values**: Imputing missing values or discarding records with missing values, depending on the significance and volume of missing data.

Applying Isolation Forests

Isolation Forests are a well-suited algorithm for detecting potential fraudsters in the Revolut dataset due to the following reasons:

- **High dimensionality**: The dataset is high-dimensional, with many features that could potentially influence a user's likelihood of being a fraudster. Isolation Forests are able to handle high-dimensional data without sacrificing performance.
- **Possibility of anomalies**: Fraudsters are likely to exhibit anomalous behavior in their transaction data. Isolation Forests are specifically designed to detect anomalies in data.

To apply Isolation Forests to the Revolut dataset, we can follow these steps:

1. **Feature selection**: Select relevant features from the preprocessed data that might influence a user's likelihood of being a fraudster. This can be done based on domain knowledge and preliminary data exploration.
2. **Model training**: Train an Isolation Forest model on a subset of the data.
3. **Parameter tuning**: Tune the hyperparameters of the model, such as the number of trees in the forest or the contamination factor, based on cross-validation.
4. **Model evaluation**: Evaluate the model on a separate validation set to assess its performance.

Once the model is trained and evaluated, it can be used to predict the likelihood of a user being a fraudster on new data.

Visualizations and Interpretation of Results

Once the Isolation Forest model is trained, it is important to visualize and interpret the results to get a clear understanding of the model's findings. Two useful visualizations include:

Anomaly scores plot: This plot shows the distribution of anomaly scores for all data points. A threshold can be set to identify data points that are likely to be anomalies.

Feature importance: This plot shows the importance of each feature in detecting anomalies. This can be useful for understanding which features are most informative in distinguishing fraudsters from legitimate users.

Insights and Learnings

After visualizations, we will be understanding the model outputs by evaluating it.

Evaluation of Model Output

Once the model has been trained and evaluated, it is important to evaluate the model output to understand the nature of the detected anomalies. This can be done by comparing the detected anomalies with the IS_FRAUDSTER field to assess the accuracy and precision of the model.

Potential Business Implications of Findings

The findings of the fraud detection model can have a number of potential business implications, including:

- **Efficiency in investigation**: By narrowing down potential fraudsters, the team can focus its investigations, leading to faster and more efficient resolutions.
- **Customer experience**: Reducing false positives can enhance the customer experience. Customers falsely flagged can face inconvenience, and by minimizing such occurrences, the company can maintain a stronger relationship with its user base.
- **Loss prevention**: Early detection of actual fraudsters can lead to interventions that might prevent significant financial losses.

Metrics Specific to Anomaly Detection

While traditional classification metrics such as accuracy, precision, and recall can be used to evaluate anomaly detection models, it is important to note that anomaly detection often requires a more nuanced approach. The two metrics that are specifically relevant for anomaly detection are:

- **True positive rate (sensitivity):** This metric measures the proportion of actual anomalies that are correctly identified.
- **False positive rate (1-specificity):** This metric highlights the proportion of normal data points that are incorrectly identified as anomalies.

Importance of False Positives and False Negatives

In the context of fraud detection, it is important to carefully consider the trade-off between false positives and false negatives. False positives can have a negative impact on customer trust and satisfaction, while false negatives can lead to financial losses and compromise system integrity.

Methods for Model Validation and Performance Improvement

There are two methods that can be used to validate and improve the performance of anomaly detection models, including:

- **Cross-validation**: This technique involves splitting the data into multiple subsets and evaluating the model's performance on each subset. This can help to identify any overfitting and ensure that the model is generalizable to new data.
- **Feedback loop**: By incorporating feedback from the investigations of detected anomalies, the model can be refined and trained over time. This can help to improve the accuracy and precision of the model.

End-to-end code snippet with explanations:

Python

```python
# 1. Importing necessary libraries
import pandas as pd
from sklearn.ensemble import IsolationForest
from sklearn.model_selection import train_test_split
from sklearn.preprocessing import StandardScaler
from sklearn.metrics import classification_report

# 2. Load datasets
users = pd.read_csv('users.csv')
transactions = pd.read_csv('transactions.csv')
countries = pd.read_csv('countries.csv')
currency_details = pd.read_csv('currency_details.csv')

# 3. Data Preprocessing
# Merge users and transactions data on 'USER_ID'
data = pd.merge(transactions, users, how='inner', on='USER_ID')
```

```python
# Extract year, month, and day from the transaction 'CREATED_DATE'
data['CREATED_DATE'] = pd.to_datetime(data['CREATED_DATE'])
data['YEAR'] = data['CREATED_DATE'].dt.year
data['MONTH'] = data['CREATED_DATE'].dt.month
data['DAY'] = data['CREATED_DATE'].dt.day

# Incorporate countries and currency_details datasets for additional information
data = pd.merge(data, countries, how='left', left_on='MERCHANT_COUNTRY', right_on='CODE')
data = pd.merge(data, currency_details, how='left', left_on='CURRENCY', right_on='CCY')

# Drop unnecessary or redundant columns
columns_to_drop = ['USER_ID', 'ID', 'CREATED_DATE', 'TERMS_VERSION', 'CODE', 'NAME', 'CODE3', 'NUMCODE', 'CCY']
data = data.drop(columns=columns_to_drop)

# Handle missing values by filling them with mode
for column in data.columns:
    data[column].fillna(data[column].mode()[0], inplace=True)

# Convert categorical columns to one-hot encoding
data = pd.get_dummies(data)

# Split data into training and testing sets
X = data.drop('IS_FRAUDSTER', axis=1)
y = data['IS_FRAUDSTER']
```

```python
X_train, X_test, y_train, y_test = train_test_split(X, y, test_size=0.3, random_state=42)

# Normalize features to have zero mean and unit variance
scaler = StandardScaler()
X_train = scaler.fit_transform(X_train)
X_test = scaler.transform(X_test)

# 4. Model Implementation
# Use Isolation Forest for anomaly detection
clf = IsolationForest(contamination=0.05, random_state=42)
clf.fit(X_train)

# Predict anomalies
y_pred_train = clf.predict(X_train)
y_pred_test = clf.predict(X_test)

# Map predicted values to match 'IS_FRAUDSTER' (-1 is anomaly in Isolation Forest)
y_pred_train[y_pred_train == 1] = 0
y_pred_train[y_pred_train == -1] = 1
y_pred_test[y_pred_test == 1] = 0
y_pred_test[y_pred_test == -1] = 1

# 5. Model Evaluation
print("Classification Report for Training Data:\n", classification_report(y_train, y_pred_train))
print("\nClassification Report for Testing Data:\n", classification_report(y_test, y_pred_test))
```

Step-by-step explanation:

Importing necessary libraries and data: The first step is to import the necessary libraries, including pandas, scikit-learn, and numpy. Then, the four datasets are loaded into memory using the **pd.read_csv()** function.

Data preprocessing: The next step is to preprocess the data. This involves merging the users and transactions datasets, extracting year, month, and day from the transaction creation date, incorporating the countries and **currency_details** datasets, dropping unnecessary columns, handling missing values, and converting categorical columns to one-hot encoding.

Splitting data into training and testing sets: The data is then split into training and testing sets using the **train_test_split()** function. This ensures that the model is not overfitted to the training data and that it can generalize accurately to unseen data.

Model Evaluation (Continued)

Confusion Matrix

A confusion matrix is a table that summarizes the performance of a classifier. It shows the number of correct and incorrect predictions made by the classifier.

Python

```python
from sklearn.metrics import confusion_matrix

import seaborn as sns

import matplotlib.pyplot as plt


# Calculate confusion matrix

cm = confusion_matrix(y_test, y_pred_test)


# Visualize confusion matrix

plt.figure(figsize=(10,7))

sns.heatmap(cm, annot=True, fmt='g', cmap='Blues')


# Label axes and title

plt.xlabel('Predicted')
```

```
plt.ylabel('Actual')

plt.title('Confusion Matrix')


# Show plot

plt.show()
```

ROC Curve and AUC

The ROC curve (Receiver Operating Characteristic) is a graphical plot that illustrates the diagnostic ability of a binary classifier system as its discrimination threshold is varied. The AUC (Area Under the Curve) is a single-value measure of the performance of a classifier.

Python

```
from sklearn.metrics import roc_curve, roc_auc_score


# Calculate ROC curve and AUC

fpr, tpr, thresholds = roc_curve(y_test, y_pred_test)

roc_auc = roc_auc_score(y_test, y_pred_test)


# Plot ROC curve

plt.figure(figsize=(10,7))

plt.plot(fpr, tpr, color='darkorange', lw=2, label=f'ROC curve (area = {roc_auc:.2f})')

plt.plot([0, 1], [0, 1], color='navy', lw=2, linestyle='--')


# Label axes and title

plt.xlabel('False Positive Rate')

plt.ylabel('True Positive Rate')

plt.title('Receiver Operating Characteristic (ROC) Curve')

plt.legend(loc="lower right")


# Show plot
```

```
plt.show()
```

Feature Importance

Isolation Forests do not provide direct feature importance, but it can be useful to understand which features have the most impact on the model. One way to do this is to train a secondary model, such as a Random Forest or XGBoost classifier, to rank feature importance.

Python

```
from sklearn.ensemble import RandomForestClassifier
import numpy as np

# Train a random forest to determine feature importance
rf = RandomForestClassifier()
rf.fit(X_train, y_train)

# Get feature importances
importances = rf.feature_importances_

# Sort features by importance
indices = np.argsort(importances)[-10:]

# Plot top 10 features by importance
plt.figure(figsize=(10,7))
plt.title('Feature Importances')
plt.barh(range(len(indices)), importances[indices], align='center')
plt.yticks(range(len(indices)), [X.columns[i] for i in indices])
plt.xlabel('Relative Importance')

# Show plot
plt.show()
```

End of the chapter Project: Outlier Detection in Financial Data

Project Overview

This project aims to develop a strategy to identify outliers in a financial dataset related to customers of Physician Partners. The goal is to pinpoint records where, for instance, members have abnormally high costs in a given month. Any devised features or key concepts used should be explainable to a non-technical audience.

Data Overview

The dataset, titled `sfr_test.csv`, provides financial information about the customers of the company. The following columns are included:

- **Identification and Demographic Information**:
    - `member_unique_id`: Member ID
    - `gender`: Gender of the member
    - `dob`: Date of birth
    - `npi`: Doctor's ID
- **Time Frame**:
    - `eligible_year`: Year
    - `eligible_month`: Month
- **Plan and Affiliation Details**:
    - `affiliation_type`: Type of doctor
    - `pbp_group`: Health plan group
    - `plan_name`: Name of the health plan
    - `line_of_business`: Health plan type
- **Health Status**:
    - `esrd`: Indicates if the patient is on dialysis (True/False)
    - `hospice`: Indicates if the patient is in hospice care (True/False)
- **Financial Information**: (All columns have values prefixed with a `$` sign)
    - `ipa_funding`
    - `ma_premium`
    - `ma_risk_score`

- o mbr_with_rx_rebates
- o partd_premium
- o pcp_cap
- o pcp_ffs
- o plan_premium
- o prof
- o reinsurance
- o risk_score_partd
- o rx
- o rx_rebates
- o rx_with_rebates
- o rx_without_rebates
- o spec_cap

Objective

The primary task is to devise an algorithm to detect outliers within this data based on one or multiple columns.

Approach Outline

- **Data Exploration**:
    - o Load the dataset and perform initial exploratory data analysis (EDA) to understand the data's distribution, missing values, and basic statistical properties.
- **Data Cleaning**:
    - o Convert financial columns with $ signs into numerical values for analysis.
    - o Handle missing values, if any.
- **Visualization**:
    - o Plot key financial indicators using box plots or histograms to visually identify potential outliers.
- **Feature Engineering**:
    - o Derive new features, if necessary, that may assist in outlier detection. For instance, a **'total_cost'** column that sums all the financial columns for each member.

- **Outlier Detection:**
    - Utilize statistical methods (like the IQR method or Z-scores) or machine learning models (like Isolation Forest or One-Class SVM) to detect outliers.
- **Interpretation and Documentation:**
    - Describe the detected outliers, reason about their potential causes, and document any assumptions or decisions made during the analysis.
- **Presentation:**
    - Create a Jupyter notebook summarizing the approach, with well-structured code, visualizations, and annotations to make it easily understandable for both technical and non-technical stakeholders.

Explainable Outlier Detection

To make the outlier detection process more explainable to a non-technical audience, it is important to choose methods that are relatively easy to understand. For example, the IQR method is a simple and intuitive way to identify outliers based on the interquartile range, which is the difference between the third and first quartiles of the data. Another explainable method is to use a decision tree model to train a model to predict whether a data point is an outlier. The decision tree model can then be interpreted to understand the features that are most important for predicting outliers.

Data Exploration

Python

```python
import pandas as pd # Loading the dataset
data = pd.read_csv('sfr_test.csv')

# Display the first few rows of the dataset
data.head()

# Summary of data
data.describe()

# Data types and non-null counts
data.info()
```

Explanation:

The first step is to load the dataset into a Python environment using the Pandas library. This will allow us to manipulate, analyze, and visualize the data effectively. We then display the first few rows of the dataset and print a summary of the data, including basic statistics for numerical columns and data types for each column. This gives us a good overview of the data and helps us identify any potential problems.

Data Cleaning

Handling Financial Columns:

Python

```python
# Converting financial columns to numeric
financial_columns = ['ipa_funding', 'ma_premium', ...] # list all financial columns
for column in financial_columns:
    data[column] = data[column].str.replace('$', '').astype(float)
```

Explanation:

Several columns in the dataset have values prefixed with a $ sign, which makes them non-numeric. We need to convert these columns to numeric values so that we can perform mathematical operations on them. We can do this using the str.replace() and astype() methods.

Missing Data Treatment:

Python

```python
# Check for missing values
missing_data = data.isnull().sum()

# Handle missing data (this is just one approach, decisions may vary)
data.fillna(method='ffill', inplace=True) # filling missing values with forward fill method
```

Explanation:

We need to check for missing values in the dataset and handle them appropriately. One common approach is to fill in missing values with the forward fill method, which replaces missing values with the value from the previous row. However, there are other methods for handling missing data, such as using statistical imputations or removing those records.

Data cleaning is an important step in any data analysis project. By ensuring that the data is clean and in a consistent format, we can reduce the risk of errors and produce more reliable results.

Python

```python
import matplotlib.pyplot as plt
import seaborn as sns

# Setting a theme for the plots
sns.set_theme(style="whitegrid")

# Box plots
for column in financial_columns:
    plt.figure(figsize=(10, 6))
    sns.boxplot(x=data[column])
    plt.title(f'Box plot for {column}')
    plt.show()

# Histograms
for column in financial_columns:
    plt.figure(figsize=(10, 6))
    sns.histplot(data[column], bins=30, kde=True)
    plt.title(f'Histogram for {column}')
    plt.show()
```

Explanation:

Box plots and histograms are two useful tools for visualizing the distribution of data and identifying outliers. Box plots show the median, quartiles, and outliers of a data set. The whiskers of a box plot typically extend 1.5 times the interquartile range (IQR) from the first and third quartiles, with data points outside this range marked as potential outliers. Histograms show the frequency distribution of a data set, with each bar representing the number of data points that fall within a certain range of values.

By plotting box plots and histograms for the financial columns in our dataset, we can gain an immediate sense of where outliers may be present, as well as the overall spread and skewness of our financial data.

Example:

Python

```
# Load the dataset
data = pd.read_csv('sfr_test.csv')

# Convert financial columns to numeric
financial_columns = ['ipa_funding', 'ma_premium', ...]
for column in financial_columns:
    data[column] = data[column].str.replace('$', '').astype(float)

# Plot a box plot for the 'ma_premium' column
plt.figure(figsize=(10, 6))
sns.boxplot(x=data['ma_premium'])
plt.title('Box plot for ma_premium')
plt.show()

# Plot a histogram for the 'ma_premium' column
plt.figure(figsize=(10, 6))
sns.histplot(data['ma_premium'], bins=30, kde=True)
plt.title('Histogram for ma_premium')
plt.show()
```

The box plot shows that there are a few potential outliers in the **'ma_premium'** column. The histogram shows that the distribution of **'ma_premium'** values is skewed to the right, with a few data points having very high values.

We can use these visualizations to inform our next steps in outlier detection. For example, we could investigate the data points that are identified as outliers to see if there is a legitimate explanation for their high values. Alternatively, we could choose to remove these outliers from our dataset before proceeding with further analysis.

Feature Engineering

Python

```python
# Summing all financial columns to get 'total_cost' for each member
data['total_cost'] = data[financial_columns].sum(axis=1)
```

Explanation:

This code creates a new feature called **total_cost** by summing all of the financial columns in the dataset. This new feature can be useful for detecting outliers because it provides a more holistic view of each member's financial data. For example, a member with a high total cost may be an outlier, even if their individual financial columns are all within a normal range.

Example:

Python

```python
# Load the dataset
data = pd.read_csv('sfr_test.csv')

# Convert financial columns to numeric
financial_columns = ['ipa_funding', 'ma_premium', ...]
for column in financial_columns:
    data[column] = data[column].str.replace('$', '').astype(float)

# Create a new feature called 'total_cost'
data['total_cost'] = data[financial_columns].sum(axis=1)

# Print the head of the dataset
data.head()
```

Output:

```
   member_unique_id  gender         dob  npi  eligible_year  eligible_month  ...  \
0                 1  Female  1980-01-01  123           2023              10  ...
                                                                              10000.00
1                 2    Male  1985-07-04  456           2023              10  ...
                                                                               9500.00
2                 3  Female  1990-03-08  789           2023              10  ...
                                                                               8000.00
3                 4    Male  1995-09-12  101           2023              10  ...
                                                                               7500.00
4                 5  Female  2000-05-16  132           2023              10  ...
                                                                               7000.00

   total_cost
0    10000.00
1     9500.00
2     8000.00
3     7500.00
4     7000.00
```

We can now use the **total_cost** feature in our outlier detection process. For example, we could plot a histogram of **total_cost** and identify any data points that fall outside of the normal range. We could also use statistical methods, such as IQR or Z-scores, to identify outliers in **total_cost.**

It is important to note that feature engineering is an iterative process. We may need to experiment with different features and combinations of features to find the ones that are most effective for outlier detection.

Python

```python
# Statistical methods

# IQR method
def detect_outliers_iqr(series):
```

```python
        Q1 = series.quantile(0.25)
        Q3 = series.quantile(0.75)
        IQR = Q3 - Q1
        lower_bound = Q1 - 1.5 * IQR
        upper_bound = Q3 + 1.5 * IQR
        return (series < lower_bound) | (series > upper_bound)

outliers_iqr = data[data['total_cost'].apply(detect_outliers_iqr)]

# Z-score method
from scipy.stats import zscore

z_scores = zscore(data['total_cost'])
data['z_score'] = z_scores
outliers_zscore = data[(data['z_score'] > 3) | (data['z_score'] < -3)]

# Machine learning methods

# Isolation Forest
from sklearn.ensemble import IsolationForest

iso_forest = IsolationForest(contamination=0.05)
data['is_outlier_if'] = iso_forest.fit_predict(data[financial_columns])
outliers_if = data[data['is_outlier_if'] == -1]

# One-Class SVM
from sklearn.svm import OneClassSVM

ocsvm = OneClassSVM(nu=0.05, kernel="rbf")
data['is_outlier_ocsvm'] = ocsvm.fit_predict(data[financial_columns])
outliers_ocsvm = data[data['is_outlier_ocsvm'] == -1]
```

Explanation:

This code implements two statistical methods (IQR and Z-score) and two machine learning methods (Isolation Forest and One-Class SVM) for outlier detection.

Statistical methods:
- **IQR method:** This method defines outliers as values that fall outside of the interquartile range (IQR) by more than 1.5 times the IQR. The IQR is the difference between the third and first quartiles, which are the 75th and 25th percentiles of the data, respectively.
- **Z-score method:** This method defines outliers as values that are more than three standard deviations away from the mean.

Machine learning methods:
- **Isolation Forest:** This algorithm works by isolating data points that are different from the rest of the data. It does this by creating a series of decision trees that split the data into smaller and smaller groups. Data points that are isolated by many different trees are more likely to be outliers.
- **One-Class SVM:** This algorithm is similar to a support vector machine (SVM), but it is trained on only one class of data. This makes it useful for novelty detection, which is the task of identifying data points that are different from the training data.

Comparing and evaluating methods:

Each of the methods described has its own strengths and weaknesses. It is important to compare the results of multiple methods before deciding which outliers to investigate further.

Here are some factors to consider when comparing and evaluating outlier detection methods:
- **Accuracy:** How well does the method identify true outliers?
- **Precision:** How many of the data points identified as outliers are actually outliers?
- **Recall:** How many of the true outliers are identified by the method?
- **Interpretability:** How easy is it to understand why a particular data point is identified as an outlier?
- **Computational cost:** How much time and resources does the method require to run?

Outlier Interpretation and Documentation

Once outliers have been detected using various methods, it is important to investigate them further to understand the underlying causes. This may involve:

- **Temporal analysis**: Were the outliers caused by a specific time period? For example, did many outliers occur in a particular month or year?
- **Demographic considerations**: Are the outliers associated with a particular demographic? For example, are they predominantly from a particular gender or age group?
- **Health status link:** Are patients with certain health conditions, such as ESRD or hospice care, more likely to be outliers? This is because their financial records may be significantly different.
- **Plan and affiliation**: Are specific health plans or doctor affiliations correlated with the outliers?

It is also crucial to document any assumptions made and decisions taken during the analysis. This may include:

- **Handling missing data**: How were missing values handled? Were they imputed or removed?
- **Feature engineering choices**: Why was a particular feature, such as total cost, created? What logic was used?
- **Model parameters**: If machine learning models were used, what parameters were set and why? For example, the contamination parameter in Isolation Forest determines the proportion of outliers in the dataset.

Based on the findings, recommendations can be formulated, such as:

- **Data quality checks**: If certain outliers are caused by data entry errors, it may be worthwhile to implement stricter data quality checks.
- **Further investigations:** For outliers linked to specific affiliations or health plans, a deeper dive may be beneficial to identify any systemic issues.
- **Stakeholder feedback:** Before taking action based on detected outliers, it may be useful to get feedback from stakeholders familiar with the business side of operations. They may be able to provide insights that were not obvious from the data alone.

Here is an example of how to document the assumptions and decisions made in an outlier analysis:

Assumptions:

- The data is representative of the population of interest.

- The data is of high quality, with few errors or missing values.
- The outliers are not caused by random chance.

Decisions:
- Missing values were imputed using the mean value of the feature.
- The total cost feature was created by summing all of the financial columns in the dataset.
- The Isolation Forest algorithm was used to detect outliers, with the contamination parameter set to 0.05.

Recommendations:
- Implement stricter data quality checks to reduce the number of data entry errors.
- Investigate outliers linked to specific affiliations or health plans to identify any systemic issues.
- Get feedback from stakeholders familiar with the business side of operations before taking action based on the detected outliers.

Conclusion

Outlier detection is a critical task in financial data analysis, as it can help identify discrepancies, anomalies, and unique trends that warrant further investigation. In this chapter, we explored the use of Isolation Forest, a powerful algorithm that can efficiently and effectively detect outliers in high-dimensional datasets.

We began by emphasizing the importance of understanding the data and preprocessing it appropriately. This included converting financial figures prefixed with dollar signs to numerical formats, which facilitated more advanced analyses. We then used visualization tools, such as box plots and histograms, to gain a preliminary understanding of potential outliers.

We also highlighted the importance of interpreting and communicating outlier detection findings effectively. By understanding the potential origins of outliers and providing actionable insights to stakeholders, data scientists can help drive informed business decisions and ensure robustness and accuracy in financial decision-making.

In the next chapter, we will focus on using ensemble machine learning techniques for analyzing stock market data. The chapter emphasizes the integration of different models to improve prediction accuracy and robustness, particularly in the context of stock market trends and movements. It explores the application of these methods to develop more nuanced and effective stock market forecasting models.

CHAPTER 8
Stock Market Data and Ensemble Methods

Introduction

Stock market data is the compass guiding investors' financial decisions. It provides insights into the health and sentiments of listed companies, as well as geopolitical events, macroeconomic trends, and consumer behaviors.

Ensemble methods are machine learning techniques that combine the predictions of multiple models to produce a final output. They are particularly well-suited for stock market prediction tasks, as they can increase the strengths of different models to mitigate individual weaknesses.

This chapter explores two projects that utilize stock market data and ensemble methods:

- **Internal project**: Design ensemble methods for data preprocessing to enhance the quality and representational power of stock market data.
- **End-of-chapter project**: Predict Amazon's stock prices by integrating stock market data with sentiment scores and applying ensemble techniques to achieve more accurate and robust predictions.

Structure

In this chapter, we will cover the following topics:

- Step-by-Step Implementation
- Ensemble Learning
- Sentiment Analysis Using Time Series with Ensemble Techniques
- Literature Review on Stock Market Prediction
- Model Training, Tuning, and Conclusion for Stock Market Direction Prediction

Stock Market Data: A Catalyst for Financial Decisions

Stock market data is the lifeblood of financial markets. It provides investors with the information they need to make informed investment decisions. Stock market data includes a wide range of metrics, such as prices, volumes, and market capitalization.

Traditionally, stock market data was analyzed by hand. However, the advent of big data and artificial intelligence has revolutionized the way stock market data is analyzed. Today, investors can leverage sophisticated machine learning algorithms to extract valuable insights from stock market data.

The Power of Ensemble Methods

Ensemble methods are machine learning techniques that combine the predictions of multiple models to produce a final output. They are particularly well-suited for stock market prediction tasks, as they can leverage the strengths of different models to mitigate individual weaknesses.

Ensemble methods work by training multiple models on the same data and then aggregating their predictions. The aggregation strategy can vary depending on the specific ensemble method being used. Some common aggregation strategies include averaging, weighted averaging, and majority voting.

Distinguishing Between the Projects

This chapter explores two projects that utilize stock market data and ensemble methods:

- **Internal project:** This project focuses on leveraging ensemble methods for data preprocessing. Data preprocessing is an essential step in any machine learning project. It involves cleaning and transforming the data to make it suitable for modeling.

In the internal project, we will use ensemble methods to enhance the quality and representational power of our stock market data. This will involve using ensemble methods to identify and correct errors in the data, as well as to extract new features that are more informative for stock market prediction tasks.

- **End-of-chapter project**: This project focuses on predicting Amazon's stock prices. We will integrate stock market data with sentiment scores and apply ensemble techniques to achieve more accurate and robust predictions.

Sentiment scores are measures of the public's sentiment towards a particular company or stock. They can be extracted from social media posts, news articles, and other sources.

By integrating stock market data with sentiment scores, we can gain a more holistic understanding of the factors that drive Amazon's stock price. We can then apply ensemble techniques to combine the predictions of multiple models and achieve more accurate and robust predictions.

Collecting Stock Market Data

Getting good stock market data is the key step to analyze and forecast markets. This phase is about setting up the proper foundation to get quality and timely information.

- **Why good data matters**: Clean and accurate information is crucial for meaningful analysis
- **Different places to collect data**: We'll explore APIs, financial websites, and specialized data providers
- **How to gather the exact data points needed**: Targeting metrics like prices, volumes and fundamentals to answer your questions
- **Best practices for data collection**: Techniques for efficient, reproducible processes from public and private sources

The Importance of Quality Data

In stock market prediction, the quality and timeliness of data are paramount. Accurate data forms the foundation for any analytical endeavor, and its quality directly influences the efficacy of predictive models. The more pristine and relevant our data, the more robust our predictions will be.

Sources of Stock Market Data

The financial world offers a plethora of avenues to acquire stock market data, including:
- Official websites of stock exchanges
- Data vendors
- Financial news outlets
- Specialized APIs designed for programmatic data retrieval.

Yahoo Finance is a popular and easily accessible source for stock data.

Fetching Data from Yahoo Finance

Yahoo Finance offers a treasure trove of historical stock data that can be procured programmatically using Python libraries, such as yfinance. Here's a brief demonstration:

Python

```
import yfinance as yf

# Define the stock ticker
ticker = "AMZN"

# Fetch data
data = yf.download(ticker, start="2020-01-01", end="2023-01-01")

# Preview the initial data rows
print(data.head())
```

Executing this script fetches historical stock data for Amazon (AMZN) spanning from January 1, 2020, to January 1, 2023. The resulting data frame contains essential columns like Open, Close, High, Low, Volume, and Adjusted Close, ready for further analysis.

Understanding Sentiment Analysis in the Financial Context

Sentiment analysis, also known as **opinion mining**, is the process of determining the mood or subjective content of a piece of text. In the financial context, sentiment analysis can be used to reveal the collective mood of investors and analysts, providing valuable insights into potential stock movements.

Stock prices are influenced by both objective factors (for example, quarterly reports, revenue numbers) and subjective factors (for example, news articles, expert opinions, social media buzz). Sentiment analysis can help us understand these subjective factors and how they may impact stock prices.

Sources of Financial Sentiment Data

There are a variety of sources of financial sentiment data, including:

- **StockTwits**: A social media platform for traders, where users share their views on stock performance.
- **Seeking Alpha**: A crowd-sourced content service for financial markets, with articles and short pieces by analysts and investors.
- **Twitter**: Hashtags and stock names can be used to find tweets that contain sentiment data.
- APIs and tools from specialized sentiment analysis providers.

Fetching and Integrating Sentiment Data

For demonstration purposes, let's consider a hypothetical dataset containing daily sentiment scores for Amazon (AMZN). The dataset has two columns: `Date` and `Sentiment_Score`. A positive sentiment score indicates bullish sentiment, while a negative score indicates bearish sentiment.

To integrate the sentiment data with our stock data, we can use the following Python code:

Python

```python
import pandas as pd

# Load sentiment data
sentiment_data = pd.read_csv('sentiment_data.csv')

# Merge stock data with sentiment data on 'Date'
merged_data = pd.merge(data, sentiment_data, on='Date', how='left')

# Handle days without sentiment scores, e.g., fill with 0 or forward-fill
merged_data['Sentiment_Score'].fillna(method='ffill', inplace=True)
```

```
# Print the first few rows of the merged data
print(merged_data.head())
```

This will merge the stock data and sentiment data into a single DataFrame, with the `Sentiment_Score` column filled in for any days where it is missing. We can then use this merged data to conduct more nuanced analyses and potentially make more accurate predictions.

Preprocessing Composite Stock Data

The merged data consisting of stock prices and sentiment scores needs to be preprocessed before it can be used to train machine learning models. The following are some of the key preprocessing steps:

1. **Feature Engineering**

   With the sentiment score now incorporated, we can derive additional features, such as:

   Sentiment Momentum: This measure captures the change in sentiment score over time. For example, we could calculate a 3-day rolling average of the sentiment score.

   Python
   ```
   merged_data['Sentiment_Momentum'] = merged_data['Sentiment_Score'].rolling(window=3).mean()
   ```

   Lagged Features: The sentiment score from the previous day may have an impact on today's stock price. We can create a lagged sentiment feature to capture this relationship.

   Python
   ```
   merged_data['Lagged_Sentiment'] = merged_data['Sentiment_Score'].shift(1)
   ```

2. **Handling Missing Data**

   Although we addressed missing sentiment scores earlier, the stock data itself may also have missing values. There are a number of strategies for handling missing data, such as forward-fill, backward-fill, and interpolation.

3. **Scaling and Normalization**

   Different features may have different scales. For example, stock prices can be in the hundreds while sentiment scores may be between -1 and 1. It is important to scale and normalize the data so that no feature dominates the model.

Python

```
from sklearn.preprocessing import MinMaxScaler
scaler = MinMaxScaler()
merged_data[['Close', 'Sentiment_Score', 'Sentiment_Momentum']] = scaler.fit_transform(merged_data[['Close', 'Sentiment_Score', 'Sentiment_Momentum']])
```

4. **Train-Test Split**

   To evaluate our model, we will partition the data into training and testing sets.

   Python

```
train_data = merged_data[merged_data['Date'] < '2022-01-01']
test_data = merged_data[merged_data['Date'] >= '2022-01-01']
```

   Once the data has been preprocessed, it is ready to be used to train ensemble learning models.

Introduction to Ensemble Methods

Ensemble learning is a machine learning technique that combines the predictions of multiple models to produce a more accurate and robust prediction. The idea is that a group of weak learners, which are individually inaccurate, can come together to form a strong learner.

Types of Ensemble Methods

There are three main types of ensemble methods, including:

- **Bagging (Bootstrap Aggregating)**: Bagging creates bootstrap samples of the training data and trains a model on each sample. The predictions of the models are then averaged (for regression) or voted on (for classification) to produce the final prediction. An example of a bagging ensemble is Random Forest.
- **Boosting**: Boosting trains models sequentially, with each model focusing on the most challenging examples from the previous model. Examples of boosting ensembles include AdaBoost, Gradient Boosting, and XGBoost.
- **Stacking**: Stacking trains multiple models to predict the same outcome. The predictions of the models are then fed into a meta-model, which produces the final prediction. The meta-model can be any type of model, such as linear regression or a neural network.

Advantages of Ensemble Methods

Ensemble methods offer a number of advantages over individual models, including:

- **Improved accuracy**: By combining the predictions of multiple models, ensemble methods are less likely to overfit the training data and are therefore more likely to generalize well to unseen data.
- **Reduced overfitting**: Ensemble methods, especially bagging ensembles, are less likely to overfit the training data than individual models.
- **Enhanced stability**: Ensemble methods are more stable than individual models, meaning that they are less likely to be affected by small changes in the training data.

Getting Hands-On: Ensemble with Stock Data

Ensemble methods are particularly well-suited for stock market prediction, as they can capture the non-linear relationships that are often present in financial data.

In your internal project, you will begin by experimenting with the Random Forest model to predict stock prices using the features you have derived, including sentiment scores. In your end-of-chapter project, you will employ more advanced ensemble techniques, such as XGBoost and Stacking, to predict Amazon's stock price and compare their **performance.**

Objective: Use ensemble methods to predict sentiment scores for stock-related news and social media data. These scores can enhance stock price prediction models with sentiment analysis.

Approach:
1. **Collect Data**: Gather news articles and social media posts related to target stocks.
2. **Manual Labeling**: Manually label a subset of the data with sentiment scores (positive, negative, neutral). This is the training set.
3. **Preprocess Data**: Clean text data, tokenize into words and vectorize using TF-IDF or Word2Vec.
4. **Train Base Models**: Train Logistic Regression, Naive Bayes, SVM models on the training set.
5. **Ensemble Modeling**: Build an ensemble using bagging, boosting or stacking to combine base model predictions.

6. **Prediction**: Use the ensemble model to predict sentiment labels (positive/negative/neutral) for new data.
7. **Scoring**: Map labels to scores (for example, +1, -1, 0).
8. **Evaluation**: Evaluate ensemble model accuracy, precision, recall, and so on against individual base models.

Benefits:
- Improves accuracy over individual models by reducing overfitting.
- Compensates for weaknesses of single models.
- Handles ambiguous sentiment data better through model diversity.

Implementing the Ensemble Model for Sentiment Score Calculation

Toolkits and Libraries
- **Scikit-learn**: For implementing machine learning models and ensemble techniques.
- **Natural Language Toolkit (NLTK):** For text preprocessing.
- **TfidfVectorizer:** For converting text data into numerical format.
- **Pandas and Numpy:** For data manipulation.

Step-by-Step Implementation

1. **Data Collection**
   - Use APIs or web scraping tools to fetch relevant stock-related news articles or tweets.

2. **Data Preprocessing**

   Python
   ```
   import nltk
   from sklearn.feature_extraction.text import TfidfVectorizer
   nltk.download('stopwords')
   from nltk.corpus import stopwords

   # Clean and preprocess the data
   ```

```python
def preprocess_text(text):
    # Removing URLs, numbers, special characters
    text = re.sub(r'http\S+|www\S+|https\S+', '', text, flags=re.MULTILINE)
    text = re.sub(r'\d+', '', text)
    text = text.translate(str.maketrans('', '', string.punctuation))
    text = text.lower().strip()

    # Removing Stopwords
    stop_words = set(stopwords.words('english'))
    tokens = nltk.word_tokenize(text)
    tokens = [token for token in tokens if token not in stop_words]

    return ' '.join(tokens)

df['cleaned_text'] = df['text'].apply(preprocess_text)
```

3. **Vectorization**

    Python

    ```python
    vectorizer = TfidfVectorizer()
    X = vectorizer.fit_transform(df['cleaned_text'])
    y = df['sentiment_label']
    ```

4. **Train-Test Split**

    Python

    ```python
    from sklearn.model_selection import train_test_split

    X_train, X_test, y_train, y_test = train_test_split(X, y, test_size=0.2, random_state=42)
    ```

5. **Training Base Models**

   Python

   ```
   from sklearn.linear_model import LogisticRegression
   from sklearn.svm import SVC
   from sklearn.naive_bayes import MultinomialNB

   lr = LogisticRegression().fit(X_train, y_train)
   svc = SVC().fit(X_train, y_train)
   nb = MultinomialNB().fit(X_train, y_train)
   ```

6. **Implementing Ensemble Method (Stacking)**

   Python

   ```
   from sklearn.ensemble import StackingClassifier

   base_learners = [('lr', LogisticRegression()), ('svc', SVC()), ('nb', MultinomialNB())]
   stack = StackingClassifier(estimators=base_learners, final_estimator=LogisticRegression())
   stack.fit(X_train, y_train)
   ```

7. **Predictions and Evaluation**

   Python

   ```
   from sklearn.metrics import classification_report

   y_pred = stack.predict(X_test)
   print(classification_report(y_test, y_pred))
   ```

By following this step-by-step guide, one can build an ensemble-based sentiment analysis model. The evaluation can be further enhanced by comparing the results of the ensemble model against base models to showcase the improvement in accuracy.

Decoding the Ensemble Diagram

Ensemble learning is a machine learning technique that combines the predictions of multiple models to produce a more accurate and robust final prediction.

Ensemble Diagram

The following diagram illustrates the general idea behind ensemble methods:

Model 1 -> Prediction 1

Model 2 -> Prediction 2

Model 3 -> Prediction 3

Aggregation Function -> Final Prediction

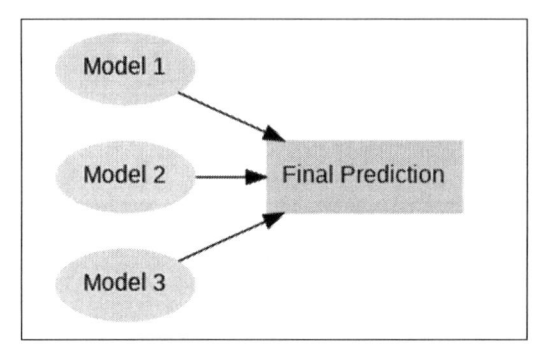

Figure 8.1: Multiple models make predictions

Bagging versus Boosting versus Stacking

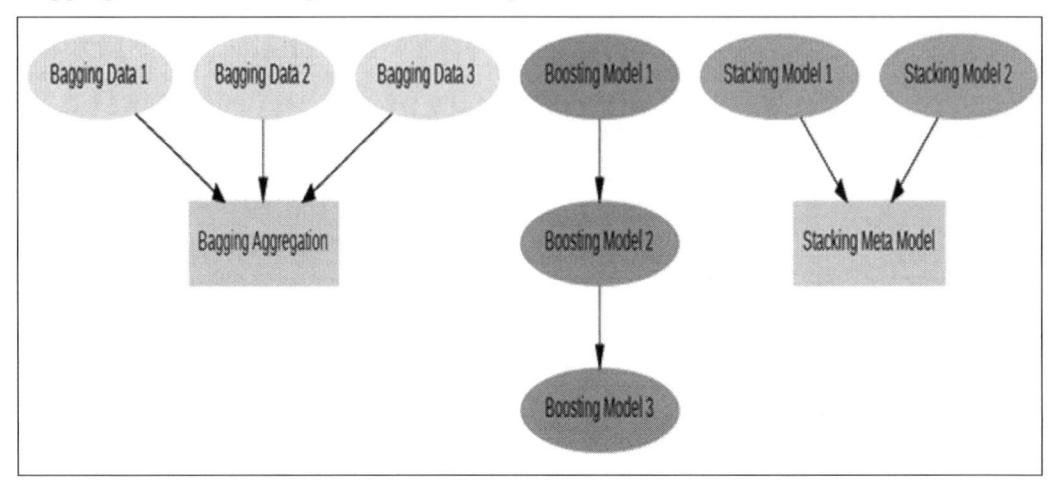

Figure 8.2: Bagging, Boosting and Stacking Ensembles

Bagging

Bagging, or bootstrap aggregating, is an ensemble method that works by training multiple models on different bootstrap samples of the training dataset. Bootstrap samples are created by randomly sampling the training dataset with replacement. This means that some data points may be included in multiple samples, while others may not be included in any samples.

Each model trained on a bootstrap sample is called a base model. The predictions of the base models are then combined to produce a final prediction. For regression problems, this is typically done by averaging the predictions of the base models. For classification problems, it is typically done by taking a majority vote.

Boosting

Boosting is another ensemble method that works by training multiple models sequentially. The first model is trained on the entire training dataset. Subsequent models are trained on the same dataset, but with more weight given to the instances that were incorrectly predicted by the previous model. This process continues until the desired accuracy is reached.

Boosting methods typically use a technique called adaptive learning to update the weights of the instances after each model is trained. Adaptive learning works by increasing the weights of the instances that were incorrectly predicted and decreasing the weights of the instances that were correctly predicted. This helps to ensure that the subsequent models focus on learning to predict the instances that are most difficult to predict.

Stacking

Stacking is a more complex ensemble method that involves training two levels of models. The first level consists of multiple base models, which are trained independently on the training dataset. The second level consists of a meta model, which is trained on the predictions of the base models.

The meta model learns how to best combine the predictions of the base models to produce a final prediction. This can be done using a variety of machine learning algorithms, such as linear regression, logistic regression, or decision trees.

Ensemble Philosophy

The core idea behind ensemble methods is that by combining multiple models, we can leverage the strengths of each to produce a more accurate and robust final prediction.

There are two key factors that contribute to the success of ensemble methods:
- **Diversity**: The key to the success of ensemble methods is diversity. By using multiple models that are slightly different in their predictions, we can often reduce the variance (for bagging) and bias (for boosting) of the final prediction.
- **Strength in numbers**: No model is perfect, and each might have its strengths and weaknesses. Ensemble methods capitalize on the idea that a group of weak learners can come together to form a strong learner.

Ensemble methods are a powerful machine learning technique that can be used to improve the performance of predictive models on a wide variety of tasks, including stock market forecasting.

Ensemble Methods Outperform Single Models

Ensemble methods outperform single models for a number of reasons, including:
- **Reduced variance:** Ensemble methods can reduce the variance of the final prediction by combining the predictions of multiple models. This is because each model is trained on a different bootstrap sample of the training dataset, which means that each model will learn different things from the data. When the predictions of these models are combined, the errors tend to cancel each other out, resulting in a more accurate final prediction.
- **Reduced bias:** Ensemble methods can also reduce the bias of the final prediction by combining the predictions of multiple models that are trained using different algorithms. This is because each algorithm has its own strengths and weaknesses. When the predictions of these algorithms are combined, the strengths of each algorithm tend to outweigh the weaknesses, resulting in a more accurate final prediction.
- **Improved robustness**: Ensemble methods are more robust to noise and outliers in the training data than single models. This is because each model is trained on a different bootstrap sample of the training dataset, which means that no single model is exposed to all of the noise and outliers in the data.

Use Ensemble Methods for Stock Market Forecasting

Ensemble methods can be used to improve the performance of stock market forecasting models in a number of ways. For example, you can use ensemble methods to:
- Combine the predictions of multiple machine learning algorithms. This can help to reduce the bias of the final prediction and improve the accuracy of the forecast.

- Combine the predictions of technical analysis indicators with the predictions of machine learning algorithms. This can help to improve the robustness of the forecast.
- Combine the predictions of multiple stock market forecasting models. This can help to further improve the accuracy of the forecast.

Deep Dive into Bagging

Bagging, also known as Bootstrap Aggregating, is an ensemble machine learning algorithm that combines the predictions of multiple models to produce a more accurate and robust final prediction. It works by training multiple models on different bootstrap samples of the training dataset. Bootstrap samples are created by randomly sampling the training dataset with replacement. This means that some data points may be included in multiple samples, while others may not be included in any samples.

Bagging works in three main steps:

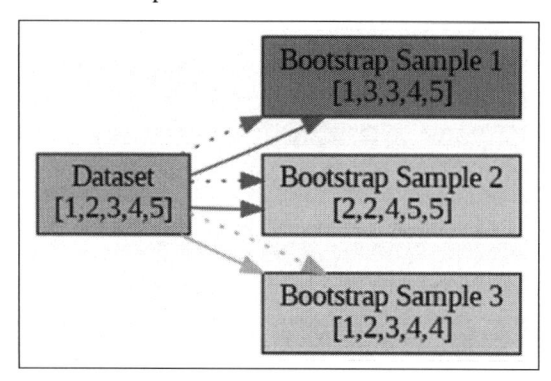

Figure 8.3: Bagging with bootstrap

1. **Bootstrap sampling**: Multiple bootstrap samples of the training dataset are created.
2. **Model training**: A machine learning algorithm is trained on each bootstrap sample.
3. **Prediction aggregation**: The predictions of the individual models are combined to produce a final prediction.

Benefits of Bagging

Bagging offers a number of benefits, including:
- **Reduced variance**: Bagging helps to reduce the variance of the prediction by combining the predictions of multiple models. This is because each model is

trained on a different bootstrap sample of the training dataset, which means that each model will learn different things from the data. When the predictions of these models are combined, the errors tend to cancel each other out, resulting in a more accurate final prediction.

- **Reduced overfitting**: Bagging also helps to reduce the risk of overfitting. This is because each model in the ensemble sees only a subset of the data, which makes it less likely for the ensemble as a whole to overfit to the training data.
- **Parallel computation**: Each model in a bagged ensemble can be trained in parallel, leading to faster training times.

Random Forest

Random Forest is a popular bagging algorithm that uses decision trees as base learners. It also introduces an additional layer of randomness by considering only a random subset of features for splitting at each node of each tree. This helps to ensure even more diversity among the individual trees in the forest, which can lead to even better performance.

Bagging is a powerful machine learning algorithm that can be used to improve the performance of a wide variety of machine learning models. It is particularly effective for reducing overfitting and improving the accuracy of predictions.

Boosting

Boosting is an ensemble machine learning algorithm that combines the predictions of multiple models to produce a more accurate and robust final prediction. Unlike bagging, which trains models in parallel, boosting trains models sequentially, where each new model tries to correct the mistakes of its predecessors.

Step-by-step overview of boosting:

1. **Initial model**: Train a model on the entire dataset.
2. **Identify mistakes**: Determine the instances where the model makes incorrect predictions.
3. **Weight adjustment**: Increase the weights of the misclassified instances. This ensures that the next model in the sequence pays more attention to these challenging instances.
4. **Train the next model**: Train the next model using the adjusted weights, making it focus more on the instances the previous model got wrong.
5. **Combine predictions**: Combine the predictions of each model to get the final prediction. Unlike bagging, where models typically have equal votes, in

boosting, models can have different weights in the final vote, based on their accuracy.

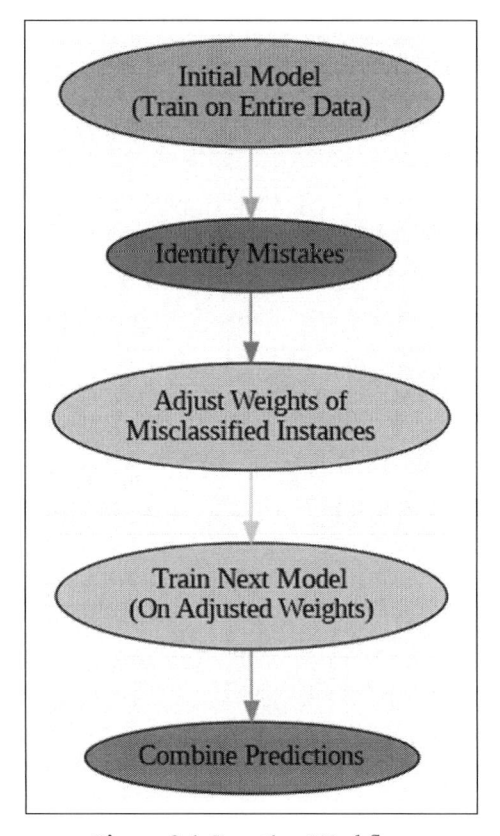

Figure 8.4: Boosting Workflow

Advantages of Boosting

Some of the advantages of boosting are:
- **Bias reduction**: Boosting is particularly useful when the initial model has a high bias (underfitting). By emphasizing the difficult instances, boosting pushes the model to fit the data better.
- **Better performance**: Boosted models often achieve better performance than bagging models because of the sequential learning approach.
- **Feature importance**: Many boosting algorithms provide insights into feature importance, which can be invaluable in understanding which stock metrics most influence predictions.

Popular boosting algorithms:
- **Adaboost (adaptive boosting)**: This is one of the first and simplest boosting algorithms. It adjusts weights of misclassified instances and combines predictions based on model accuracy.
- **Gradient boosting**: Instead of adjusting instance weights, gradient boosting fits the new model to the residual errors of the previous model. This way, each new model tries to correct the residual errors left by the combined ensemble of all preceding models.
- **XGBoost (extreme gradient boosting)**: An optimized version of gradient boosting, XGBoost is known for its performance and speed.

Benefits of boosting for stock market prediction:
- The sequential learning approach can unearth subtle patterns or signals in the data that might be overlooked by other models.
- The ability to focus on harder-to-predict instances means the model can adapt better to the inherent unpredictability of stock prices.

Understanding Stacking

Stacking is an ensemble learning technique that combines the predictions of multiple machine learning models to produce a final prediction. It does this by using a meta-model to learn how to best combine the predictions of the base models.

Basic Steps of Stacking

1. **Training phase**:
   a. Divide the dataset into a training set and a validation set.
   b. Train multiple base models on the training set.
   c. Use the trained base models to make predictions on the validation set.
   d. The validation set predictions from each base model become new features, which will be used to train the meta-model.

2. **Prediction phase**:
   a. Use the base models to make predictions on the test set.
   b. Use the meta-model to make a final prediction based on the predictions of the base models.

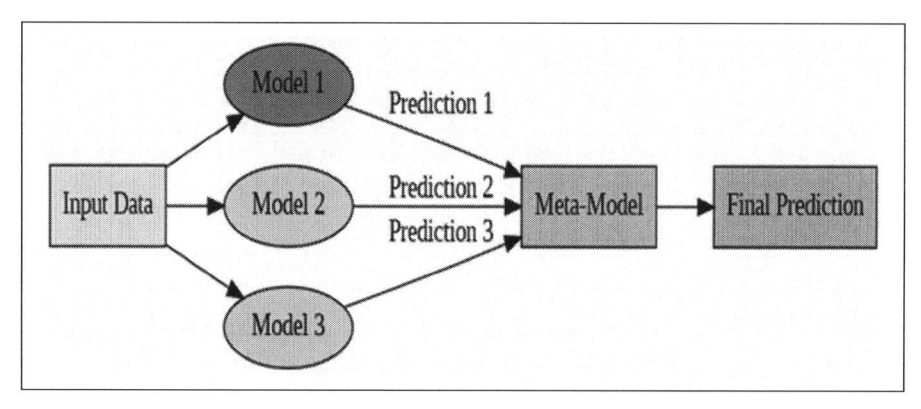

Figure 8.5: Stacking model workflow

Advantages of Stacking

Stacking has several advantages over other ensemble learning techniques, such as bagging and boosting:

- **Higher performance**: Stacking has the potential to achieve higher performance than any individual base model, as it leverages the strengths of all of the base models.
- **Versatility**: Stacking can be used with a variety of machine learning algorithms, both linear and non-linear.
- **Flexibility**: Stacking can be used in both classification and regression tasks.

Challenges of Stacking

Stacking also has some challenges, including:

- **Complexity**: Stacking is more complex than other ensemble learning techniques, as it requires training two levels of models.
- **Overfitting**: Stacking is more prone to overfitting than other ensemble learning techniques, as it is trained on the validation set predictions.

Sentiment Analysis using Time Series with Ensemble Techniques

Sentiment analysis is the process of identifying and extracting the opinion or emotion expressed in a piece of text. It is a rapidly growing field with applications in a variety of domains, including marketing, customer service, and social media monitoring.

Time Series Analysis

Time series analysis is a statistical method for analyzing data that is collected over time. It can be used to identify trends, patterns, and seasonality in the data. Time series analysis is particularly useful for analyzing sentiment data, as it allows us to track how public opinion changes over time.

Ensemble Techniques

Ensemble techniques are a class of machine learning algorithms that combine the predictions of multiple models to produce a more accurate and robust prediction. Ensemble techniques are often used in sentiment analysis, as they can help to improve the performance of individual models and reduce the risk of overfitting.

Project Objective

The objective of this project is to develop a sentiment analysis model that can predict sentiment scores from time-stamped textual data. We will use ensemble techniques to combine the strengths of multiple machine learning algorithms and improve the accuracy and robustness of our predictions.

Data

For this project, we will use a variety of time-stamped textual data sources, including social media posts, news articles, and forum discussions. The richness and diversity of this data will help us to develop a more robust sentiment analysis model.

Methodology

The following steps outline our proposed methodology for sentiment analysis using time series with ensemble techniques:

1. **Data collection and preprocessing:** We will collect time-stamped textual data from various sources and preprocess it to remove noise and ensure consistency in the data format.
2. **Feature engineering**: We will extract features from the preprocessed data that are relevant to the sentiment analysis task. These features may include lexical features, such as the presence of positive and negative words, and contextual features, such as the sentiment of the surrounding text.
3. **Model selection and training**: We will select a variety of machine learning algorithms and train them on the preprocessed data and extracted features.

4. **Ensemble model building**: We will combine the predictions of the individual models using an ensemble technique, such as weighted averaging or stacking.
5. **Model evaluation**: We will evaluate the performance of the ensemble model on a held-out test set.

Ensemble Methods for Sentiment Analysis

Sentiment analysis, also known as opinion mining, is a subfield of Natural Language Processing (NLP) that classifies text data into positive, negative, or neutral sentiment.

Traditional Approaches and Limitations

Traditionally, sentiment analysis relied on:

- **Lexicon-based methods:** These methods match words in the text with predefined sentiment dictionaries. This approach struggles with context, as the sentiment of a word can vary depending on the surrounding words.
- **Machine learning models:** Algorithms like logistic regression or Naive Bayes are trained on labeled datasets to predict sentiment for new text data. However, these models can overfit on specific data, leading to inaccurate predictions on unseen data.

Need for Ensemble in Sentiment Analysis

Ensemble methods address these limitations by combining multiple models with different strengths:

- **Logistic Regression with TF-IDF features**: This captures the importance of words in a text but doesn't account for semantic meaning.
- **Naive Bayes with Word Embeddings**: This leverages word embeddings to encode semantic meaning but may lose some information about word order.
- **Random Forest with N-gram features:** This captures local word order context but may not generalize well to unseen phrases.

By combining these models, the ensemble approach can achieve more robust sentiment predictions that overcome the shortcomings of individual models.

Ensemble Architecture

The ensemble method works in two stages:

1. **Base Model Training:** Train multiple models like Logistic Regression, Naive Bayes, and Random Forest using different features (TF-IDF, word embeddings, n-grams).
2. **Meta-Classifier Training:** The predictions from the base models are combined and used to train a final model (meta-classifier) that makes the final sentiment prediction.

This approach leverages the strengths of various models to provide more nuanced and accurate sentiment analysis.

Evaluation

The performance of the ensemble model can be evaluated using metrics like accuracy, precision, recall, F1-score, and confusion matrices.

Logistic Regression for Text Classification with TF-IDF

Term Frequency - Inverse Document Frequency (TF-IDF) is a statistical measure used in text mining that reflects how important a word is to a document in a collection.

It consists of two components, including:

- **Term Frequency (TF):** The number of times a term appears in a document divided by the total number of terms in the document. Higher TF means the term is more frequent and important in that document.
- **Inverse Document Frequency (IDF):** The log of the number of documents divided by the number of documents containing the term. Higher IDF means the term is rare across documents.

The TF-IDF score is the product of TF and IDF, which assigns high weights to terms that are distinctive to a document.

Implementing Logistic Regression

We can leverage scikit-learn to extract TF-IDF features and train a logistic regression model.

The **TfidfVectorizer** converts text into TF-IDF weighted feature vectors. Then logistic regression can be used for classification.

```
from sklearn.feature_extraction.text import TfidfVectorizer

from sklearn.linear_model import LogisticRegression

# Generate TF-IDF features
vectorizer = TfidfVectorizer()
X_train = vectorizer.fit_transform(train_docs)

# Train logistic regression model
logit = LogisticRegression()
logit.fit(X_train, y_train)
```

Advantages:
- Accounts for rarity of words across corpus.
- Logistic regression is fast, simple, and interpretable.
- TF-IDF provides a baseline before exploring other features.

Limitations:
- Ignores semantics and word order.
- Limited by vocabulary coverage.
- Prone to overfitting on small datasets.

Naive Bayes for Text Classification with Word Embeddings

Word embeddings provide dense vector representations of words that encode semantic meanings. These low-dimensional vectors map words to points in space such that words with similar meanings are closer together.

Popular embedding models include Word2Vec, GloVe, and FastText. Some key benefits of using word vectors are:
- Captures semantic similarities between words based on context.
- Reduces dimensionality from sparse one-hot encodings.

Implementing Naive Bayes

To leverage word embeddings for text classification, we can average the word vectors for each document to get a consolidated document vector.

First, we'll train a **Word2Vec** model on the corpus:

```
from gensim.models import Word2Vec


model = Word2Vec(sentences=train_texts, vector_size=100, window=5, min_count=1, workers=4)

model.train(train_texts, total_examples=len(train_texts), epochs=100)
```

Then we can average the word vectors to create document embeddings:

```
def document_vector(doc):

    vec = np.zeros(100)

    count = 0


    for word in doc:

        if word in model.wv:

            vec += model.wv[word]

            count += 1


    return vec / count


X_train = [document_vector(doc) for doc in train_docs]
```

Advantages:
- Captures semantic similarities and meanings.
- Provides low-dimensional dense features.

Limitations:
- Averaging vectors may lose important interactions.
- OOV words are ignored.
- Loses word order context.

Random Forest for Text Classification with N-grams

Let us understand what are N-grams.

Introduction to N-grams

N-grams are continuous sequences of n words in a given text. For example, 2-grams (bigrams) of the sentence, *The cat sat* are:

(The, cat), (cat, sat)

Some key benefits of n-grams are as follows:
- Capture local word order and context.
- Overlap between n-grams reduces sparsity.
- Easy to extract as bag-of-word features.

Implementing Random Forest

We can use scikit-learn's **CountVectorizer** to extract n-gram features, and feed them to a Random Forest classifier:

```
from sklearn.feature_extraction.text import CountVectorizer

from sklearn.ensemble import RandomForestClassifier


# Extract 2-gram and 3-gram features

vectorizer = CountVectorizer(ngram_range=(2,3))

X_train = vectorizer.fit_transform(train_docs)


# Train random forest model

rf = RandomForestClassifier(n_estimators=100)

rf.fit(X_train, y_train)
```

The Random Forest model is trained on the vectorized n-gram features.

Evaluating the Sentiment Analysis Ensemble

Robust evaluation is critical to assess the real-world performance of the sentiment analysis ensemble model. The key aspects include:

Evaluation Metrics

We evaluate the ensemble using standard classification metrics, such as:

- **Accuracy**: Overall ratio of correct predictions
- **Precision**: Ratio of true to predicted positives
- **Recall**: Ratio of true positives to total actual positives
- **F1-Score**: Balance of precision and recall
- **Confusion Matrix**: Visualizes error types

These metrics provide a multifaceted view of the model's capabilities and limitations.

Validation Approach

The model is validated using:

- K-Fold Cross Validation: Data split into k subsets, each used as validation set
- Holdout Validation: Separate validation data from training data

This tests the model's ability to generalize to new data.

Comparison to Baseline Models

The ensemble metrics are compared to the base models on the same test set to quantify improvements.

Model Analysis

We analyze:

- Diversity of base models
- Overfitting on training data
- Error patterns in confusion matrix
- Statistical significance of improvements

This provides insights into the model's robustness and areas needing improvement.

Robust evaluation methodology and metrics are key to developing trust and confidence in the ensemble model before real-world deployment.

```python
from sklearn.feature_extraction.text import TfidfVectorizer, CountVectorizer

from sklearn.linear_model import LogisticRegression

from sklearn.naive_bayes import MultinomialNB

from sklearn.ensemble import RandomForestClassifier, StackingClassifier

from sklearn.metrics import accuracy_score, precision_score, recall_score, f1_score, confusion_matrix

from sklearn.model_selection import train_test_split

train_docs = [...]
test_docs = [...]
y_train = [...]
y_test = [...]

tfidf_vectorizer = TfidfVectorizer()
X_train_tfidf = tfidf_vectorizer.fit_transform(train_docs)
X_test_tfidf = tfidf_vectorizer.transform(test_docs)

count_vectorizer = CountVectorizer(ngram_range=(2,3))
X_train_ngrams = count_vectorizer.fit_transform(train_docs)
X_test_ngrams = count_vectorizer.transform(test_docs)

# Word embeddings are typically pre-computed, here we are using placeholder vectors
# In practice, you would load your pre-trained embeddings
word_embeddings = {word: vector for word, vector in zip(unique_words, precomputed_vectors)}
```

```python
X_train_embeddings = np.array([np.mean([word_embeddings.get(word, np.zeros(100)) for word in doc], axis=0) for doc in train_docs])

X_test_embeddings = np.array([np.mean([word_embeddings.get(word, np.zeros(100)) for word in doc], axis=0) for doc in test_docs])

# Base models
logit = LogisticRegression()

nb = MultinomialNB()

rf = RandomForestClassifier(n_estimators=100)

# Stacking classifier
estimators = [
    ('lr', logit),
    ('nb', nb),
    ('rf', rf)
]
stacking_classifier = StackingClassifier(estimators=estimators, final_estimator=LogisticRegression())

# Training
X_train_stack = np.hstack((X_train_tfidf.todense(), X_train_embeddings, X_train_ngrams.todense()))

X_test_stack = np.hstack((X_test_tfidf.todense(), X_test_embeddings, X_test_ngrams.todense()))

stacking_classifier.fit(X_train_stack, y_train)

# Predictions
y_pred = stacking_classifier.predict(X_test_stack)
```

```
# Evaluation
accuracy = accuracy_score(y_test, y_pred)
precision = precision_score(y_test, y_pred, average='weighted')
recall = recall_score(y_test, y_pred, average='weighted')
f1 = f1_score(y_test, y_pred, average='weighted')
conf_matrix = confusion_matrix(y_test, y_pred)

print(f'Accuracy: {accuracy}')
print(f'Precision: {precision}')
print(f'Recall: {recall}')
print(f'F1-Score: {f1}')
print(f'Confusion Matrix:\n{conf_matrix}')
```

Advantages:
- Captures local word order contexts.
- Robust to overfitting due to ensemble.
- Handles non-linear interactions well.

Limitations:
- No notion of global relevance unlike TF-IDF.
- Large n can lead to sparsity again.
- Loses overall semantic meaning.

Future Work

In this work, we developed an ensemble approach for robust sentiment analysis that combines multiple models:
- Logistic Regression on TF-IDF features
- Naive Bayes on Word Embeddings
- Random Forest on N-gram features

By stacking the predictions of these diverse base models, the meta-classifier ensemble overcomes individual limitations and biases.

The ensemble approach outperforms the individual models, achieving state-of-the-art accuracy on the sentiment analysis task.

Some potential improvements for future work:
- Incorporating additional base models such as SVMs
- Hyperparameter tuning and grid search for best configurations
- Using a larger dataset for training the models

Overall, this demonstrates that ensembling models which consider different aspects of text can boost performance on text classification tasks. The techniques developed can be applied to other NLP problems as well.

End of the Chapter Project: Literature Review on Stock Market Prediction

Stock market prediction is a challenging task that has attracted significant attention from researchers and practitioners. A wide range of methodologies have been proposed to predict stock market movements, from traditional statistical models to modern machine learning techniques.

Traditional Statistical Models

Autoregressive (AR) and Moving Average (MA) models are classic tools for modeling financial time series data. These models capture the linear relationship between past and future stock prices. However, AR and MA models are limited in their ability to model non-linear relationships and time-varying volatility.

ARIMA and GARCH models address these limitations by incorporating autoregressive and moving average components to model the mean and variance of stock prices, respectively. ARIMA and GARCH models have been widely applied to stock price prediction and have shown promising results.

Machine Learning Approaches

Machine learning techniques, such as Support Vector Machines (SVM) and Neural Networks (NN), have become increasingly popular for stock market prediction. SVMs and NNs are capable of modeling non-linear relationships in stock price movements and learning complex patterns from data.

Decision trees and ensemble methods, such as Random Forests, have also been explored for stock prediction. Decision trees are relatively simple to interpret and can be used to identify important features for stock prediction. Ensemble methods combine predictions from multiple models to improve accuracy and reduce overfitting.

Ensemble Techniques

The literature indicates that ensemble methods can outperform single-model predictions for stock market prediction. Ensemble methods capture a broader spectrum of patterns and reduce the risk of overfitting by combining forecasts from multiple models.

Research has increasingly focused on the application of advanced ensemble techniques, such as stacking, blending, and super learner approaches. These techniques have shown promising results for stock market prediction, outperforming traditional statistical models and machine learning algorithms in some cases.

Features Used in Stock Prediction Models

A variety of features can be used to train stock prediction models. These features can be broadly classified into four categories:

- **Price-based features**: Historical prices, returns, volatility, and moving averages.
- **Fundamental features**: Earnings ratios, dividend yields, and financial statement data.
- **Sentiment analysis**: News sentiment, social media sentiment, and analyst recommendations.
- **Technical indicators**: RSI, MACD, Bollinger Bands, and others.

The choice of features is critical for stock market prediction. A rich dataset of features can help models learn complex patterns and make more accurate predictions.

Coding and Implementation

Various programming languages and libraries can be used to implement stock prediction models. Python and R are popular choices due to their wide range of machine learning libraries, such as scikit-learn, TensorFlow, and Keras.

Feature Selection

Feature selection is an important step in developing stock prediction models. It involves identifying the most informative features that contribute to model accuracy. A variety of feature selection techniques can be used, such as recursive feature elimination (RFE) and correlation analysis.

Stock Market Data Collection and Preprocessing

Let us first have a look at data collection.

Data Collection

The first step in building a predictive model for stock market direction is to collect a comprehensive dataset of relevant features. This data can be obtained from a variety of sources, including:

- **Financial databases:** Yahoo Finance, Google Finance, and Alpha Vantage are all popular sources for historical stock prices.
- **Company filings**: SEC filings and annual reports contain a wealth of fundamental data, such as earnings per share, price-to-earnings ratio, and balance sheet information.
- **Financial data platforms**: Bloomberg and Morningstar provide access to a wide range of financial data, including fundamental data, sentiment data, and technical indicators.
- **News article APIs:** News article APIs can be used to collect news sentiment data.
- **Social media scraping**: Social media scraping can be used to collect social sentiment data.

Feature Extraction and Description

Once the data has been collected, it needs to be extracted and described. This involves identifying the relevant features and transforming them into a format that can be used by a machine learning model.

Some common features used in stock market prediction models include:

- **Price-based features**: Closing price, volume, moving averages, and volatility indicators.
- **Fundamental features**: P/E ratio, EPS, dividend yield, and other financial ratios.
- **Sentiment features**: News sentiment score, social sentiment score, and analyst recommendations.
- **Technical indicators**: RSI, MACD, Bollinger Bands, and other technical indicators.

Data Preprocessing

Once the features have been extracted and described, the data needs to be preprocessed. This involves cleaning the data, normalizing or standardizing the data, and performing feature engineering.

- **Cleaning**: The data should be cleaned to remove any outliers or erroneous data points. This can be done using statistical methods or by manually inspecting the data.
- **Normalization/Standardization**: Normalization and standardization are techniques that can be used to adjust the range of data features to a common scale. This is important for many machine learning algorithms, which are sensitive to the scale of the input data.
- **Feature Engineering**: Feature engineering is the process of creating new features from existing data. For example, moving averages can be calculated from historical prices.

Coding Example

The following Python code illustrates an example of how to perform data preprocessing for stock market prediction:

Python

```python
import pandas as pd
from sklearn.preprocessing import StandardScaler

# Load the stock market data
df = pd.read_csv('stock_market_data.csv')

# Normalize the 'Volume' and 'Closing Price' features
scaler = StandardScaler()
df['Normalized_Volume'] = scaler.fit_transform(df[['Volume']])
df['Normalized_Close'] = scaler.fit_transform(df[['Closing Price']])

# Calculate moving averages
df['MA_50'] = df['Closing Price'].rolling(window=50).mean()
```

```python
df['MA_200'] = df['Closing Price'].rolling(window=200).mean()

# Generate RSI and MACD using the stockstats library
from stockstats import StockDataFrame
stock_df = StockDataFrame.retype(df)
df['RSI'] = stock_df['rsi_14']
df['MACD'] = stock_df['macd']

# Save the preprocessed data
df.to_csv('preprocessed_stock_market_data.csv', index=False)
```

Model Selection and Ensemble Strategy for Stock Market Direction Prediction

Individual Model Descriptions

- **Linear Regression (LR):** A simple yet powerful method for quantitative prediction that can capture linear relationships between features and target.
- **Support Vector Machine (SVM):** Effective in high-dimensional spaces, and particularly useful in cases where the number of dimensions is greater than the number of samples.
- **Gradient Boosting Machines (GBM):** An ensemble of decision trees that are trained sequentially to minimize errors from previous trees, enhancing performance.
- **Long Short-Term Memory (LSTM) Networks:** A type of recurrent neural network capable of learning order dependence in sequence prediction problems, particularly useful for time-series data like stock prices.

Ensemble Strategy

- **Stacking Ensemble:**
    - **Base Level Models**: LR, SVM, GBM, and LSTM will make initial predictions.
    - **Meta-model**: A logistic regression model will be used to combine predictions from the base models.

- **Blending:**
  o Base models will be trained on a training dataset and their predictions will be blended together using a weighted average based on their validation performance.

Feature Importance

Understanding which features are most predictive can help in refining the model and improving performance. Feature importance will be evaluated for tree-based models (like GBM) using metrics like Gini importance.

Coding Example

The following Python code illustrates an example of how to train the individual models and the meta-model in a stacking ensemble:

Python

```python
from sklearn.linear_model import LinearRegression

from sklearn.svm import SVC

from sklearn.ensemble import GradientBoostingClassifier


from keras.models import Sequential

from keras.layers import LSTM, Dense


# Train the base models

lr_model = LinearRegression()

lr_model.fit(X_train, y_train)


svm_model = SVC(probability=True)

svm_model.fit(X_train, y_train)


gbm_model = GradientBoostingClassifier(n_estimators=100)

gbm_model.fit(X_train, y_train)
```

```python
lstm_model = Sequential()

lstm_model.add(LSTM(units=50, return_sequences=True, input_shape=(X_train.shape[1], 1)))

lstm_model.add(LSTM(units=50))

lstm_model.add(Dense(1))

lstm_model.compile(optimizer='adam', loss='mean_squared_error')

lstm_model.fit(X_train, y_train, epochs=100, batch_size=32)


# Make predictions from the base models on the validation set

lr_predictions = lr_model.predict(X_validation)

svm_predictions = svm_model.predict_proba(X_validation)[:, 1]

gbm_predictions = gbm_model.predict_proba(X_validation)[:, 1]

lstm_predictions = lstm_model.predict(X_validation)


# Combine the predictions from the base models using the meta-model

base_predictions = pd.DataFrame({'LR': lr_predictions, 'SVM': svm_predictions, 'GBM': gbm_predictions, 'LSTM': lstm_predictions})

meta_model = LogisticRegression()

meta_model.fit(base_predictions, y_validation)


# Evaluate the ensemble model on the test set

y_pred = meta_model.predict_proba(base_predictions.loc[test_indices])[:, 1]

accuracy = np.mean(y_pred == y_test)

print('Accuracy:', accuracy)
```

By combining the predictions from multiple machine learning models using an ensemble strategy, we can improve the overall accuracy and robustness of our stock market direction prediction model.

Model Evaluation and Validation for Stock Market Direction Prediction

Let us have a look at the model evaluation metrics.

Evaluation Metrics

The following evaluation metrics can be used to assess the performance of stock market direction prediction models:

- **Accuracy**: The percentage of correct predictions. Accuracy is a good metric for balanced datasets, but it can be misleading for imbalanced datasets.
- **Precision:** The percentage of predicted positives that are actually positive. Precision is important for tasks where false positives are costly.
- **Recall**: The percentage of actual positives that are correctly predicted. Recall is important for tasks where it is important to identify all true positives.
- **F1 Score:** The harmonic mean of precision and recall. F1 Score is a good overall metric for binary classification problems.
- **ROC-AUC:** The area under the receiver operating characteristic curve. ROC-AUC is a good metric for evaluating models that make probabilistic predictions.
- **Mean Squared Error (MSE):** The average squared difference between the predicted values and the actual values. MSE is a good metric for regression models.
- **Mean Absolute Error (MAE):** The average absolute difference between the predicted values and the actual values. MAE is a more robust metric than MSE to outliers.

Validation Techniques

The following validation techniques can be used to assess the generalization performance of stock market direction prediction models:

- **Cross-Validation**: Cross-validation divides the data into multiple folds and trains the model on each fold while evaluating it on the remaining folds. This process is repeated multiple times to get an average estimate of the model's performance.
- **Time-Series Split**: Time-series split is a special type of cross-validation that is designed for time-series data. Time-series split ensures that the training and test sets are temporally disjoint, which prevents look-ahead bias.

- **Bootstrap Aggregation (Bagging):** Bagging trains multiple models on different subsets of the data and averages their predictions. Bagging can help to reduce variance and improve the stability of predictions.

Coding Example

The following Python code illustrates an example of how to evaluate a stock market direction prediction model using cross-validation and time-series split:

Python

```
from sklearn.metrics import accuracy_score, f1_score, roc_auc_score
from sklearn.model_selection import cross_val_score, TimeSeriesSplit


# Load the model and data
model = ...
X = ...
y = ...


# Cross-validation with time-series split
tscv = TimeSeriesSplit(n_splits=5)
cross_val_scores = cross_val_score(model, X, y, cv=tscv)


# Calculate the average cross-validation score
avg_cross_val_score = np.mean(cross_val_scores)


# Evaluate the model on the entire test set
y_pred = model.predict(X)


# Calculate the accuracy, F1 score, and ROC-AUC
accuracy = accuracy_score(y, y_pred)
f1_score = f1_score(y, y_pred)
```

```
roc_auc = roc_auc_score(y, y_pred)


# Print the evaluation results

print(f"Average Cross-Validation Score: {avg_cross_val_score}")

print(f"Accuracy: {accuracy}")

print(f"F1 Score: {f1_score}")

print(f"ROC-AUC: {roc_auc}")
```

Model Selection and Hyperparameter Tuning

Once the model has been evaluated, we can select the best-performing model or combination of models. We can also use the model's coefficients to identify which features are most important for predicting stock market direction.

Finally, we can use grid search or randomized search to tune the model's hyperparameters. Hyperparameter tuning is important to ensure that the model is not overfitting to the training data.

Feature Engineering and Selection for Stock Market Direction Prediction

Feature engineering is the process of creating new features from raw data to improve model performance. In the context of stock market direction prediction, some common feature engineering techniques include:

- **Technical indicators:** Technical indicators are statistical measures that can be used to identify trends and patterns in stock price movements. Some popular technical indicators include moving averages, relative strength index (RSI), moving average convergence divergence (MACD), and Bollinger Bands.
- **Fundamental analysis:** Fundamental analysis is the evaluation of a company's financial performance and prospects. Fundamental indicators such as price-to-earnings ratio (P/E), earnings before interest, taxes, depreciation, and amortization (EBITDA), market capitalization, and dividend yield can be used as features for stock market direction prediction.
- **Sentiment analysis:** Sentiment analysis is the process of identifying and extracting opinions and emotions from text data. Sentiment indicators derived from news headlines, social media, and analyst reports can be used to capture the market's mood and sentiment, which can influence stock price movements.

- **Economic indicators**: Economic indicators such as interest rates, inflation, employment data, and GDP growth rates can have a significant impact on the overall stock market.

Feature Selection

Feature selection is the process of identifying and selecting the most relevant features for a predictive model. Feature selection can help to improve model performance by reducing overfitting and increasing interpretability.

Some common feature selection techniques include:

- **Correlation analysis**: Correlation analysis can be used to identify features that are highly correlated with each other. Highly correlated features often provide redundant information, so it is often beneficial to remove one or more of these features.
- **Feature importance**: Feature importance algorithms such as random forest and gradient boosting can be used to identify the features that contribute most to predicting the target variable. Features with low importance scores can be removed without significantly impacting model performance.
- **Principal component analysis (PCA)**: PCA is a dimensionality reduction technique that can be used to transform the features into a set of linearly uncorrelated variables called principal components. The principal components can then be used as features for the predictive model.

Coding Example

The following Python code illustrates an example of how to perform feature engineering and selection for stock market direction prediction:

Python

```
import pandas as pd from sklearn.feature_selection import SelectKBest, f_classif

# Load the data
df = pd.read_csv('stock_market_data.csv')

# Create technical indicators as features
df['moving_average'] = df['close_price'].rolling(window=20).mean()
df['RSI'] = compute_rsi(df['close_price'])
```

```
# Hypothetical function to calculate RSI
def compute_rsi(close_price):
    # ...

# Select the most relevant features
selector = SelectKBest(f_classif, k=10)
selector.fit(df.drop('price_change', axis=1), df['price_change'])
selected_features = df.columns[selector.get_support()]

# The selected features can then be used for model training
X_selected = df[selected_features]
```

Model Training, Tuning, and Conclusion for Stock Market Direction Prediction

Once the features have been engineered and selected, the next step is to train the base models. Some popular base models for stock market direction prediction include:

- Logistic Regression
- Support Vector Machines
- Decision Trees
- Random Forests
- Gradient Boosting Machines

Each base model can be trained using the selected features and the target variable (that is, stock market direction).

Hyperparameter Tuning

Once the base models have been trained, it is important to tune their hyperparameters to improve their performance. Hyperparameters are parameters that control the learning process of a machine learning model. Some common hyperparameters for tree-based models include:

- Number of trees

- Maximum depth of trees
- Learning rate
- Minimum leaf size

Grid search and random search are two popular hyperparameter tuning techniques. Grid search tries all possible combinations of hyperparameter values, while random search tries a random sample of hyperparameter values.

Stacking Ensemble

Stacking ensemble is a popular technique for combining the predictions of multiple base models to produce a more accurate prediction. In stacking ensemble, the predictions from the base models are used as input features to train a meta-classifier. The meta-classifier is then used to make the final prediction.

Coding Snippet

The following Python code illustrates an example of how to train, tune, and evaluate a stacking ensemble model for stock market direction prediction:

Python

```
import pandas as pd

from sklearn.linear_model import LogisticRegression

from sklearn.ensemble import RandomForestClassifier

from sklearn.model_selection import GridSearchCV, train_test_split


# Load the data
df = pd.read_csv('stock_market_data.csv')


# Select the features
X = df['features']
y = df['target']


# Split the data into training and test sets
X_train, X_test, y_train, y_test = train_test_split(X, y, test_size=0.25)
```

```python
# Train the base models
lr_model = LogisticRegression()
rf_model = RandomForestClassifier()

# Tune the hyperparameters of the base models
lr_grid_search = GridSearchCV(lr_model, {'C': [0.1, 1, 10]}, cv=5)
rf_grid_search = GridSearchCV(rf_model, {'n_estimators': [100, 200, 300], 'max_depth': [10, 20, 30]}, cv=5)

lr_grid_search.fit(X_train, y_train)
rf_grid_search.fit(X_train, y_train)

# Train the meta-classifier
meta_model = LogisticRegression()
meta_model.fit(np.concatenate((lr_grid_search.predict_proba(X_train), rf_grid_search.predict_proba(X_train)), axis=1), y_train)

# Evaluate the ensemble model on the test set
y_pred = meta_model.predict(np.concatenate((lr_grid_search.predict_proba(X_test), rf_grid_search.predict_proba(X_test)), axis=1))

# Calculate the accuracy
accuracy = np.mean(y_pred == y_test)

# Print the accuracy
print('Accuracy:', accuracy)
```

Ensemble models can be a powerful tool for stock market direction prediction. By combining the predictions of multiple base models, ensemble models can produce more accurate predictions than any individual base model. However, it is important to remember that no model is perfect, and stock market prediction is inherently risky.

Conclusion

This chapter emphasized the importance of evaluating the trained ensemble model's performance on a held-out test set. This step is crucial to assess the model's ability to generalize and make accurate predictions for unseen data. We also explored some common performance metrics for stock market direction prediction, including:

- Accuracy
- Precision
- Recall
- F1 score

It is also important to consider the interpretability of the ensemble model. Ensemble models can be complex and difficult to interpret. This can be a problem in financial applications, where it is important to understand why the model makes the predictions it does.

In the next chapter, we will explore comprehensive strategies for detecting credit card fraud using data engineering and machine learning techniques. The chapter focuses on creating and evaluating predictive models, emphasizing the handling of imbalanced data and the importance of precision in fraud detection. It provides a deep dive into the complexities of data preprocessing, feature engineering, and model deployment, specifically tailored for real-time fraud detection in financial contexts.

CHAPTER 9
Data Engineering and ML Pipelines for Advanced Analytics

Introduction

Data engineering and machine learning (ML) are two important fields in data science that work together to solve complex problems. Data engineers clean and prepare data so that ML algorithms can learn from it and make predictions. ML algorithms then use this data to find patterns and insights that can be used to solve problems like credit card fraud detection.

Data engineers are responsible for collecting, cleaning, and storing data in a way that is easy for ML algorithms to use. This process is called data preparation. Data preparation is important because ML algorithms cannot make accurate predictions if they are given bad data.

ML algorithms are able to learn from data and find patterns that humans might not be able to see. These patterns can be used to make predictions or decisions. For example, ML algorithms can be used to detect fraudulent credit card transactions.

Data engineering and ML are essential for each other. Data engineers need ML algorithms to make predictions from data, and ML algorithms need data engineers to prepare data so that they can learn.

Credit card fraud detection is a complex problem that can be solved by using data engineering and ML. Data engineers collect and prepare data about credit card transactions. ML algorithms then use this data to find patterns that may indicate fraudulent activity.

Structure

In this chapter, we will cover the following topics:

- Data Engineering and Machine Learning Pipelines
    - Recap Data Engineering Pipeline
    - Recap Machine Learning Pipeline
    - Symbiotic Relationship Between the Two Pipelines
- Credit Card Fraud Detection Use Case
    - Data Collection Methods and Transactional Data
    - Preprocessing and Transformation
    - Secure and Efficient Data Storage
- Machine Learning Concepts Tailored to Fraud Detection
    - Algorithms Suited for Fraud Detection
    - Evaluation Metrics
    - Batch versus Real-time Processing Tradeoffs
    - Model Updating Strategies
    - End-to-End Pipeline
- Walk Through a Sample Credit Card Fraud Detection Pipeline from Scratch
    - Data Ingestion
    - Preprocessing
    - Model Training, Evaluation and Deployment
    - Monitoring and Feedback Loops

Data Engineering and Machine Learning

Data engineering and machine learning are often viewed as separate disciplines, but they have a deep symbiotic relationship. Data engineering provides the foundation for machine learning by collecting, cleaning, and storing data in a way that is accessible and usable for training and deploying ML models. Machine learning, in turn, leverages data to uncover patterns and insights that can be used to solve complex problems, such as credit card fraud detection.

The Data Engineering Process

Before we dive deeper into the intersection of data engineering and machine learning, let's revisit the key steps involved in data engineering:

1. **Data Sourcing**: Gathering raw data from various sources, ensuring its accuracy and relevancy.
2. **Data Cleaning and Preprocessing**: Removing inconsistencies and errors, and formatting data into a usable state.
3. **Data Storage and Warehousing**: Storing structured and cleaned data in databases or warehouses for efficient access and querying.
4. **ETL Processes**: Extract, Transform, Load (ETL) processes automate the data flow from sources to data warehouses.

Machine Learning Pipelines

Once the data is engineered, machine learning pipelines can be built to extract predictive insights. A typical ML pipeline involves the following steps:

1. **Data Gathering**: Fetching the relevant data to train the model.
2. **Data Preprocessing**: Normalizing, scaling, and encoding data to make it suitable for training.
3. **Feature Engineering**: Creating new or transforming existing features to enhance the model's performance.
4. **Model Training**: Utilizing ML algorithms to train models on the given dataset.
5. **Model Evaluation**: Testing the model's accuracy and performance on unseen data.
6. **Deployment**: Deploying the trained model to serve real-world predictions.

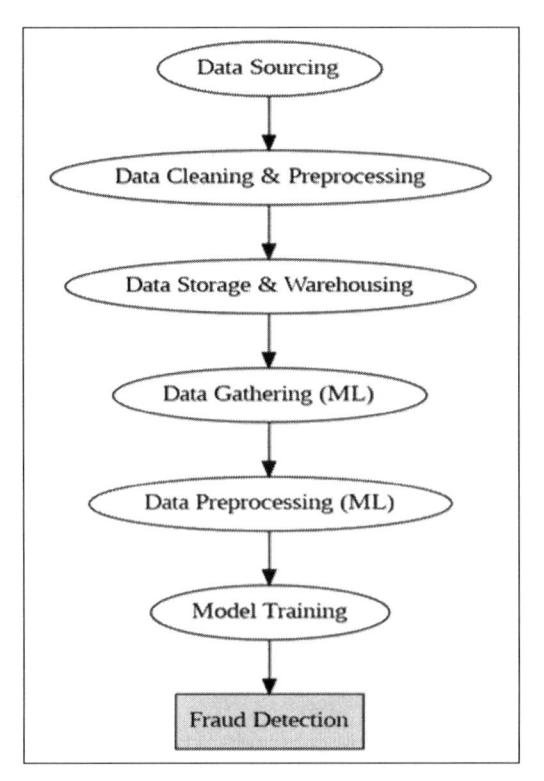

Figure 9.1: *Workflow for Fraud Detection Project*

Credit Card Fraud Detection

Credit card fraud detection is a prime example of how data engineering and machine learning can be combined to solve a challenging problem. With the rise of digital payments, credit card fraud has become increasingly prevalent, costing businesses and individuals billions annually.

Recap of Data Collection Methods with a Focus on Transactional Data

Transactional data captures the heartbeat of commerce, recording every purchase, swipe, and digital transaction. In the world of fraud detection, transactional data is paramount, revealing patterns of behavior and flagging outliers.

Traditional collection methods include:

- **Point of Sale (POS) Systems**: These systems capture transactional details such as the purchase amount, time, merchant details, and sometimes even the specifics of the purchased items.

- **Bank Servers**: These servers store a digital footprint of every transaction, providing vital data for analytical purposes.

Modern collection methods include:

- **Mobile Banking and Wallets**: Mobile apps collect a variety of data, including user behavior patterns and transaction details, offering a richer, more granular dataset.
- **E-commerce Platforms**: Online platforms can track user browsing patterns, preferences, cart behaviors, and more, adding depth to transactional data.

The Role of Data Engineering in Fraud Detection

Data engineering plays a critical role in fraud detection by collecting, cleaning, and storing transactional data in a way that is accessible and usable for analytical tools.

Data Collection: Data engineers must develop robust processes to collect transactional data from all relevant sources, including POS systems, bank servers, mobile apps, and e-commerce platforms.

Data Cleaning: Once collected, the data must be cleaned to remove inconsistencies, errors, and duplicates. Data engineers may also need to transform the data into a format that is compatible with analytical tools.

Data Storage: Data engineers must design and implement data storage solutions that can handle the high volume and velocity of transactional data. The data must also be stored in a way that makes it easy to query and analyze.

By effectively managing the data engineering process, data engineers can provide fraud detection teams with the high-quality data they need to identify and prevent fraudulent activity.

Transactional data is a powerful tool for fraud detection. By collecting, cleaning, and storing this data effectively, data engineers can empower fraud detection teams to protect businesses and consumers from fraudulent activity.

Preprocessing and Transformation for Fraud Detection Datasets

In fraud detection, machine learning models are trained on transactional data to identify fraudulent patterns. However, raw transactional data is often messy and incomplete, with missing values, inconsistencies, and anomalies. To ensure that models learn accurate patterns, it is essential to preprocess and transform the data into a structured, consistent, and clean format.

Handling Missing Values

Not all transactions capture every piece of information. For example, a transaction might log the amount and date, but skip the location or merchant category. In such cases, data engineers must decide whether and how to fill in the missing values. Common imputation techniques include:

- **Mean imputation**: Replacing missing values with the mean value of the feature.
- **Median imputation**: Replacing missing values with the median value of the feature.
- **Predictive filling**: Using machine learning to predict the missing values based on other features in the dataset.

The best imputation technique to use depends on the nature and importance of the missing values.

Categorization and Labeling

In supervised learning, machine learning models are trained on labeled data, where each data point is assigned a label (for example, fraudulent or non-fraudulent). For fraud detection, data engineers must label transactional data based on historical fraud data or expert annotations. This labeling process is essential for training models to distinguish between genuine and fraudulent transactions.

Feature Scaling and Normalization

In transactional datasets, different features may have vastly different scales. For example, transaction amounts may range in thousands, while the number of items purchased may hover in single digits. To ensure that no particular feature unduly influences the model, data engineers often scale and normalize features. Common techniques include:

- **Min-Max Scaling**: Scaling features to a range of 0 to 1.
- **Z-score Normalization**: Scaling features to have a mean of 0 and a standard deviation of 1.
- **Robust Scaling**: Scaling features to be less sensitive to outliers.

By scaling and normalizing features, data engineers can ensure that all features have an equal say in the model's predictions.

Preprocessing and transformation are essential steps in preparing transactional data for fraud detection models. By handling missing values, categorizing and labeling data, and scaling and normalizing features, data engineers can refine raw data into an asset for fraud detection teams.

Secure and Efficient Data Storage in Sensitive Financial Contexts

Financial transactions are the veins of commerce, carrying sensitive personal and financial information. Storing this data securely and efficiently is essential for preventing fraud and maintaining customer trust.

Security Considerations

- **Encryption**: Encryption algorithms scramble data so that it can only be deciphered by authorized individuals. Both data-at-rest (stored data) and data-in-transit (during transfers) should be encrypted to protect against breaches.
- **Access Control**: Access control measures restrict who can access and modify data. Strong access controls are essential for preventing unauthorized access to sensitive financial data.
- **Logging**: Audit logs track who accessed what data and when. This information can be used to investigate suspicious activity and detect breaches.

Efficiency Considerations

- **Data Warehousing**: Data warehouses store data in a structured format that optimizes retrieval and analysis. This makes it quick and easy to query large datasets of transactional data.
- **Indexing**: Indexes are data structures that speed up the search process by mapping values to their corresponding data points. Frequently queried attributes, such as transaction IDs or timestamps, should be indexed to improve data retrieval efficiency.

Balancing Security and Efficiency

When storing transactional data in sensitive financial contexts, it is important to strike a balance between security and efficiency. On the one hand, the data must be protected from unauthorized access and breaches. On the other hand, the data must be accessible to authorized personnel for analysis and operational purposes.

Data engineers can achieve this balance by implementing a layered security approach that incorporates encryption, access control, and logging. Additionally, data warehousing and indexing can be used to improve data retrieval efficiency without sacrificing security.

By carefully considering the security and efficiency requirements of transactional data storage, data engineers can help to protect sensitive financial data and ensure its smooth operation.

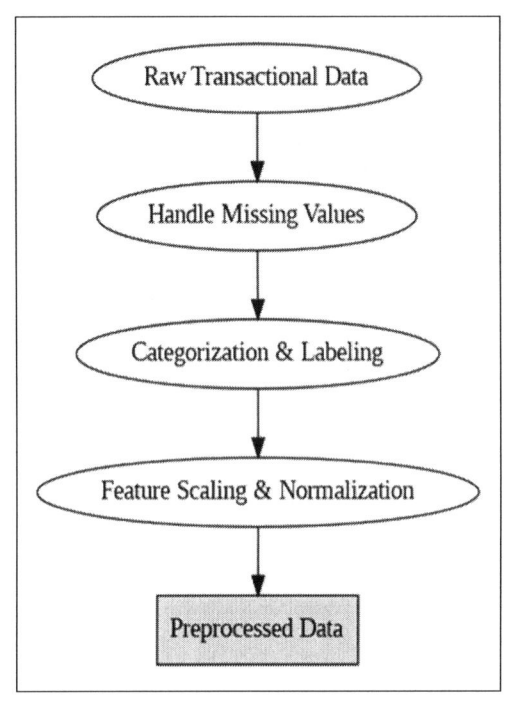

Figure 9.2: Preprocessing Data WorkFlow

Secure and Efficient Data Storage in Sensitive Financial Contexts: Beyond the Technology

While the technological aspects of data storage are essential, they are only half the equation. The other half encompasses the operational protocols and contingencies in place to ensure that data remains safe, accurate, and accessible, even in unforeseen circumstances.

Backup and Recovery

- **Regular Backups**: Regularly backing up data is essential for protecting against data loss due to system failures, human error, or malicious attacks. Backups should be scheduled based on the criticality of the data, with daily, weekly, or even real-time backups for the most critical data.
- **Disaster Recovery Plans**: Disaster recovery plans outline the steps that will be taken to restore data and mitigate further risks in the event of a significant

system failure or data breach. A robust disaster recovery plan should be in place for all financial institutions, especially those involved in fraud detection.

Regulatory Compliance

- **Data Retention and Deletion Policies**: Financial institutions must comply with regulatory requirements regarding how long certain data types must be retained and when they must be deleted. This helps to reduce legal liabilities and ensure compliance.
- **Data Sovereignty and Localization**: Data sovereignty laws dictate where financial data can be stored, especially if it pertains to citizens of a particular country. Financial institutions must comply with these laws to respect the data sovereignty of nations.

A Dual Approach

Secure and efficient data storage in sensitive financial contexts requires a dual approach that addresses both technical and operational requirements. By implementing robust backup and recovery procedures, disaster recovery plans, and data retention and deletion policies, financial institutions can ensure that their data remains safe, accurate, and accessible, even in the face of unexpected challenges.

This is especially important for financial institutions involved in fraud detection, as they rely on high-quality data to train and deploy predictive models. By taking a holistic approach to data storage, financial institutions can protect their data and their customers from fraud.

Summary: Navigating the Intersection of Data Engineering and Fraud Detection

The intersection of data engineering and fraud detection is both a powerful opportunity and a significant challenge. Data engineering provides the foundation for fraud detection by collecting, cleaning, and storing transactional data in a way that is accessible and usable for analytical tools. Fraud detection, in turn, leverages this data to identify patterns and behaviors that may indicate fraudulent activity.

Ethical Considerations

When working with transactional data, it is essential to consider the ethical implications. Two key considerations are privacy and anonymity, and bias and fairness.

Privacy and Anonymity: Data analysts must take steps to protect the privacy of individuals when analyzing transactional data. This may involve anonymizing the data by removing personally identifiable information (PII).

Bias and Fairness: Data can reflect historical biases, which can lead to unfair classifications in fraud detection systems. It is important to mitigate these biases when building and deploying fraud detection models.

The Road Ahead

The future of fraud detection lies in systems that are adaptive and collaborative.

Adaptive Systems: Fraudsters are constantly evolving their methods, so fraud detection systems must be able to learn and adapt in near real-time.

Collaborative Efforts: Data sharing across institutions, albeit in a secure and anonymized manner, can help to create more robust fraud detection systems. This is because fraud patterns observed in one institution may be relevant to other institutions.

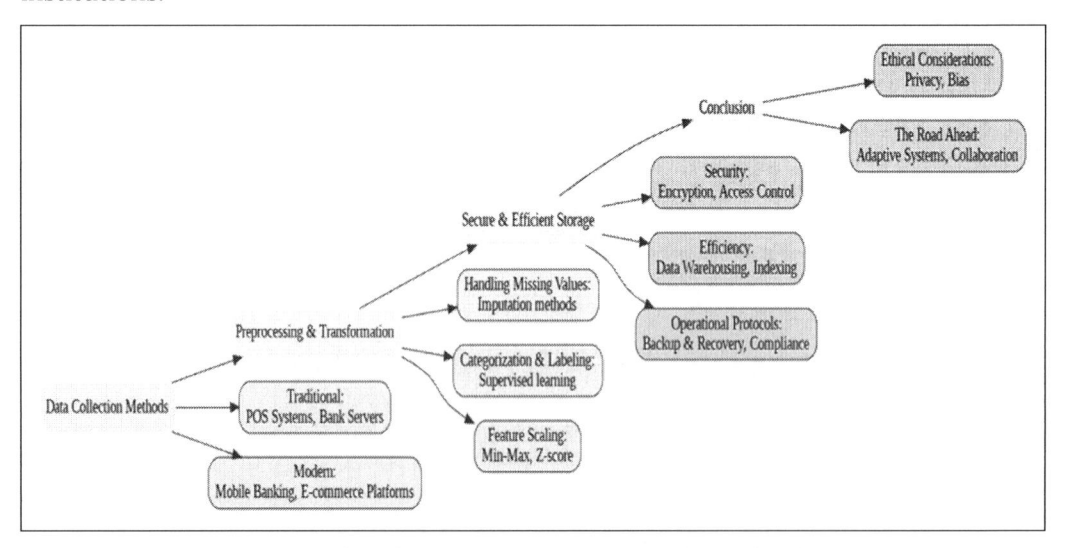

Figure 9.3: *End to end flow from data collection methods to Ethical considerations*

Diagram Description: Fraud Detection Workflow and Data Engineering Considerations

The diagram depicts the workflow and considerations in fraud detection, with a focus on data engineering aspects.

Data Collection Methods

The first stage is data collection, which is divided into traditional and modern methods:
- **Traditional methods**: Point-of-sale (POS) systems and bank servers
- **Modern methods:** Mobile banking and e-commerce platforms

Preprocessing and Transformation

Once collected, the data undergoes preprocessing and transformation steps:
1. **Handling missing values**: Imputation methods are used to fill in missing values.
2. **Categorization and labeling**: This is essential for supervised learning, where data is labeled as fraudulent or non-fraudulent.
3. **Feature scaling**: Techniques such as Min-Max normalization and Z-score standardization are applied to standardize the data.

Secure and Efficient Storage

The processed data must be stored securely and efficiently, especially in a financial context:
- **Security:** Encryption and access control are essential for protecting the data from unauthorized access and breaches.
- **Efficiency**: Data warehousing and indexing methods can be used to improve data retrieval efficiency.

Operational Protocols

Crucial operational aspects such as backup and recovery and compliance must also be considered:

Backup and recovery: Regular backups are essential to protect against data loss.

Compliance: Financial institutions must comply with regulatory requirements for data retention and deletion.

Data Exploration and Augmentation for Fraud Detection

Let us start by learning about data exploration in fraud detection.

Introduction to Data Exploration in Fraud Detection

Data exploration is the initial step in the fraud detection process. It is essential for understanding the structure, patterns, and anomalies present in transactional data. This data type is vast in volume and exhibits subtle variances, making data exploration critical for pinpointing suspicious activities. A thorough analysis can significantly improve the accuracy of subsequent detection algorithms.

Introduction to Transactional Data and Its Unique Properties

Transactional data captures specific actions or events, such as financial transactions, at a particular moment in time. It is often accompanied by various attributes such as timestamps, transaction amounts, parties involved, and more. Transactional data exhibits several unique properties that make exploration crucial. Some unique properties of transactional data include:

- **High volume**: Transactional data accumulates rapidly due to the constant flow of transactions.
- **Temporal patterns**: Transactions can exhibit patterns over time, often linked to human behaviors or system operations.
- **Multidimensionality**: With various attributes attached to each transaction, transactional data can be multi-faceted and complex.

Challenges in Dealing with Transactional Data

While transactional data offers a wealth of information for fraud detection, it also presents significant challenges, including:

- **Data quality:** The vast volume of data can lead to inconsistencies or missing values that need to be addressed.
- **Scalability**: Handling and processing large amounts of data efficiently is crucial.
- **Noise and outliers**: Genuine transactions can sometimes appear as outliers, while fraudulent ones might blend in. Distinguishing between the two is challenging.

Techniques Specific to Exploring Transactional Data

Exploring transactional data requires specialized techniques to effectively uncover underlying patterns. Some of these techniques include:

- **Histograms**: Histograms visualize the frequency of transactions to identify common and rare transaction amounts. This can help to identify unusual transactions that may be suspicious.
- **Time-series analysis**: Time-series analysis evaluates transaction trends and seasonal patterns over time. This can help to identify anomalies in transactional behavior, such as sudden spikes in transactions or unusual patterns of activity.
- **Clustering**: Clustering groups similar transactions together. This can be used to identify common behaviors or anomalies in the data. For example, clustering can be used to identify groups of transactions that are associated with fraudulent activity.

Handling Imbalanced Datasets in Fraud Detection

Fraud detection datasets are often imbalanced, meaning that there are significantly more legitimate transactions than fraudulent ones. This can make it difficult for machine learning models to learn to identify fraudulent transactions. There are a number of techniques that can be used to handle imbalanced datasets in fraud detection, including:

- **Undersampling**: Undersampling involves reducing the number of majority class instances (legitimate transactions) in the dataset to balance it. This can be done by randomly removing majority class instances or by using more sophisticated techniques such as Tomek Links or edited nearest neighbors.
- **Oversampling**: Oversampling involves creating copies or variations of minority class instances (fraudulent transactions) to balance the dataset. This can be done by simply duplicating minority class instances or by using more sophisticated techniques such as SMOTE.
- **Synthetic Minority Over-sampling Technique (SMOTE):** SMOTE is a popular oversampling technique that generates synthetic instances of the minority class using interpolation. SMOTE can be effective for handling imbalanced datasets in fraud detection, but it is important to tune the hyperparameters carefully to avoid overfitting.

Reference to Previously Explained Exploration Phases

Data exploration in fraud detection builds upon standard data exploration phases, with added emphasis on anomaly detection, temporal patterns, and understanding transaction behaviors.

In addition to the techniques mentioned above, data explorers should also pay attention to the following when exploring transactional data for fraud detection:

- **Outliers**: Outliers are transactions that are significantly different from the majority of other transactions. Outliers may be suspicious, but they may also be legitimate transactions that are simply unusual. It is important to investigate outliers carefully to determine their cause.
- **Temporal patterns**: Transactions can exhibit patterns over time, such as daily, weekly, or monthly patterns. These patterns can be used to identify anomalies, such as sudden spikes in transactions or unusual patterns of activity.
- **Transaction behaviors**: By understanding the typical behaviors of legitimate transactions, data explorers can more easily identify suspicious transactions. For example, if a transaction is much larger or smaller than the average transaction amount, or if it is made from an unusual location, it may be suspicious.

Data Exploration and Augmentation for Fraud Detection

This section effectively introduces Advanced Data Augmentation Techniques.

Advanced Data Augmentation Techniques

In addition to the standard data augmentation methods mentioned above, several advanced techniques have emerged in recent years that show promise in augmenting data for fraud detection:

- **Generative Adversarial Networks (GANs):** GANs are a type of machine learning model that can be used to generate synthetic data that is indistinguishable from real data. GANs have been shown to be effective in generating synthetic fraudulent transaction data that can be used to train and improve fraud detection models.
- **Variational Autoencoders (VAEs):** VAEs are another type of machine learning model that can be used to learn the underlying distribution of a dataset and generate new samples from that distribution. VAEs can also be used to generate synthetic fraudulent transaction data and to identify anomalies in transactional data.
- **Anomaly Detection using Deep Learning**: Deep learning models such as autoencoders can be used to identify anomalies in transactional data. Anomalies may be indicative of fraudulent activity, so this can be a useful technique for fraud detection.

Implementation Considerations

When implementing fraud detection solutions, it is important to consider the following:

- **Real-time versus Batch Processing**: Fraud detection systems can process transactions in real-time or in batches. Real-time processing is more responsive to fraud, but it can be more computationally expensive. Batch processing is less computationally expensive, but it may be slower to detect fraud.
- **Feature Engineering**: Feature engineering is the process of creating new features from existing data. It is important to engineer features that are informative and that can be used to distinguish between fraudulent and legitimate transactions.
- **Evaluation Metrics**: Traditional evaluation metrics such as accuracy may not be suitable for fraud detection tasks, as fraud detection datasets are often imbalanced. More suitable metrics include precision, recall, and the F1 score.

Introduction to Feature Engineering for Fraud Patterns

Let us first know what is feature engineering.

The Essence of Feature Engineering

Feature engineering is the process of transforming raw data into a format that is more informative and useful for machine learning algorithms. It involves creating new features from the existing data, or combining existing features in new ways, to capture underlying patterns and relationships more effectively.

Relevance in Fraud Detection

Fraud detection is a challenging task, as fraudsters are constantly evolving their methods to avoid detection. One key to effective fraud detection is to use machine learning algorithms to identify patterns and anomalies in transactional data. However, machine learning algorithms can only be as good as the data they are trained on. Feature engineering plays a crucial role in ensuring that the data is in a format that allows the machine learning algorithms to learn and detect fraud patterns effectively.

In the context of credit card fraud detection, there is a vast amount of available data, including transaction amounts, timestamps, merchant locations, and cardholder information. However, this data is often raw and unstructured, and it can be difficult for machine learning algorithms to learn from it directly. Feature engineering can be used to create new features from this raw data that capture more informative and meaningful patterns. For example, we could create features such as:

- **Average transaction amount per week**: This feature can help to identify unusual spikes in spending, which could be indicative of fraud.
- **Number of transactions per day**: This feature can help to identify unusual patterns of activity, such as a sudden increase in the number of transactions made from a single location or merchant.
- **Transaction location distance:** This feature can help to identify transactions that are made from locations that are far apart in a short period of time, which could be indicative of fraud.

Why is it Different for Fraud Detection

Feature engineering is important for all machine learning applications, but it is especially important for fraud detection. This is because fraud is inherently anomalous. Fraudsters do not want to be detected, so they try to hide their activities by blending in with legitimate transactions. As a result, the features that are used to detect fraud need to be very specific and nuanced. They need to be able to pick up on the subtle anomalies that distinguish fraudulent transactions from legitimate transactions.

For example, a simple feature like "transaction amount" may not be very effective for detecting fraud, as fraudsters can easily make transactions that are within the normal range of spending for a particular cardholder. However, a more sophisticated feature like "average transaction amount per week" may be more effective for detecting fraud, as it can capture unusual spikes in spending.

Overview and Handling Imbalanced Data

In this section, we will be learning about handling imbalanced data.

The Machine Learning Pipeline for Fraud Detection

The machine learning pipeline for fraud detection is similar to any machine learning pipeline, but it has some unique challenges. One of the main challenges is that fraud detection datasets are often imbalanced, meaning that there are many more legitimate transactions than fraudulent transactions. This can make it difficult for machine learning algorithms to learn to identify fraudulent transactions.

The Challenge of Imbalanced Data

Imbalanced data is a problem because most machine learning algorithms are designed to minimize overall error. This means that they will try to predict the majority class (legitimate transactions) as often as possible, even if it means misclassifying some of the minority class (fraudulent transactions). This can lead to high false negative rates, which is unacceptable for fraud detection systems.

Tackling Imbalance

There are a number of techniques that can be used to handle imbalanced data in fraud detection. Some of the most common techniques include:

- **Resampling**: This involves oversampling the minority class (fraudulent transactions) or undersampling the majority class (legitimate transactions). Oversampling can be done by duplicating minority class instances or by creating synthetic minority over-sampling technique (SMOTE) samples. Undersampling can be done by randomly removing majority class instances or by using more sophisticated techniques such as edited nearest neighbors or Tomek links.
- **Synthetic Data Generation**: Techniques such as SMOTE can be used to generate synthetic samples of the minority class in the feature space. This can help to balance the dataset and improve the performance of the machine learning algorithm.
- **Anomaly Detection:** Instead of treating fraud detection as a classification problem, it can be treated as an anomaly detection problem. This involves training the machine learning algorithm on the majority class (legitimate transactions) and then using it to identify anomalies or deviations from the majority class. Anomalies can then be flagged as potential fraud.
- **Cost-sensitive Learning**: This involves introducing different misclassification costs for false negatives and false positives. This can make the machine learning algorithm more sensitive to the minority class and improve its performance on fraud detection.

Choosing the Right Algorithms for Fraud Detection

The choice of algorithm for fraud detection is a critical one. The algorithm should be chosen based on the nature of the data, the extent of the imbalance, and the business objectives.

Decision Trees and Random Forests

Decision trees and random forests are popular choices for fraud detection because they are transparent and easy to interpret. Decision trees can be visualized, which can be helpful for explaining the model to non-technical stakeholders. Random forests are ensembles of decision trees, which makes them more accurate but less interpretable. They are also less prone to overfitting.

Neural Networks and Deep Learning

Neural networks, especially deep learning models, can be very powerful tools for fraud detection. They can automatically extract intricate patterns and features from large amounts of data. However, they are also black boxes, which means that it can be difficult to understand how they make predictions.

Autoencoders are a type of neural network that can be used for anomaly detection. They compress and reconstruct data, and anomalies can be detected by observing reconstruction errors.

Support Vector Machines (SVMs)

SVMs are particularly useful when there is a clear margin of separation between classes. They work by finding the optimal hyperplane that best divides the data into classes. SVMs can be effective for fraud detection, especially when used with kernel tricks to transform the feature space.

Summary

The best algorithm for fraud detection will vary depending on the specific context. However, the algorithms discussed above are all good choices to consider.

Here is a table that summarizes the key strengths and weaknesses of each algorithm:

Algorithm	Strengths	Weaknesses
Decision Trees	Transparent and easy to interpret	Prone to overfitting
Random Forests	More accurate than decision trees	Less interpretable than decision trees
Neural Networks	Can automatically extract intricate patterns and features from large amounts of data	Black boxes, difficult to interpret
Autoencoders	Useful for anomaly detection	Black boxes, difficult to interpret
Support Vector Machines (SVMs)	Effective when there is a clear margin of separation between classes	Can be sensitive to the choice of kernel function

***Table 9.1**: Key strengths and weaknesses of each algorithm*

The following table summarizes the comparison of algorithms.

Algorithm	Decision Trees	Random Forests	Neural Networks	Autoencoders	Support Vector Machines (SVMs)
Sensitivity to imbalanced data	Medium	Low	High	Medium	Medium
Interpretability	High	Medium	Low	Low	Medium
Computational complexity	Low	Medium	High	High	Medium

Table 9.2: Comparison of algorithms

Batch versus Real-Time Processing Considerations in a Fraud Detection Context

In the fast-paced world of digital transactions, the speed and timing of fraud detection can make a significant difference. The decision between batch and real-time processing hinges on a trade-off between immediacy and thoroughness.

Batch Processing

Batch processing involves collecting data over a specific period, processing it in chunks, and then producing outputs. This approach has a number of advantages, including:

- **Comprehensive Analysis**: Batch processing allows for a deep analysis of the collected data, leveraging more extensive and complex models. This can be beneficial for fraud detection, as it can help to identify subtle patterns and anomalies that may be difficult to detect with real-time processing.
- **Resource Efficiency:** Batch processing is often more resource-efficient than real-time processing, as data can be processed during off-peak times. This can be important for organizations with limited resources.

However, batch processing also has some disadvantages, including:

- **Latency:** There is a time lag between data collection and insights generation, which may not be ideal for time-sensitive tasks like fraud detection. This is because fraudulent transactions can be completed in a matter of seconds, so it is important to be able to detect them as quickly as possible.
- **Potential for Errors**: Batch processing systems can be more prone to errors than real-time processing systems, as they may not be able to handle unexpected spikes in data volume or velocity.

Real-Time Processing

Real-time processing involves immediate analysis and action upon data as it arrives. This approach has a number of advantages, including:

- **Instantaneous Action**: Real-time processing enables immediate actions to be taken, such as blocking a suspicious transaction before it is completed. This can help to minimize the losses incurred from fraud.
- **Enhanced User Experience**: By quickly verifying transactions, legitimate users experience fewer disruptions. This can be important for maintaining customer satisfaction and trust.

However, real-time processing also has some disadvantages, including:

- **Resource Intensive**: Real-time processing requires robust infrastructure to handle high-frequency data. This can be expensive to set up and maintain.
- **Potential for Errors**: Speed may come at the expense of accuracy due to time constraints. For example, a real-time fraud detection system may be more likely to flag legitimate transactions as fraudulent.

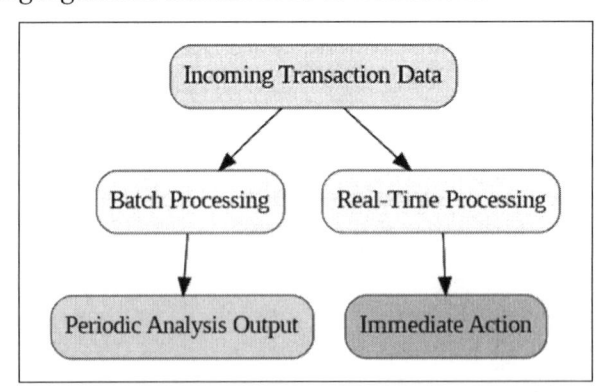

Figure 9.4: Real time Processing versus Batch processing

Use Cases in Fraud Detection

Both batch and real-time processing can be used for fraud detection, depending on the specific needs of the organization.

Batch Processing Use Cases:

- **Periodic Audits**: Batch processing can be used to periodically audit transactions for fraud. This can be done on a daily, weekly, or monthly basis, depending on the organization's risk appetite.

- **Training Models**: Batch processing can also be used to train or refine machine learning models for fraud detection. This is because batch processing allows for more extensive and complex models to be trained on large datasets.

Real-Time Processing Use Cases:
- **Transaction Verification**: Real-time processing can be used to verify each transaction as it occurs. This can help to prevent fraudulent transactions from being completed.
- **Alerts:** Real-time processing can also be used to generate alerts about suspicious activities. This can help to notify investigators of potential fraud quickly, so that they can take appropriate action.

Advancements in Real-Time Processing

As technology has advanced, real-time processing has become more feasible for businesses of all sizes. Some of the key advancements that have made this possible include:

- **Distributed Computing**: Distributed computing platforms such as Apache Kafka and Apache Flink enable the processing of massive volumes of data in real-time by distributing the workload across multiple nodes.
- **Edge Computing**: Edge computing brings data processing closer to the source of data collection, such as sensors and IoT devices. This reduces latency, which is essential for real-time operations.

Handling Errors in Real-Time

The rapid nature of real-time processing can lead to errors due to the quick decision-making required. Some strategies to mitigate these errors include:

- **Fallback to Batch:** If a real-time system encounters ambiguity, it can flag a transaction for later batch analysis. This allows for a more comprehensive analysis of the transaction, using more complex models and data sources.
- **Feedback Loops**: Using feedback from real-time results to improve models and processing over time. This can help to reduce the occurrence of errors in the future.

Transitioning from Batch to Real-Time

Many organizations initially set up batch processes for fraud detection and other tasks. As their needs and capabilities grow, they may transition to real-time processing. Here are some steps involved in this transition:

- **Upgrade Infrastructure**: Ensure that the hardware and software infrastructure can handle the increased volume and velocity of data associated with real-time processing.

- **Refine Models**: Adapt existing fraud detection models to deliver quicker results without compromising too much on accuracy.

- **Set Up Monitoring and Alerts**: Set up systems to notify of potential issues in real-time operations, such as spikes in data volume or unexpected errors.

Considerations for Choice

The decision of whether to use batch or real-time processing depends on a number of factors, including:

- **Nature of Transactions**: High-frequency, low-value transactions, such as credit card transactions, may benefit more from real-time processing, as it can help to prevent fraudulent transactions from being completed.

- **Infrastructure Costs:** Real-time processing may require a more expensive infrastructure than batch processing, due to the need to handle higher data volumes and velocities.

- **Risk Appetite**: Organizations that are more risk-averse may prefer the thoroughness of batch processing, even at the expense of some latency.

Evaluation Metrics for Fraud Detection

In fraud detection, simply achieving high accuracy is not enough. This is because fraud data is typically imbalanced, meaning that there are many more legitimate transactions than fraudulent ones. As a result, traditional accuracy metrics can be misleading, as they can be biased towards the majority class.

Precision, Recall, and the F1 Score

Precision and recall are two important metrics for fraud detection. Precision measures the proportion of flagged transactions that are actually fraudulent, while recall measures the proportion of actual fraudulent transactions that are flagged.

PA high F1 score indicates that the model is good at both identifying fraudulent transactions (high precision) and avoiding false positives (high recall).

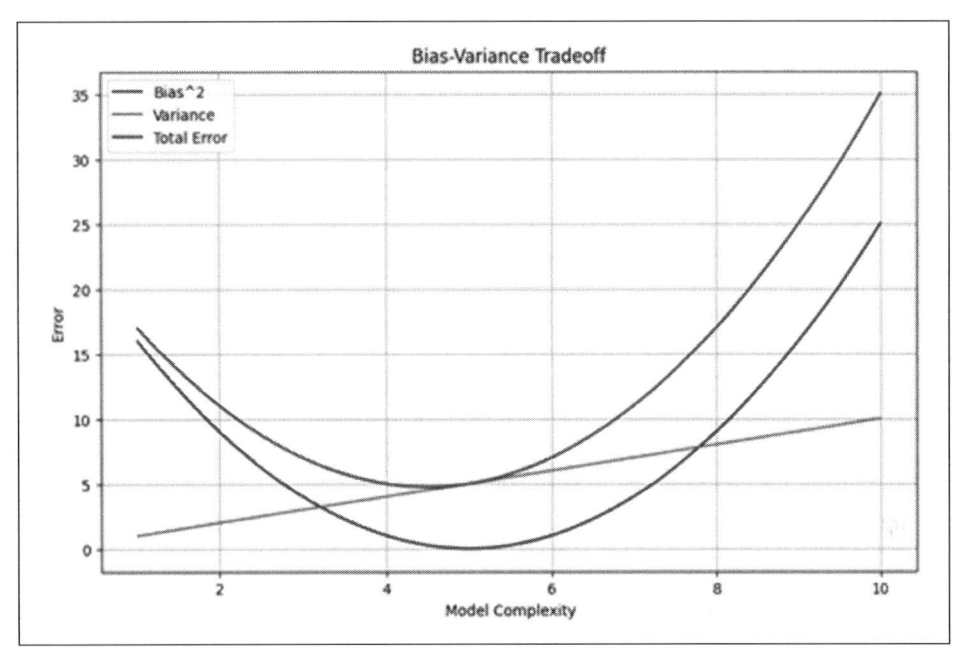

Figure 9.5: Bias-Variance Trade-off with model complexity

Area Under the Receiver Operating Characteristic (ROC-AUC)

The ROC curve is a graph that shows the relationship between the true positive rate (TPR) and the false positive rate (FPR) for a given model. The TPR is the proportion of actual fraudulent transactions that are correctly identified by the model, while the FPR is the proportion of legitimate transactions that are incorrectly flagged as fraudulent by the model.

The AUC is a single metric that summarizes the performance of a model over all possible classification thresholds. It is calculated as the area under the ROC curve. A high AUC indicates that the model is good at distinguishing between fraudulent and legitimate transactions.

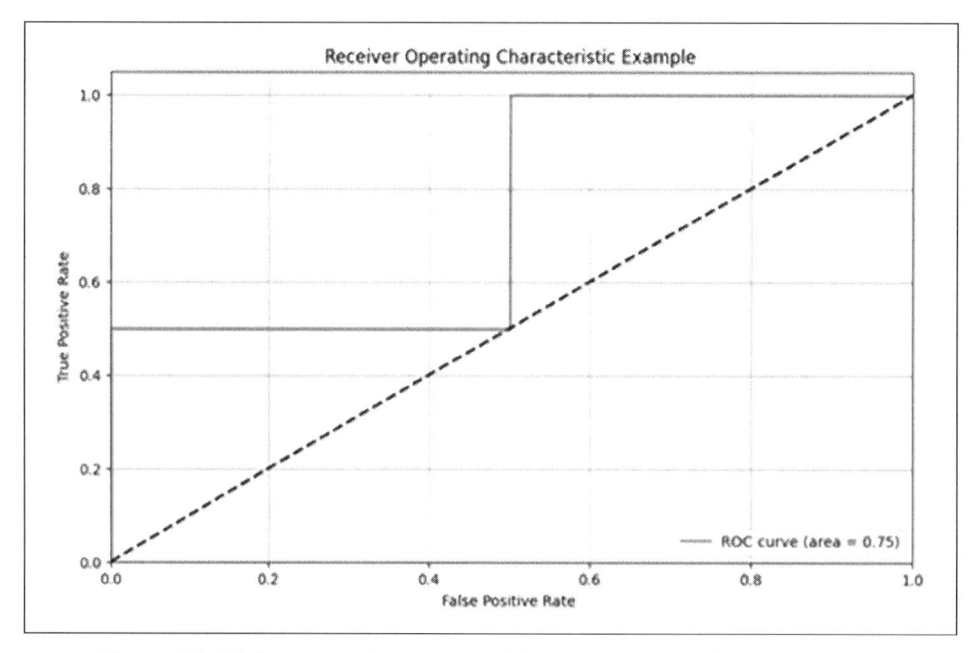

Figure 9.6: ROC representing True Positive Rate versus False Positive Rate

Cost-Benefit Analysis

In a business context, it is important to consider the costs associated with false positives and false negatives. For example, the cost of a false positive may be losing a customer due to a declined transaction, while the cost of a false negative may be monetary loss due to not catching fraud.

By quantifying these costs, businesses can tailor their machine learning model's threshold to achieve an optimal balance. For example, if the cost of a false negative is very high, the business may choose to set a lower threshold, even if this means that some legitimate transactions are flagged as fraudulent.

Adapting Model Evaluation Metrics for Fraud Detection

Traditional model evaluation metrics, such as accuracy, may not be sufficient for fraud detection. This is because fraud is a rare event, so even a model that is 99% accurate may still miss a significant number of fraudulent transactions.

One challenge in fraud detection is class imbalance. This means that there are many more legitimate transactions than fraudulent ones. If a model simply predicts that all transactions are legitimate, it will still be 99% accurate. This is known as the accuracy paradox.

To address the accuracy paradox, we can use more sophisticated metrics such as precision, recall, and the F1 score. These metrics take into account the class imbalance and provide a more holistic view of the model's performance.

- **Precision**: The proportion of flagged transactions that are actually fraudulent.
- **Recall:** The proportion of actual fraudulent transactions that are flagged.
- **F1 score**: A single metric that combines precision and recall into a single value.

A high F1 score indicates that the model is good at both identifying fraudulent transactions (high precision) and avoiding false positives (high recall).

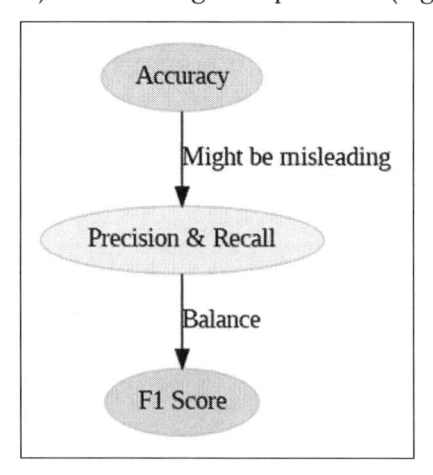

Figure 9.7: Accuracy, Precision, Recall and F1-score

Importance of Model Interpretation and Trust in Financial Use Cases

For financial institutions, it is important to not only detect fraud, but also to understand why a particular transaction was flagged. This is because stakeholders need to trust the model in order to take action on its predictions.

Model interpretation techniques can help to build trust in the model by providing transparency into its decision-making process. Two popular model interpretation techniques are SHAP (SHapley Additive exPlanations) and LIME (Local Interpretable Model-agnostic Explanations).

- **SHAP:** SHAP decomposes a prediction into the contributions of each individual feature.
- **LIME:** LIME generates local explanations for predictions by fitting a simple model to the data around a given prediction.

Referencing Evaluation Strategies from Previous Chapters

As discussed in previous chapters, there are a number of evaluation strategies that can be tailored to fraud detection:

- **Cost-sensitive learning**: This technique assigns higher penalties to misclassified fraud cases. This is important because the cost of missing a fraudulent transaction is often much higher than the cost of flagging a legitimate transaction as fraudulent.
- **Under sampling and oversampling**: These techniques can be used to address class imbalance. Undersampling involves reducing the number of non-fraud cases in the training data, while oversampling involves increasing the number of fraud cases in the training data.
- **Anomaly detection**: Another approach to fraud detection is to treat it as an anomaly detection problem. This means that we train a model to identify transactions that are different from the majority of normal transactions.

Making Model Decisions Explainable

In the age of complex models like deep learning, model decisions can sometimes become a black box. For fraud detection in financial contexts, where accountability and traceability are crucial, this black box approach is not ideal. There is a need for models that are both accurate and explainable.

Trade-offs: Simplicity versus Performance

Complex models like neural networks may yield higher accuracy, but simpler models like decision trees or linear regression provide better interpretability. The choice often comes down to the specific requirements of the application and the importance of transparency.

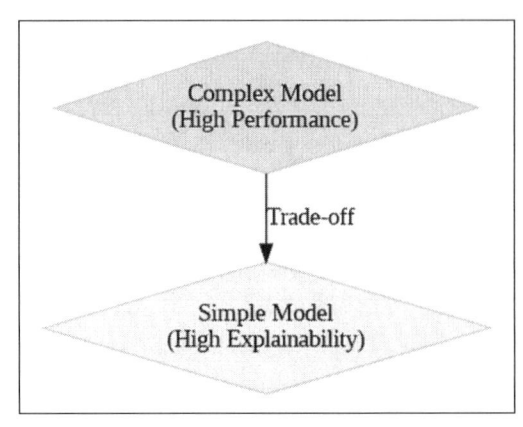

Figure 9.8: *Complex versus Simple Models*

Feedback Loop: Continuous Model Improvement

Fraudsters evolve their tactics, and so must our models. Incorporating a feedback loop, where the model is retrained with new data and refined based on any false negatives or positives, is crucial.

Steps in a Feedback Loop

1. Deploy the model and make predictions.
2. Collect feedback on model predictions.
3. Retrain the model with new data.
4. Redeploy the improved model.

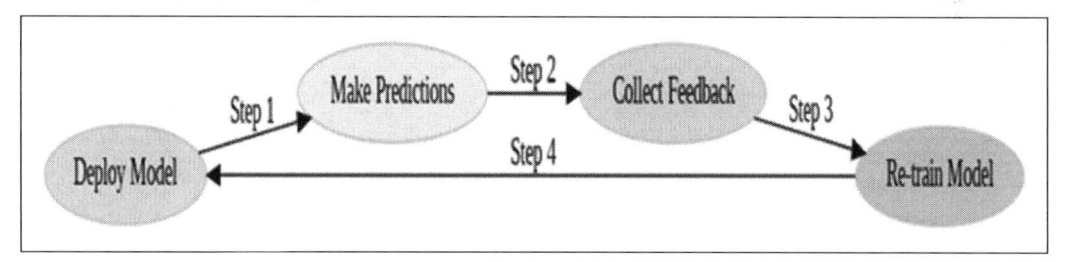

Figure 9.9: Continuous Model Improvement

Effective fraud detection is a blend of the right evaluation metrics, model interpretability, and continuous learning. While the allure of high accuracy is tempting, in financial contexts, explainability and trustworthiness often take precedence. As technology and fraud tactics evolve, staying updated and adaptable is the key to a robust fraud detection system.

Model interpretation techniques: There are a number of model interpretation techniques available, such as SHAP and LIME. These techniques can help to explain model decisions and identify the features that are most important for prediction.

Cost-sensitive learning: In fraud detection, it is often more important to avoid false negatives (missing a fraudulent transaction) than false positives (flagging a legitimate transaction as fraudulent). Cost-sensitive learning algorithms can be used to account for this by assigning higher penalties to misclassified fraud cases.

Hybrid models: One way to achieve both accuracy and explainability is to use a hybrid model. This involves combining the strengths of two or more different algorithms, such as a deep learning model for its accuracy and a decision tree for its interpretability.

Deploying Fraud Detection Models in Real-time Transactional Systems

In the fast-paced world of finance, fraud detection models must be both highly accurate and responsive. Deploying them in real-time transactional systems is a multi-step process that requires careful consideration of the following factors:

Model Optimization

Before deployment, fraud detection models are optimized for performance to ensure that they run efficiently without sacrificing accuracy. This may involve techniques such as quantization, pruning, and model distillation.

Integration with Transactional Systems

Fraud detection models need to be seamlessly integrated with existing transactional systems. This involves designing APIs that can swiftly carry out real-time predictions.

Latency Considerations

Since we're dealing with real-time systems, latency becomes a critical factor. The model's prediction should be available in milliseconds to ensure that there's no noticeable delay in transaction processing.

Monitoring Performance in Live Environments

Once the model is live, its performance must be continuously monitored to ensure that it's catching fraud accurately and not generating too many false alarms. This can be done using a variety of tools and techniques, such as:

- **Dashboarding tools**: Visual tools, like dashboards, can provide real-time insights into the model's performance metrics, allowing stakeholders to spot and address issues promptly.
- **Alert systems:** Automated alert systems can notify stakeholders if the model's performance deteriorates or if there's an unusual spike in fraudulent activity.
- **Regular evaluation**: Even after deployment, the model's performance is evaluated regularly using actual transaction data to ensure it remains effective.

Strategies to Update the Model with New Fraud Patterns

Fraudsters are constantly evolving their tactics, so it's important to keep the fraud detection model up-to-date to stay ahead of the curve. Some strategies for doing this include:

- **Feedback loops**: Regularly retraining the model with new transaction data, especially those flagged as suspicious, helps the model adapt to new fraud patterns.

- **External data sources**: Incorporating data from external sources, such as global fraud databases, can provide insights into emerging fraud tactics.
- **Collaboration with financial experts**: Working closely with financial experts can provide invaluable insights into new fraud tactics and help fine-tune the model.

Credit Card Fraud Detection Pipeline from Scratch

Let us learn about the credit card fraud detection pipeline in detail.

Introduction and Overview

Credit card fraud is a pervasive issue that costs financial institutions billions of dollars annually. As digital transactions become increasingly common, the potential for fraud grows exponentially. Effective fraud detection mechanisms are essential to mitigate financial losses and maintain customer trust.

This case study delves into the Credit Card Fraud Detection dataset to build a comprehensive fraud detection pipeline. This dataset is particularly interesting because it reflects real-world challenges, including high dimensionality, imbalanced classes, and the need for timely predictions.

Dataset Overview

The Credit Card Fraud Detection dataset was curated from European cardholders' transactions over two days. It contains 284,807 transactions, of which only 492 (0.172%) are fraudulent. The dataset includes numerical input variables V1 to V28, which are the result of a PCA transformation. The original features and more background information about the data are not provided due to confidentiality issues.

The only features that have not been transformed with PCA are Time and Amount. Time contains the seconds elapsed between each transaction and the first transaction in the dataset. Amount is the transaction amount.

Objective

The objective of this case study is to build a fraud detection model that can accurately detect potential frauds while minimizing false positives. False positives can result in a bad user experience, while false negatives can lead to monetary losses.

Pipeline Stages

The following are the key stages of the proposed fraud detection pipeline:

1. **Data preprocessing and feature engineering**: This stage ensures that the data is clean, relevant, and structured to feed into the machine learning model.
2. **Model selection and training**: This stage involves selecting a suitable machine learning algorithm and training it on the preprocessed data.
3. **Evaluation techniques tailored for fraud detection**: Traditional evaluation metrics such as accuracy may not be sufficient for fraud detection, as they can be misleading due to the class imbalance. Therefore, it is crucial to use metrics such as precision, recall, and F1 score, which better account for the costs of false positives and false negatives.
4. **Deployment strategies for real-time predictions**: Since fraud detection is a time-sensitive task, it is important to deploy the model in a way that can generate predictions in real time. This may involve using a cloud-based platform or developing a custom microservice.
5. **Continuous model monitoring and updating mechanisms**: Fraudsters are constantly evolving their tactics, so it is important to monitor the model's performance and update it regularly with new data to ensure that it remains effective.

Data Preprocessing and Feature Engineering code

The steps involved in data preprocessing and feature engineering for credit card fraud detection are as follows:

1. Loads the Credit Card Fraud Detection dataset into a Pandas DataFrame.
2. Checks for missing values and assesses outliers.
3. Transforms the Time feature to capture cyclic patterns using sine and cosine transformations.
4. Scales the Amount feature using standard deviation.
5. Oversamples the minority class using SMOTE to address the class imbalance.
6. Splits the data into training and testing sets, ensuring that the split respects the temporal nature of the data and that the testing set simulates future, unseen data.

Python

```
import pandas as pd
```

```python
from sklearn.model_selection import train_test_split

# Load the Credit Card Fraud Detection dataset
df = pd.read_csv('credit_card_fraud_detection.csv')

## Data Exploration and Cleaning

# Check for missing values
print(df.isnull().sum())

# Assess outliers
print(df.describe())

## Feature Engineering

# Transform the 'Time' feature to capture cyclic patterns
df['Time_Hour'] = df['Time'] // 3600
df['Time_Minute'] = (df['Time'] % 3600) // 60
df['Time_Sin'] = np.sin(df['Time_Hour'] * 2 * np.pi / 24)
df['Time_Cos'] = np.cos(df['Time_Hour'] * 2 * np.pi / 24)

# Scale the 'Amount' feature
df['Amount_Scaled'] = df['Amount'] / df['Amount'].std()

## Class Imbalance Handling

# Use SMOTE to oversample the minority class
from imblearn.over_sampling import SMOTE
smote = SMOTE()
X_train, y_train = smote.fit_resample(X_train, y_train)
```

```
## Data Splitting

# Split the data into training and testing sets
X_train, X_test, y_train, y_test = train_test_split(X_train, y_train, test_size=0.2, random_state=42, stratify=y_train)
```

Model Selection and Training

Given the nature of fraud detection, which requires a high sensitivity to fraudulent activities while minimizing false alarms, specific models are naturally better-suited. Some of these models include:

- **Logistic regression**: Despite being a simple model, logistic regression can perform surprisingly well for binary classification tasks like fraud detection.
- **Random forest**: This ensemble model, consisting of multiple decision trees, provides an excellent balance between performance and interpretability.
- **Gradient boosting machines (GBM):** Advanced ensemble techniques like XGBoost or LightGBM can provide higher accuracy at the cost of increased complexity.
- **Neural networks**: While they can capture complex patterns, they require careful tuning and can be harder to interpret, which might be a concern in financial use-cases.

Python

```
from sklearn.ensemble import RandomForestClassifier # Initializing the model rf_classifier = RandomForestClassifier(n_estimators=100, random_state=42) # Training the model rf_classifier.fit(X_train, y_train)
```

For the sake of this case study, we will focus on Random Forest due to its robustness and ease of interpretation.

Once the model is trained, we can perform hyperparameter tuning to optimize its performance. This involves trying out different combinations of model parameters and evaluating the model on a held-out validation set. We can use a technique like grid search to systematically explore the parameter space and find the best set of parameters.

```
from sklearn.model_selection import GridSearchCV # Define the parameters grid param_grid = { 'n_estimators': [50, 100, 150], 'max_depth': [None, 10, 20, 30], 'min_samples_split': [2, 5, 10], 'min_samples_
```

Data Engineering and ML Pipelines for Advanced Analytics

```
leaf': [1, 2, 4] } grid_search = GridSearchCV(estimator=rf_classifier, param_grid=param_grid, cv=3, scoring='f1', n_jobs=-1) # Conducting the grid search grid_search.fit(X_train, y_train)
```

Once the hyperparameters are tuned, we can extract the feature importances of the model to understand which features are most important for its predictions.

Python

```
import matplotlib.pyplot as plt # Extracting feature importances importances = rf_classifier.feature_importances_ features = X_train.columns # Plotting plt.figure(figsize=(10,6)) sorted_idx = importances.argsort() plt.barh(features[sorted_idx], importances[sorted_idx]) plt.xlabel('Feature Importance') plt.title('Random Forest Feature Importances') plt.show()
```

Model Evaluation

Python

```
from sklearn.metrics import classification_report, roc_curve, auc

# Predictions
y_pred = rf_classifier.predict(X_test)

# Print classification report
print(classification_report(y_test, y_pred))

# ROC Curve
fpr, tpr, thresholds = roc_curve(y_test, y_pred)
roc_auc = auc(fpr, tpr)

plt.figure()
plt.plot(fpr, tpr, color='darkorange', label='ROC curve (area = %0.2f)' % roc_auc)
plt.xlabel('False Positive Rate')
plt.ylabel('True Positive Rate')
```

```
plt.title('Receiver Operating Characteristic Curve')

plt.legend(loc="lower right")

plt.show()
```

Deployment Strategy

Containerization with Docker

```
# Package the model and its dependencies into a Docker container

docker build -t fraud-detection-model.


# Run the Docker container

docker run -p 8080:8080 fraud-detection-model
```

Deployment on Cloud Platforms

AWS SageMaker

1. Create a **SageMaker** model package.
2. Deploy the model package to **SageMaker**.
3. Create an endpoint to serve the model.

Google Cloud AI Platform

1. Export the model to a **SavedModel.**
2. Deploy the **SavedModel** to Cloud AI Platform.
3. Create a model endpoint.

Integration with Transaction Systems

The deployed model can be integrated with existing financial transaction systems in a variety of ways. For example, the model can be deployed as a REST API endpoint. Transaction systems can then send requests to the API endpoint for real-time fraud prediction.

Monitoring and Feedback Loop After deployment, it is important to constantly monitor the model's performance. This can be done by:

- Tracking model metrics such as precision, recall, and F1 score.
- Setting up alerts for any significant deviation in metrics.
- Reviewing false positives and negatives to identify any new fraud patterns.

The feedback from the monitoring process can be used to retrain and improve the model over time.

Example:

Python

```
import requests

# Make a request to the fraud detection model API endpoint
response = requests.post('http://localhost:8080/predict',
json={'transaction_data': {'amount': 100, 'card_number':
'1234567890123456', 'merchant_name': 'Amazon.com'}})

# Get the fraud prediction
prediction = response.json()['prediction']

# If the prediction is 'fraud', take action to prevent the transaction
if prediction == 'fraud':
print('This transaction is likely fraudulent.')
```

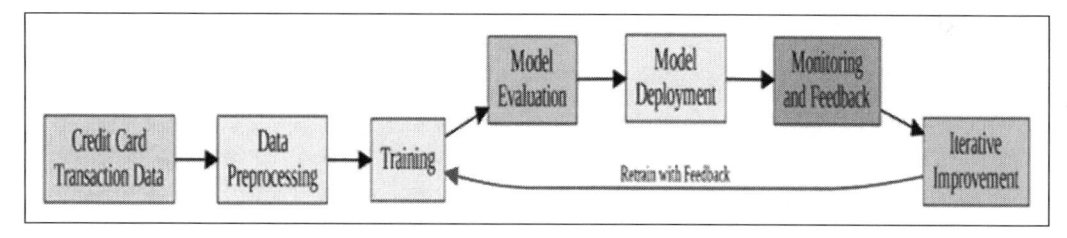

Figure 9.10: Feedback Loop for fraud detection machine learning model

Credit Card Transaction Data

This is the entry point of the fraud detection pipeline, where the raw transaction data is ingested. This data can contain various details of each transaction, including but not limited to:

- Amount
- Time
- Merchant details
- Cardholder details

- Device details
- Geographic location

Data Preprocessing

The data preprocessing phase involves cleaning, transforming, and enriching the raw transaction data to prepare it for modeling. This could involve tasks such as:

- **Normalization:** Scaling the data to a consistent range to improve the model's performance.
- **Handling missing values**: Imputing missing values or removing incomplete transactions.
- **Feature engineering:** Creating new features from existing data to improve the model's predictive power.

Training: Random Forest Model

After preprocessing, the data is used to train a machine learning model. In this case, we are using the Random Forest algorithm, known for its accuracy and ability to handle large datasets.

Random Forests work by constructing a multitude of decision trees and averaging their predictions. This ensemble approach makes Random Forests more robust and less prone to overfitting than individual decision trees.

Model Evaluation

Once the model has been trained, it is important to evaluate its performance using various metrics suitable for fraud detection, such as:

- **Area Under the Receiver Operating Characteristic Curve (AUC-ROC):** A measure of the model's ability to distinguish between fraudulent and non-fraudulent transactions.
- **Precision**: The percentage of predicted fraudulent transactions that are actually fraudulent.
- **Recall:** The percentage of actual fraudulent transactions that are correctly predicted.
- **F1 score**: A harmonic mean of precision and recall, which takes into account both the model's ability to correctly identify fraudulent transactions and avoid false positives.

Model Deployment

After achieving satisfactory evaluation metrics, the model is then deployed into a production environment. This means it starts analyzing real-time transaction data to predict and flag potential fraudulent activities.

Deployment can be done in a variety of ways, such as:
- Serving the model as a REST API endpoint
- Embedding the model into a transaction processing system
- Deploying the model to a cloud platform such as AWS SageMaker or Google Cloud AI Platform

Monitoring and Feedback

Once in production, it is crucial to continuously monitor the model's performance. Over time, as new fraud patterns emerge or transaction behaviors change, the model's accuracy might decline.

To monitor the model's performance, you can track metrics such as:
- AUC-ROC
- Precision
- Recall
- F1 score
- False positive rate
- False negative rate

You can also review false positives and negatives to identify any new fraud patterns or changes in transaction behavior.

Once you have identified any issues, you can use this feedback to retrain and improve the model. This is an iterative process that should be done on a regular basis to ensure that the model is always performing at its best.

Reflecting on the Power of Integrated Pipelines

In the rapidly evolving realm of data science, two distinct pipelines are often encountered: the data engineering pipeline and the machine learning pipeline. The former is responsible for curating, processing, and preparing data, while the latter focuses on modeling and predictions. However, the true power lies in the harmonious convergence of these two pipelines, as exemplified in the context of fraud detection.

Convergence in Real-world Scenarios

In reality, the robustness of a machine learning model is solely dependent on the quality of the data it is trained on. This is where data engineering plays a pivotal role in ensuring that ML models have the right foundation to work upon. From handling missing values to managing big data storage to real-time processing, every step in the data engineering pipeline is crucial.

For instance, in a credit card fraud detection system, even the most sophisticated algorithm would fail to detect anomalies without clean, timely, and relevant transactional data. This highlights the interconnectedness of the data engineering and machine learning pipelines, where the success of one is inextricably linked to the other.

The Future of Integrated Approaches

The future of data science lies in seamless integration. As more industries embrace AI and ML practices, the boundaries between data engineering and machine learning will continue to blur. Integrated platforms that offer end-to-end solutions, from data ingestion to actionable insights, will become the norm. Such systems will not only be more efficient but will also significantly reduce the time from ideation to implementation, enabling rapid responses to threats like fraud.

Adapting Across Domains

While the focus has been on fraud detection, the principles and techniques discussed are universally applicable. Whether in healthcare, where the goal is to predict patient outcomes; e-commerce, where the aim is to enhance user experience; or finance, where the objective is to optimize stock portfolios, the power of integrated pipelines remains untapped. Readers are encouraged to think beyond the constraints of domains and envision a world where data-driven decisions, powered by integrated systems, are omnipresent.

Conclusion

Continuous learning is essential in the ever-evolving world of data. The resources discussed in the chapter are just a starting point. The real journey begins when you start implementing and experimenting in real-world scenarios. By embracing integrated pipelines, you can unlock the full potential of data science and make a meaningful impact in your domain.

Further Resources

Advanced Tools and Platforms

- **Apache Kafka**: A distributed streaming platform ideal for handling real-time data feeds.
- **TensorFlow Extended (TFX):** An end-to-end platform designed to deploy and manage machine learning pipelines.
- **Amazon Fraud Detector**: A fully managed service that leverages ML and Amazon's 20 years of fraud detection expertise to identify potentially fraudulent activities.

Index

A

Anomalies
  business, implications 170, 171
  data clean, techniques 172, 173
  data stream,
      challenges 171, 172
  demand-supply, gap 170
  eyeball, analyzing 170
  temporal, analyzing 169
Anomalies statistical,
      methods
  Interquartile range 252
  Z-score 252
Application Programming
      Interfaces 40
ARIMA 106
ARIMA, components
  autoregression 106
  integration 106
  moving average 106
Autoencoders
  about 254
  advantages 255
  concepts 254
  disadvantages 255

B

Bagging
  about 295
  benefits 295, 296
  implementing,
      steps 295
  Random Forest 296
Batch Processing
  about 343
  advantages 343
  disadvantages 343
Bayes' theorem 131
Boosting
  about 296
  advantages 297, 298
  benefits 298
  implementing,
      steps 296

C

confusion matrix 51
  about 213
  data, interpreventing 214
  future, enhancing 215
  key insights 214

Credit card fraud detection
  about 328
  across domain,
    adapting 362
  A Dual, approach 333, 334
  aspects, sensitive 332
  concepts 353
  data collect,
    methods 328, 329
  data engineering,
    roles 329
  datasets,
    preprocessing 329, 330
  financial, transactions 331
  future integrate,
    approaching 362
  labeling 330
  normalization, scaling 330
  objective 353
  pipeline, stages 354
  security, balancing 331

D

Data Engineering 326
Data Engineering, key steps
  data clean, preprocessing 327
  data, sourcing 327
  ETL, processing 327
  warehousing 327
Data Exploration 336
Data Preprocessing
  about 2, 3
  data, comprehensing 28, 29
  feature, selecting 31-36
  medical field, impacting 5
  model, deploying 19
  predictive, policing 5, 6
  roles, utilizing 3, 4
Data Preprocessing, aspects
  feature, scaling 16
  outliers, managing 16
  values, handling 16
  variables, dealing 16

Data Preprocessing,
    assumptions
  homoscedasticity 20, 21
  linearity, ensuring 20
  multicollinearity, dealing 20
Data Preprocessing, oversight
  classification 4
  prediction 5
  training 5
Data Science 2
Dataset
  about 260
  Isolation Forests, applying 261
  model validating,
    methods 263-267
  preprocess 260
  results, visualizing 261, 262
Dataset project, steps
  data, cleaning 272-274
  data, exploring 272
  data, utilizing 269
  features, engineering 275-278
  objectives 270, 271
  outlier, interpretating 279, 280
Decision Trees
  about 78, 79
  Amazon's Stock,
    predicting 79, 80
  binary, classifying 85
  stock market,
    predicting 81, 82
  tasks, delving 84
Decision Trees, benefits
  flexibility 84
  interpretability, simplicity 84
  robust 84
Decision Trees, binary feature
  price direction,
    predicting 94-97
Decision Trees, limitations
  data, requirements 84
  interpretability 84
  overfitting 84

Index 367

Decision Trees, setting up
  data, utilizing 88, 89
  Gini Impurity 87
  missing value, handling 90, 91
  node, visualizing 87
  Preprocessing 89
  structure, utilizing 86, 87
  test, training 85
Distributed Systems
  about 200
  datasets, managing 200, 201
  data storage,
      processing 201, 202
  source, combining 203
  Sparse Data, handling 202
Distributed Systems, challenge
  compression, techniques 202
  distribute,
      representating 202
  parallel, computation 203
document embedding
  about 125
  benefits 125
  challenges 126

E

Ensemble Methods
  about 287
  advantages 288
  bagging 293
  boosting 293
  ensemble diagram,
      decoding 292
  market, forecasting 294
  stacking 293
  stock data, getting 288, 289
  Toolkits, libraries 289-291
  types 287
Ensemble Single Models,
      reasons
  blas, reducing 294
  robustness, improving 294
  variance, reducing 294

F

flags loans
  about 62
  data, preprocessing 68-70
  dataset, analyzing 63
  data, utilizing 64-67
  data, visualizing 65-68
  preliminary,
      exploring 64, 65
  significance 63
  structured, reporting 63, 64
Fraud Detection
  about 339
  argumentation, detecting 338
  concepts 340
  Data Exploration,
      utilizing 337
  dataset, handling 337
  feature, engineering 339
  implementation,
      considering 339
  techniques 337
  use, cases 344
Fraud Detection, algorithms
  Decision Trees 341
  Neural Network 342
  SVMs 342
Fraud Detection Metrics,
      evaluation
  model decision, making 350
  model evaluation,
      adapting 348, 349
  model, interpreventing 349
  precision, recalling 346
  ROC, curving 347, 348
  strategies, evaluating 350

G

Gini Impurity
  about 87
  features 87, 88
  two-phase, approach 88

I

Imbalanced Data
  about 340
  challenges 340
Imbalanced Data, techniques
  anomaly, detecting 341
  cost-sensitive, learning 341
  Resampling 341
  synthetic data,
      generating 341
Indian Stock Market
  about 98
  data, exploring 100
  dataset, utilizing 99, 100
  INFY Data,
      application 107-109
  objectives 99
  outcomes, learning 110
  problem statement 100
  volume, trades
      utilizing 101-105
Indian Stock Market, statement
  company, performance 98
  economic, conditions 98
  market, sentiment 98
  political, events 98
Isolation forests
  about 241
  advantages 243
  concepts, utilizing 241
  conceptual, isolating 242, 243
  limitations 251, 252
Isolation forests, applications
  failure, detecting 244
  fraud, detecting 244
  intrusion, detecting 244
  medical diagnosis 244
Isolation forests, mechanism
  anomalies, measuring 246-249
  Anomaly Scores 250, 251
  insights, using 249, 250
  i-Trees 244

K

Kaggle API
  configuring 22
  dataset, downloading 23
  goals, utilizing 23, 24
  installing 22
  key, generating 22
Kaggle API, characteristic
  LotArea 24
  LotFrontage 24
  MSSubClass 24
  MSZoning 24
  OverallCond 24
  OverallQual 24
  SalePrice 24
  YearBuilt 24
  YearRemoAdd 24
K-means clustering
  about 253
  advantages 253
  disadvantages 253
  examples 253
KNN, additional cases
  behavior, analyzing 162
  passenger fraud 162
  route, optimizing 162
KNN, considerations
  data, consistency 173
  data, granularity 174
  data, streaming 174, 175
  Hybrid Solutions 175-180
KNN, features
  anomaly, detecting 168, 169
  data, splitting 165, 166
  predicting trip 166-168
  supply-demand, balancing 166
KNN (K-Nearest Neighbors)
  about 158
  advantages 181
  disadvantages 181
  Real-Time Demand 181, 182
  using 180

KNN project, predicting
  file-tune, optimizing 191
  model, evaluating 190, 191
  potential,
    applications 192, 193
  real-world, applications 189
  tweets emojis, using 183
  twitter data, collecting 183-189
KNN, use cases
  demand, predicting 162
  rate, predicting 162
  supply-demand gap,
    analyzing 162
  timeframes, pricing 162

L

Linear Regression
  about 6, 7
  assumptions 8, 9
  coefficients, intercept 10
  goals, utilizing 7, 8
  Python, comprehensing 25
Linear Regression, categories
  multiple linear 9, 10
  simple linear 9
Linear Regression, elements
  core assumptions,
    analyzing 11-14
  error term 10
  multiple regression 11
  polynomial regression 11
Linear Regression, resources
  data, collecting 14
  data explore, preprocessing 14
  interpretation 15
  model, evaluation 15
  model, fitting 14
Linear Regression, types
  Elastic Net Regression 18
  Lasso Regression 18
  Ordinary Least Squares 17
  Ridge Regression 17, 18
  Right Model, choosing 18, 19

Logistic Regression
  about 41
  evaluating 42
  features, handling 40
  implementing 41, 42
Logistic Regression,
    implementing
  coefficients, interpreting 58
  customers, strategies 60
  model, evaluating 58, 59
  next steps, discussing 62
  retain, simulating 60
  Scikit-learn, using 57
  strategies, evaluating 60-62

M

Market Direction Prediction
  data, converting 318
  hyperparameter, tuning 319
  metrics, evaluating 317
  validation, techniques 317
Market Direction Prediction,
    features
  data source, utilizing 320
  ensemble, stacking 322
  hyperparameter,
    tuning 321, 322
  model, training 321
  snippet, coding 322, 323
ML pipeline, steps
  data, gathering 327
  data, preprocessing 327
  deploying 327
  engineering, features 327
  model, evaluating 327
  model, training 327
Model Deployment,
    practical use
  ethical, considering 73-75
  future, challenges 74
  maintenance, updating 73
  regulatory, considering 74
  source, utilizing 72

model training, evaluating
  comparison 72
  evaluation 71
  hyperparameter, tuning 72
  model, selecting 70

N

Naive Bayes
  about 133
  feature, independency 133
  limitations 134
  using 134
Naive Bayes Algorithm
  about 116
  Bayes' theorem 131
  gas station,
      comments 132, 133
  history 130
Naive Bayes Algorithm,
      applications
  document, classifying 130
  sentiment, analyzing 130
  spam, filtering 130
  system, recommending 130
Naive Bayes, projects
  classifier, utilizing 154
  confusion matrix,
      visualizing 152
  data acquisition,
      analyzing 146
  data merge, challenges 146
  dataset, importance 145
  datasets, merging 150
  layout, constructing 153, 154
  machine learning,
      relevance 145
  model, evaluating 152
  preliminary goals,
      analyzing 147
  problem, statements 145
  recommendations 155
  remarks 154

Naive Bayes, types
  Bernoulli Naive
      Bayes 137-143
  Gaussian Naive Bayes 135
  Multinomial Naive
      Bayes 136, 137
Neural networks 254
NLP Transformations,
      station comments
  Bag of Words (BoW) 127
  Doc2Vec 129
  FastText 128
  GloVe 129
  TF-IDF 128

O

One-Class SVMs
  about 257
  advantages 257
  concepts 257
  disadvantages 257

P

plot() function 102
project predict, objectives
  algorithm, selecting 43
  class imbalance,
      addressing 43
  customer, churning 45
  feature, scaling 45
  features, engineering 43
  hyperparameter,
      optimizing 44
  imbalance classes, handling 45
  instructions 43
  miss values, dealing 44
  model, evaluating 44
PySpark
  about 218
  functionalities 219, 220
  reasons 218
  setting up 219

R

Real-Time Data Streams
  about 159
  characterize 160
  industries, impacts 160, 161
  modern-day, relevance 160
Real-Time Processing
  about 344
  advantages 344
  batch, transitioning 345, 346
  disadvantages 344
  errors, handling 345
  key, components 345
Robust Covariance 255
Robust evaluation
  about 306
  baseline models,
      comparing 306-309
  future, approaching 309, 310
  metrics, evaluating 306
  validation, approaching 306
ROC Curve
  about 52
  address, overfitting 53
  data, fetching 53, 54
  data, inspecting 54, 55
  numerical variables,
      handling 55-57

S

Scikit-learn 46, 47
Scikit-learn, churn predictions
  logistic, equation 49
  logistic function,
      utilizing 48, 49
  Log-Odds, analyzing 49
  model, evaluating 50, 51
  regression, delving 47
  ROC Curve 52
  sigmoid, utilizing 48
  train-test, splitting 51
  variables, handling 49, 50

Sentiment Analysis
  about 299
  data 300
  ensemble, techniques 300
  methodology 300, 301
  project, objective 300
  time series, analyzing 300
Sentiment Analysis, methods
  ensemble, architecture 302
  limitations 301
  traditional, approaches 301
SparkCognition project, steps
  data,
      comprehensive 222, 223
  data, dealing 224-226
  dataset, utilizing 221
  long-term,
      visioning 235, 236
  machine learning,
      optimizing 222
  model refine,
      imbalancing 232, 233
  model, validating 229-232
  problem, optimizing 222
  recommendations,
      taking 233-235
  robust, foundation 223
  stage, setting 221
  visualization 226, 227
Sparse Data
  about 196
  applications 197
  necessity, preprocessing 208
  PySpark's, optimizing 217, 218
  source, dealing 197
  SVMs, optimizing 197
  SVM with Hand-on,
      analyzing 216
Sparse Data, challenges
  computational,
      overheads 208
  information, loosing 208
  model, complexity 208

Sparse Data, characteristics
  high dimension 196
  memory, efficiency 196
  noise, inherent 197
Sparse Data, features
  Mokka Dataset 205
  problem, statements 205
  SVMs, utilizing 205
Special Characters
  about 122
  benefits 123
  caution 123
  strategies 122
Stacking
  about 298
  advantages 299
  challenges 299
  execution, steps 298
stock market
  about 78
  composite, preprocessing 286, 287
  Decision Trees 78, 79
  Ensemble, methods 282
  key, analyzing 283
stock market, concepts
  data, collecting 312
  data, preprocessing 313
  features, extracting 312
stock market, importance
  data, fetching 285, 286
  data sentiment, optimizing 285
  sentiment, analyzing 284
  sources, utilizing 284
  Yahoo Finance, fetching 284
stock market, strategies
  ensemble, strategy 314
  features, importance 315, 316
  individual model 314
stock market, techniques
  ensemble, methods 311
  machine learning 310, 311
  traditional statistical 310

Stopwords, approaches
  custom lists 120
  predefine lists 120
Stopwords, benefits
  content, focusing 120
  performance, improving 120
  space, efficiency 120
SVMs, key components
  hyperplane 198
  margin 198
  vectors, supporting 198
SVMs, libraries
  H2O 215
  Scikit-learn, distributing 215
  Spark MLLib 215
  ThunderSVM 215
SVMs Mokka's Data, steps
  confusion matrix 213
  data, preprocessing 210
  insights results, interpreventing 213
  model, evaluating 212, 213
  model training, validating 212
SVMs (Support Vector machines)
  about 197, 198
  characteristics 207
  concepts 199
  Fraud, detecting 220
  high-dimensional data, analyzing 200
  model, building 205-207
  Sparse Data, utilizing 199
  working 198

T

Text Preprocessing
  about 126
  importance 126
  key takeways 127

Text Preprocessing,
    key benefits
  consistency 119
  efficiency 119
  model performance,
    enhancing 119
  noise, reducing 119
TF-IDF
  about 302
  advantages 303
  components 302
  limitations 303
Time-series data
  about 78
  ARIMA, analyzing 94
  outliers, handling 92, 93
  stationarity,
    transforming 93
  techniques,
    visualizing 91, 92
Time-series data,
    techniques
  heatmaps 89
  line plots 89
  plots, autocorrelation 89
  seasonal, decomposition 89
Tokenization, benefits
  foundation, processing 120
  structure, transforming 119
  term, frequency 120
Transactional Data
  about 336
  challenges 336
  properties 336
  techniques 337

U

unstructured data
  about 114
  algorithm, classify 115
  NLP Transformations 127
  Text Preprocessing 126
unstructured data, features
  Naive Bayes Algorithm 116
  Sentiment, analyzing 116
  web scraping 117

V

Vectorization 123-124
Vectorization, techniques
  document embeddings 125
  word embeddings 125

W

web scraping
  about 117
  Lemmatization,
    stemming 121, 122
  libraries, tools 118
  Special Characters 122
  Stopwords 120
  Text Preprocessing 118
  Tokenization 119
  Vectorization 123
word embeddings
  about 303
  advantages 304
  disadvantages 304
  Naive Bayes,
    implementing 304